"Nathan Finn and Keith Whitfield are to be commended for assembling this fine group of scholars and practitioners to address these timely topics around the shared theme of the Great Commission. The chapters connect and cohere well, enabling readers to think in fresh ways about the implications of the Great Commission for various areas of study, ministry, and leadership. The book is a worthy tribute to my good friend Danny Akin. I am pleased that he could be appropriately honored by the thoughtful and insightful contributions found in this volume. I count it a joy to recommend this important work."

—**David S. Dockery**, president, Southwestern Baptist Theological Seminary

"Nothing could be more appropriate as the subject of a Festschrift for my friend Danny Akin than the topic of the Great Commission. Every beat of the man's heart is about the spread of the gospel. He will be more delighted if this book moves us to fulfill the Great Commission than if it brings attention to him. His happiness in the Lord, his faithfulness to the Word, and the focus of his life, leadership, and ministry bless me and thousands of others. So, take up and read, and *go*!"

—**Ligon Duncan**, chancellor, Reformed Theological Seminary

"One of the great friendships of my life has been the one I share with Danny Akin, and I can tell you there is no one whose heart beats more for the Great Commission. Danny would say, just like Peter responding to Jesus, "Lord, to whom would we go?" This book captures his passion, his sold-out commitment, and his life's dedication to the Great Commission. I hope you can read it, as I have, with a love for the man and a renewed allegiance to carrying this mission forward."

—**Kevin Ezell**, president, North American Mission Board

"Ever since William Carey first riveted the Christian church to the missionary imperative, Jesus's Great Commission has been at the heart of world evangelization. The same passion that moved Carey also motivates Dr. Danny Akin. This volume is a worthy tribute to his remarkable vision and gospel work."

—**Timothy George**, distinguished professor at Beeson Divinity School

"Danny Akin has been a consistent Acts 1:8 disciple of Jesus Christ, first with his family and second with the scores of Christians he has influenced both personally and professionally. This Festschrift, which reflects the breadth of people he has influenced, is an appropriate honor for a brother dearly beloved. I love Danny Akin and his zeal for the Great Commission (and the Great Commandment)."

—**Kevin Smith**, pastor, Family Church Village, West Palm Beach, Florida

FULFILLING THE GREAT COMMISSION

FULFILLING THE GREAT COMMISSION

Essays in Honor of

DANIEL L. AKIN

EDITORS
NATHAN FINN AND KEITH WHITFIELD

B&H
ACADEMIC
BRENTWOOD, TENNESSEE

Fulfilling the Great Commission: Essays in Honor of Daniel L. Akin

Published by B&H Academic
Brentwood, Tennessee

ISBN: 978-1-0877-8532-5

Dewey Decimal Classification: 269.2
Subject Heading: GREAT COMMISSION \
EVANGELISTIC WORK \ MISSIONS

Cover design by Emily Keafer Lambright. Cover etching: "The Ascension" by Jacques Callot, from the series The Mysteries of the Passion, c. 1631, courtesy National Gallery of Art, Washington. Additional images sourced from olaser/iStock and AskinTulayOver/iStock.

Printed in China

29 28 27 26 25 24 RRD 1 2 3 4 5 6 7 8 9 10

CONTENTS

FOREWORD

DANIEL L. AKIN: GOD'S HAPPY WARRIOR

R. Albert Mohler Jr.

Following the tragic death of Admiral Lord Nelson at the Battle of Trafalgar, William Wordsworth wrote a tribute to the admiral, defining the late hero as a "happy warrior." The honorific has made its way into our popular culture, describing a leader who, while called to do hard things, maintains his joyful disposition to life.

Danny Akin is a genuine happy warrior. To know him is to see his joy and to see it spread. I came to see that disposition as the key to Danny Akin's leadership.

Almost thirty years ago, I needed to find a new senior vice president for academic administration who would simultaneously serve as dean of the School of Theology at The Southern Baptist Theological Seminary. That was a time of crisis for our school, as we were amid the conservative resurgence in the Southern Baptist Convention. I needed a solid leader of great ability, and I needed a colleague with whom I could work toward the great goal of building the institution. I needed a Southern Baptist leader who honored God, loved the church, faithfully served Christ, and would take this major responsibility within the Southern Baptist Convention at a moment of tumult and opportunity.

Given the passage of time, I can safely recount the fact that individuals with the requisite experience lacked the necessary convictions and those with the convictions lacked the experience. Most also lacked the passion and resilience that were required. I needed a colleague who could leap aboard a fast-running train and lead, relishing the opportunity.

At the time, I had only one man in mind, and I hardly knew him. But I had observed that he had what I was looking for. I had met Danny Akin but had not held a major conversation with him. The only problem was that he seemed quite happy where he was, at Southeastern Seminary serving as dean of students. As a courtesy, I asked Southeastern's president at the time, Paige Patterson, for permission to call Danny and ask him to consider the position at Southern. That was a two-sided danger. Paige graciously gave permission and then informed Danny of my interest in him, simultaneously seeking to prevent Danny from leaving Southeastern. Fair play.

Thus, my first call with Danny Akin was not as warm as I had hoped it would be. I played the long game and threw theology at him, underlining the fact that he was spiritually obligated to consider Southern's opportunity. He came for a visit, and the rest was history. He called his wife, Charlotte, who was completely happy in Wake Forest with their four boys, and he told her he sensed God's leading. Within weeks, the Akins were in Louisville, and I had a new dean and vice president. And I gained a friend for life. The Mohlers and the Akins became like family.

I have seen Danny Akin work and lead in nearly every situation imaginable, and some we could never have imagined. I knew I could count on him to tell the truth and do the right thing. I learned that his face simply cannot lie, and that a smile always meant all was well (or would be well) and that clenched teeth always meant we faced trouble (as in, God help us all). From 1996 to 2004 we had the great experience of working together, teaching together, learning together, and navigating rapids together.

I learned several truths about Danny Akin.

First, his teaching style is infectious, and he is a passionate professor. The man was made to teach. He just gets before a class and sets himself loose. Students flocked to his classes, even if they had a tough time keeping up with his lectures, which were always delivered at full throttle. He was a teacher first and foremost, and it showed. He is a true theologian who combines academic excellence and biblical fidelity.

Second, he is a skilled preacher. That is essential to effective leadership in the Southern Baptist Convention and, to an even greater degree, as a model for students training for the pastorate. Danny Akin is more at home in the pulpit than most anywhere else, and congregations sense it. He loves the Bible, and he loves to preach the Bible. He preaches as he teaches, at full throttle and with full intensity.

Third, Danny is a natural magnet for talent. He deserves much credit for helping Southern Seminary find and recruit an epic faculty. We aimed high and scored high, and a remarkable faculty was built. Those faculty members became friends as well as colleagues. We taught together, worked together, and grew up together, even as our families grew close. Later, of course, Danny would take those same skills to Southeastern Seminary as its president.

Fourth, Danny Akin loves students, and they know it. As Kierkegaard understood, the truest teaching comes as an exchange of passion. Danny Akin is a conduit for the right kind of passion to be injected into students. He cannot relate without passion. If you do not want to share his passions, you had better stay far away.

Finally, Danny Akin is a one-man catalyst for one specific passion: Great Commission faithfulness. The Great Commission has been on Danny's heart his entire Christian life. But by the time he went to Southeastern Seminary as president, I could see that passion within him about to explode. Predictably, Danny Akin has thrown his life into Southeastern Seminary, and it shows. Over the last two decades, Danny has demonstrated remarkable leadership on the global scene as a passionate promoter of the Great Commission. That passion has translated into missionaries serving all over the world, churches planted across the landscape, and congregations more committed and involved in missions, evangelism, and church planting.

With skill and intentionality, Danny has transfused that passion into the lives of others and extended it throughout the Southern Baptist Convention and beyond. To know him is to know that passion, and the legacy of Danny Akin will show up on the Day of the Lord in men and women who have heard the gospel of Jesus Christ, believed, and been saved.

This is Danny Akin's greatest gift to theological education. He gets right to the Great Commission and does not let up. The call of Christ to the nations shapes his entire vision. It shapes the institution he leads. It shapes his understanding of life. It is his gift to the Southern Baptist Convention and to this generation of students and pastors.

Much more can be said, and this reflection has barely scratched the surface. Knowing Danny Akin as colleague and friend has been one of the great gifts of God to my life, to Mary, and to our entire family.

But that brings me to a final and essential point. Danny Akin would likely be a total failure in life and a menace to society except for Charlotte Akin. Danny and Charlotte are made for each other, and it shows. Charlotte has been Danny's companion, wife, and inspiration for their entire adult lives together. She is sweet, kind, and indispensable. They have raised a remarkable family, starting with four sons—all deeply involved in Christian ministry and leadership—and then their wives and a boisterous harvest of grandchildren, who adore both Danny and Charlotte. Together they are a great gift from God and a picture of the kingdom's promise. One of their sons, Paul, is now serving at Southern Seminary in the very same role once filled by his father, senior vice president for academic administration and provost.

Mary and I are incredibly thankful for Danny and Charlotte Akin as friends, colleagues, and cherished companions on life's way. I pray that God will extend Danny Akin's leadership and influence within the Southern Baptist Convention (SBC) and the evangelical world for many years to come. We need God's happy warrior on the field of battle.

PREFACE

Nathan A. Finn and Keith S. Whitfield

Authors write some books because they have to, others because they need to, and still others because they simply want to. This is a book we have wanted to edit and contribute to for a decade. We first discussed this book when we were both faculty members at Southeastern Baptist Theological Seminary, sometime around 2013 or 2014. In the ensuing years, we revisited the topic periodically, pondered the appropriate timeline, and considered possible contributors. There were a lot of phone calls, emails, and face-to-face conversations. We did it all because we love Danny Akin.

Our own friendship began over two decades ago, and for the entirety of that time, Dr. Akin has been a part of that story. We met at Southern Baptist Theological Seminary, where Keith was working on the ThM and Nathan was pursuing the MDiv. At the time, Keith's wife, Amy, was Dr. Akin's administrative assistant in his role as Southern's vice president of academic administration. When there was an opening for a receptionist in the Office of Academic Administration, Amy hired Nathan's wife, Leah, for the job. Leah soon became Dr. Akin's administrative assistant in his role as dean of the School of Theology.

Because of God's kind providence—and two immensely gifted wives—we were blessed to spend time around Dr. and Mrs. Akin. We saw behind closed doors that not only was Dr. Akin a good leader; he was a godly man. He was not arrogant. He told the truth. He was kind. He was devoted to his wife and sons. He loved Jesus, loved the church, and loved the lost. He taught both of us what it looks like to give one's life tirelessly to serve King Jesus. He was the real deal. And he was also funny. Very funny. During these years when we were students who were blessed to be in his orbit, Dr. Akin taught us so much about what it means to be a man of God. We have continued to learn from him in the years since.

Dr. Akin became the president of Southeastern Baptist Theological Seminary in January 2004. Eventually, both our families followed him to Wake Forest, North Carolina. Nathan completed the MDiv and earned a PhD from Southeastern, joining the full-time faculty from 2007 to 2015. He has continued to teach adjunctively in the PhD program since leaving Wake Forest. Keith also completed his PhD from Southeastern, joining the full-time faculty in 2012. He has subsequently served in several key administrative roles at Southeastern, including provost.

It is one of the great joys of our lives to edit this Festschrift in honor of Dr. Akin's twentieth anniversary as president of Southeastern Seminary and nearly five decades of gospel ministry. Though we briefly considered several themes for this book, early on we settled on the centrality of the Great Commission for all of life and ministry. This has been a consistent theme of Dr. Akin's personal walk with Christ, his institutional leadership of Southeastern Seminary, and his wider leadership within the Southern Baptist Convention. It was the only theme that made sense for this volume.

We are grateful to the men and women who contributed chapters to this Festschrift. Some, like us, are former students and/or faculty members who served under his leadership. Others are his longtime peers and colleagues. Some contributors have been among his closest personal friends for decades. Four of the contributors are his sons. We think it worth noting that not a single person whom we invited to contribute turned down the invitation. We are confident we could have invited many others who would not have rejected the opportunity. There are so many people who love and respect Dr. Akin.

We would also like to thank Madison Trammel and his team at B&H Academic for publishing this volume. From the beginning, our friends at B&H Academic have seen the value of this book and been supportive of its publication. We also want to thank Ryan Hutchinson, who serves as executive vice president for operations at Southeastern Seminary and contributed a chapter to this Festschrift. As we worked with B&H, he supported this volume and helped us think through how this volume could be a blessing to the Southeastern Seminary family.

We always thank our wives and children in these sorts of prefaces, but our wives deserve particular thanks for this book. Not only have they been enthusiastic supporters of this volume, and not only did Amy contribute a chapter, but we remain keenly aware this book would not exist had Danny Akin not liked our wives enough that he was willing to spend time with us! Leah and Amy—thanks for being awesome. We would not be here without you. Literally.

Finally, we thank the Lord that he saw fit to allow us to get to know Dr. Akin. It is impossible to adequately articulate everything he means to us, how much he has influenced us, and how much we have learned from him. But the Lord knows. We hope this volume is one small way to demonstrate our tremendous love and respect for Dr. Akin, as well as to help cultivate his commitment to holistic Great Commission faithfulness among everyone who reads this book.

Nathan A. Finn and Keith S. Whitfield
December 17, 2022

INTRODUCTION

THE LIFE OF DANIEL L. AKIN

Jonathan Akin, Nathan Akin,
Paul Akin, and Timothy Akin

At commencement services, our father typically preaches a familiar story or verse from the Bible because the diverse crowd ranges from unbelievers to missionaries going to countries that cannot be named. For example, on one occasion, he preached perhaps the most famous verse in the Scriptures, John 3:16. In typical Danny Akin style, his exposition went word by word to explain this magnificent verse. That is his practice at graduation. He models in those messages, as he has done throughout his years in ministry, faithful exposition combined with a strong gospel appeal.

Writing the introduction to a book written in our father's honor is a daunting task, especially since he is our hero. We thought one appropriate approach was to attempt something we have been trying our entire lives: be like our dad. One way we can honor our hero in a work on the Great Commission dedicated to him is to walk phrase by phrase through the best-known Great Commission passage, Matt 28:18–20, pointing out how Danny Akin has exemplified its truths. Not only has he taught us the Great Commission in his preaching, but he has modeled it for us with his integrity, grit, passion, leadership, and joy.

Our father is passionate about the Great Commission. He loves the Lord Jesus and desires Jesus's Lordship in his life above all things. He loves the nations; he loves the cause. So, he has spent his life on the "go" (see Matt 28:19)!

"All authority has been given to me in heaven and on earth."

"All that matters is that you please Jesus." This was the straightforward way our dad taught us about the Lordship of Christ. As friends often do, one of ours mimics (mocks?) our dad's Southern voice while saying, "I'd do anything for Jeee-sus." We have also heard Keith Getty mimic our dad, and it does not sound as sarcastic when spoken with a Northern Irish accent.

The Great Commission begins and ends with Jesus. It begins with his authority and culminates in his glory. Jesus establishes for his disciples the fact that he is sovereign. He can give this commission and call his followers to a cause this great because he is the only one who possesses the power to make it happen. And rightfully so! His power does not derive solely from who he is, but also from what he has done. His authority rests on who he is—the One who is fully God and truly man. But he also has this authority because he saved humanity from sin. His obedience to the Father on the cross and the Father's vindication of his Son through the resurrection is to be proclaimed in this commission. He has authority to save us and call us to his cause because of what he accomplished.

So, it begins and ends with Jesus. All that matters is that you please him who has done so much for you. You then can trust him for the task because he possesses all you need for it. Our dad reminded us of this often, and he modeled it by his faith. We are not prone to worry because we trust in Jesus. Our father instilled that trust in us by his deep, abiding faith in Jesus's sovereign lordship over all things.

"Go . . . [to] all nations."

This great news reminds us of his grand authority and propels us because the cause is massive. We go because of impetus and scope. The impetus is the glory of this great King and love of neighbor. The scope is the globe. All peoples!

In this regard, our father led by instruction and example. When we were young, he had us join Royal Ambassadors to learn the work of Southern Baptists in the Great Commission. Our father taught us about missionary heroes and the lessons in Matthew 28:18–20, Mark 16:14–18, Luke 24:46–49, and John 20:30–31.

He also led by example. Our dad took short-term mission trips to Australia and to Thailand when we were young boys. We remember the stories he told about opportunities to share the gospel, teach the Bible, and encourage missionaries serving in those locations.

This visible example of a Great Commission life continues: our dad has now ministered in more than twenty countries around the world. He loves the nations. He desires the salvation of all peoples. He desires for Jesus to receive the reward of his suffering (see Rev 5:9–10) and his inheritance of nations (see Ps 2:8).

Our father works for the cause and gives to the cause. For many years, our parents have given almost 20 percent of their yearly income to ministry and mission. They are passionate about funding mission efforts among the most unreached and underserved peoples.

He passed on this love to his children and grandchildren as well. Two of us (Paul and Tim) lived and served among Muslims with the International Mission Board. All of us have served shorter terms in several different contexts around the world. The passion and love for God's mission that define the life of Danny Akin was passed from one generation to the next. Today, his grandchildren bear the names Elliot and Judson—also the names of famous missionaries.

It is fitting that he is also ensuring that his passion for the nations extends beyond his life and ministry. Beyond teaching his children and grandchildren about the Great Commission, he funded and supported their missions. Several years ago, he started a mission fund for his grandchildren. Every month, a little money is designated to give his grandchildren the opportunity to serve the Lord in another culture after high school. He does not intend to only teach his children and grandchildren about the Great Commission—he is committed to fund and support their going to the nations.

"Make disciples . . ."

The central imperative of the commission is not to make converts; it is to make disciples. Danny Akin is not just concerned with decisions for Jesus, but also with Christ's people submitting to his lordship. This lordship will be apparent to all one day but now is confessed and lived out in the lives of the King's own. To that end, our father has devoted his life to seeing men and women shaped into disciples of Jesus Christ.

Danny Akin has trained scores of people for gospel ministry through the local church and through formal theological education in SBC seminaries. Many of those students are serving as pastors, missionaries, and leaders in North America and around the world. Yet without hesitation, he would state that his priority in ministry was always first his own family. In other words, discipleship started in the home with his wife and children.

He writes in *Raising Kids with a Heart for Mission* that "obeying the Great Commission should begin in the home, though it should certainly not end there."[1] Danny Akin was entrusted by God to shepherd a wife and four sons. For him, disciple making would begin with those five people. Prayerfully before the Lord, he strived to model and demonstrate what it really means to follow Jesus Christ.

He writes, "Most children look up to, admire, and follow in their parents' footsteps. What you love they will love. What you value they will value. What you have a passion for, they will have a passion for. After all, you are their heroes!"[2] All of us learned how to be disciples by watching our dad. All of us learned how to pray for the nations by watching our dad. All of us learned how to share the gospel, teach and love the Bible, disciple people, and engage in Great Commission work by watching our father.

". . . baptizing . . ."

Believer's baptism is the visible sign associated with someone becoming a follower of Christ. Our father has been a staunch defender of this integral part of the commission. He devoted his ministry to being a Baptist theologian because he believes a plain reading of the text demands it. Baptism is applied only to believers because this command testifies to a believer's new birth and union with Christ in his death, burial, and resurrection. He believes in immersion because it can re-enact that death and resurrection. He believes the church testifies to the baptized that they are sinners who deserve death but, by virtue of their faith in Jesus Christ, what is true of Christ is now true of them. They already died, they have already been buried, and they have already been raised to walk in new life. Thus, this sign should only be given to those who are disciples.

---

[1] Daniel Akin, *Raising Kids with a Heart for Mission* (Leyland, UK: 10 Publishing, 2020), 8.

[2] Akin, 9.

Not only does he hold this conviction theologically, but he carried out baptism of disciples personally with us, his four sons. We were blessed with parents who read the Bible and shared the gospel with us most nights. As a result, my dad had the blessing of leading us as children to saving faith in Jesus.

On a Sunday morning in Dallas, Texas, at the Audelia Road Baptist Church, two of us (Nathan and Jonathan) decided during the invitation to trust Jesus as Savior. We were young, so our dad took his time to make sure we understood what was happening. He said, "Let's go home, eat lunch, take a nap, and then, if you still want to talk about this, come out to my study and let's talk." We did, and after he explained the gospel more carefully to us, we trusted Christ. Next, he took his time in assessing our spiritual state and making sure we understood the nature of baptism. Then, he baptized us. Paul and Tim also both trusted Christ on the same day and were baptized together by dad.

". . . teaching them to observe [obey] . . ."

Discipleship is connected to sanctification, and sanctification is connected to teaching. Jesus says, "[Father,] sanctify them in the truth, your Word is truth" (John 17:17). This saying of Jesus is consistent with his command in the Great Commission. Our father is committed in this regard.

Danny Akin has embodied this part of the commission as an excellent teacher. He has committed his life to preaching books of the Bible in the local church. Through the Wednesday night Bible study at his church, he has preached through numerous books of the Bible, including Genesis, Ruth, Nehemiah, Psalms, Song of Songs, Daniel, Jonah, and the entire New Testament except for Luke's Gospel. He has also committed himself to being a theologian in the academy, a journey that included seminary, then a doctor of philosophy from a university, before becoming a theological educator. We can remember running into his home study, walking into our basement, or stepping in his bedroom, and most of the time he had a book and highlighter in hand, studying to show himself approved.

However, Dad is more than an intellectual theologian and teacher in the church and the academy: he is a practical instructor who used our home as the classroom. From the time we were young boys, our father taught us much about theology, the Bible, Jesus, and the church. The instruction that was most impactful was our father's instruction in having the right priorities. He taught us this early and often. It has been said that repetition is the mother of all learning. Like a coach, our father looked for teachable moments to remind us to order our lives according to God's design.

First, he instilled in us the priority to love Jesus. He would often say, "Boys, if you put Jesus first, if he is Number One in your life, then all of the other priorities will fall into place." He taught us to love the Lord with all our heart, mind, soul, and strength. He taught this and he modeled it. I can remember all four of us running with him one day at a track. On the last lap he sprinted as fast as he could. When we were finished, we asked him, "How did you finish like that?" I will never forget his words: "If Jesus could suffer for me on the cross for hours, I can suffer for a few minutes." Danny Akin has committed his life to making Jesus his top priority and passed this down to his sons.

Next, Dad taught us the importance of loving our wives. For nearly three decades, Danny Akin has traveled the country teaching and preaching about marriage and family. As his sons, we can say that he practices what he preaches. He has been a faithful and committed husband to our mother for nearly five decades, and he has loved her as Christ loved the church. He taught us to do the same.

The third priority he taught was to be fathers who love their children. He can eloquently expound Ephesians 6:1–4 and mine the deep biblical riches in that wonderful text, but his most powerful teaching was his unconditional love for each of his sons. We are often asked,

"What is it like to be Danny Akin's son? Is it a burden?" Our answer has never wavered. We always respond, "Being his son is a privilege that I do not take lightly." He disciplined out of love and with the purpose of correction and restoration. He was patient, kind, and gracious. All four of us now have children of our own, and by God's grace, we have a wealth of knowledge from simply watching our dad over the years.

Finally, Dad prioritized love for the local church and her mission. Danny Akin has been in Christian ministry for nearly five decades. He has experienced the good, the bad, and the ugly of the church. However, he never—and we mean ever—brought dissension or conflict issues into our home. He shielded us so that we could grow up to love the bride of Christ. All four Akin boys are in Christian ministry today in large part because of the example set by our father.

A work honoring our father would be incomplete without also honoring his wife and our mother, Charlotte Akin. Dad has instructed aspiring ministers for years on the importance of choosing the right spouse. He said, "A great woman can take a mediocre man and make him great, but a mediocre woman can take a great man and make him mediocre." Our mom is that great woman! Danny Akin would not be the man he is without her. We would not be the men we have become without her loving and instructive care. She has modeled Christlike service to us and to others time and again. She has been Dad's helpmate from the time he was in Bible college until becoming a seminary president. She has been a constant source of encouragement and counsel—even reminding him kindly, following his Sunday sermon on Philippians 2 and *kenosis,* to teach the Bible in a way the entire congregation can understand. We are so thankful to contribute to this work that honors our mother as well as our father. We love them very much.

We write this introduction in hopes that you will be confident that Danny Akin is personally and privately the person that you see publicly. We believe he is rightly honored by this work. In an era when church leaders fail and scandals regularly challenge the church's reputation, know that our dad is who he appears to be. He loves Jesus. He is a theologian. He is a practitioner. He is a preacher. He is a professor. He is an author. He is a grandad. He is a missionary.

Danny Akin has lived his life in service to the cause of the Great Commission. He has lived under the authority of the Lordship of Jesus Christ. He has gone to the nations. He has made disciples. He has baptized us and taught us to obey the commands of Christ.

He has passed this on to his sons, and by God's grace we are now passing this on to our children, students, and members of our local churches. We do not miss the kindness of the Lord in this recalling. He has taught countless seminary students. He has taught countless pastors. Yet the greatest beneficiaries of his love of the Great Commission have been the four of us. We pray we steward it well!

CHAPTER ONE

THE BIBLE AND THE GREAT COMMISSION

Charles L. Quarles

Danny Akin has often described the Great Commission that appears in Matt 28:18–20 as the "final marching orders of King Jesus" to his church. This Great Commission is the primary inspiration for the efforts of the churches that form the Southern Baptist Convention. Under Dr. Akin's leadership, the Great Commission has become a central focus of the mission of Southeastern Baptist Theological Seminary, which exists to equip students "to serve the church and fulfill the Great Commission."

This fervor to fulfill the Great Commission is necessary for genuine Christian living. The Great Commission is no novel idea that only occurred to the Lord Jesus in the final moments of his earthly ministry. God's passion for the nations pulses throughout the whole Bible, the books of Moses, the Prophets, the Psalms, the Gospels, Acts, the Epistles, and the book of Revelation. God's love for the nations is apparent throughout biblical history, and the salvation of the nations is clearly part of his eternal plan for his world.[1]

The Old Testament and the Great Commission

Although the Old Testament focuses primarily on God's relationship to Israel, there is evidence in all major sections of the Old Testament of his intention to save people of all nations. The theme especially stands out in the direct messianic prophecies. God loudly and clearly announced his intention to include the nations in his redemptive plan in even the earliest books of the Hebrew Scriptures.

Books of Moses

The books of Moses promise the coming of an "offspring," a personal descendant of important figures in Israel's history. This "seed" of Adam and Eve (Gen 3:15) is identified with increasing specificity in the Pentateuch.[2] He is the "seed" of Abraham (Gen 22:17), of Isaac (Gen 26:4), of Jacob (Gen 28:14; Num 24:15–19), and of Judah (Gen 49:8–12). These prophecies repeatedly insist that this descendent will be one "by whom all nations of the earth will be blessed." This promise made first to Abraham is restated to Isaac, and then again to Jacob. The restatement of this promise elevates it to a place of prominence. The promise of God's blessing through the Messiah on "all nations of the

---

[1] For more detailed examination of the Great Commission in biblical theology, see the excellent treatments in Daniel Akin, Benjamin Merkle, and George Robinson, *40 Questions about the Great Commission* (Grand Rapids: Kregel Academic, 2020), 207–68.

[2] See Daniel Block, "My Servant David: Ancient Israel's Vision of the Messiah," in *Israel's Messiah in the Bible and the Dead Sea Scrolls*, ed. Richard S. Hess and M. Daniel Carroll R. (Grand Rapids: Baker Academic, 2003), 56.

earth" demonstrates that God's kindnesses and mercies to Israel are not exclusive. God loves the people of all nations.

Examples reinforce God's compassion for people of other nations in the Pentateuch. The account of Sodom and Gomorrah is typically remembered for God's outpouring of wrath on Gentiles. But remember, too, that Abraham interceded urgently on their behalf and God would have spared the cities if only ten righteous people could be found in them (Gen 18:16–33). God's compassion to people of other nations continues throughout Genesis with the healing of Abimelech's family (Gen 20:17–18). God showed mercy to Hagar, Sarah's Egyptian slave, by hearing her "cry of affliction" and sparing the lives of her and her son Ishmael (Gen 16:1, 11). This foreign woman, despised by Sarah, praised Yahweh as "El-roi," that is, "the One who sees me" (Gen 16:13). Through Joseph's revelatory dream in prison (Gen 41), God exalted Joseph and spared Israel from starvation; it also saved the nation of Egypt from certain death in the seven-year famine that struck the whole land. Thus, the very first book of the Bible powerfully displays God's compassion, not only to his chosen people, but to the other nations as well, even peoples such as the Canaanites, who later emerge in the biblical narrative as the Israelites' archenemy. Abraham's intercession for the people of Sodom and Gomorrah and for Abimelech serve as models to Israel in its mission as a light to the nations.

Prophets

The theme of God's love for the nations is even more explicit and pronounced in the Old Testament prophets. In fact, the writings of the Prophets are so rich with references to God's love for and intention to save the nations that space will not permit a full exploration here. We must limit our attention to just one of the prophets, Isaiah, chosen since this book stands at the head of the major prophets.

Isaiah 2 records a vision of the prophet in which he beholds what will occur "in the last days" (Isa 2:2). The vision reveals that "all nations will stream" to the Lord's house to learn from him. God will teach the nations "about his ways" so they may "walk in his paths" (Isa 2:3). God will also establish peace among the nations so they reforge their swords and spears into farming tools and "they will never again train for war" (Isa 2:4). The great messianic promise in Isa 11:1–10 confirms that the Messiah will guide "the nations" (Isa 11:10). Yet other texts promise that he will "bring justice to the nations" (Isa 42:1) and "establish justice on earth" (Isa 42:4).

Perhaps the clearest and most striking description in Isaiah of God's love for the nations appears in the messianic prophecy in Isaiah's second Servant Song (Isa 49:1–6). The Messiah will restore national Israel (Isa 49:5). Thus, Yahweh remained committed to his promise to Abraham to gather both through the great nation that would come from Abraham and the nations that would be blessed through his seed. It is "not enough" for him to merely raise up the tribes of Jacob. Yahweh promises: "I will also make you a light for the nations, to be my salvation to the ends of the earth" (Isa 49:6b). This salvation is clearly a spiritual salvation, and it also has implication for the life one lives. The cry, "This is our God . . . and he has saved us" (Isa 25:9) shows that this salvation entails destroying death (Isa 25:8) and wiping every tear from the eyes of his people (Isa 25:8). This salvation involves the forgiveness of iniquity and the healing of all sickness (Isa 33:22, 24; see 35:4–6); the removal of shame (Isa 45:17; see Isa 42:17; 44:9, 11); and the justification and glorification of God's people (Isa 45:22–25).

The Song of the Suffering Servant (Isa 52:13–53:12) explains how God will grant salvation to the nations. The Messiah who "was pierced because of our rebellion, crushed because of our iniquities," who died as a "guilt offering" that "bore the sin of many," will also "sprinkle many nations" (Isa 52:15). This sprinkling is a priestly act that purifies and cleanses the nations so that they may approach God.

This brief treatment limited to just one prophetic book barely scratches the surface of this important prophetic theme. Other important messianic prophecies declare that the Messiah's kingdom will include "all the nations that bear my name" (Amos 9:11–12) and that "those of every people, nation, and language" will serve the Son of Man (Dan 7:14).

Psalms

The messianic psalms continue this theme by proclaiming that the Messiah will crush the rebellion of the nations against his authority with an iron scepter (Ps 2:9). God promises the Anointed One "Ask of me, and I will make the nations your inheritance and the ends of the earth your possession" (Ps 2:8). Although the psalm strongly warns of the consequences of defying the Messiah's authority, it also promises "All who take refuge in him are happy" (Ps 2:12), and this "all" clearly includes the nations, peoples, kings, and rulers, and very ends of the earth mentioned in the preceding context.

Yet another messianic psalm confirms that the Messiah's kingdom will include people of all nations:

> May he rule from sea to sea and from the Euphrates to the ends of the earth. May desert tribes kneel before him and his enemies lick the dust. May the kings of Tarshish and the coasts and islands bring tribute, the kings of Sheba and Seba offer gifts. Let all kings bow in homage to him, all nations serve him. (Ps 72:8–11)[3]

---

[3] For a more detailed discussion of these important OT texts and others, see John Hammett and Charles L. Quarles, *The Work of Christ*, Theology for the People of God (Nashville: B&H Academic, forthcoming).

The New Testament and the Great Commission

In the New Testament, the familiar theme of God's love for the nations and his desire to save them escalates. Just as the horn blast from an oncoming vehicle increases in volume and rises in pitch as it approaches, the declaration of God's passion for the peoples of the world increases in volume, pitch, and frequency as we turn to the New Testament. Literally, from the very first chapter of the New Testament to the very last, God announces his intention to save the nations.

Matthew

It is an understatement to say that the very first chapter of the New Testament announces God's intention to save the nations. That intention is proclaimed in the very first *verse* of the first New Testament book. Matthew 1:1 presents Jesus as "son of Abraham." Matthew is not merely describing Jesus as a true Israelite. He is identifying Jesus as the promised "seed" or "offspring" of Abraham through whom all nations on earth will be blessed in fulfillment of the promises to Abraham (Gen 12:3; 22:17), Isaac (Gen 26:4), and Jacob (Gen 28:14).

It is no accident that Matthew then includes only four mothers (other than Mary) in Jesus's genealogy (Matt 1:3, 5, 6). These mothers serve as representatives of the nations because they all share a Gentile identity. Tamar and Rahab were Canaanites. Ruth was a Moabite. Bathsheba may seem to break this pattern since she was an Israelite. However, rather than identifying Bathsheba by name, Matthew identifies her as the wife of Uriah, who is well-known as a Hittite (2 Sam 11:3, 6, 17, 21, 24; 12:9–10; 23:39; 1 Kgs 15:5; 1 Chron 11:41) and thus assumes a Hittite identity herself. Matthew likely mentions these four women, and only these, to emphasize the presence of Gentiles in Jesus's family line and to hint that "his people," whom Jesus came to save from their sins (Matt 1:21), includes Gentiles from among the nations.

Even in his infancy, Jesus draws Gentiles from distant lands to worship him. Although the chief priests and scribes are told of the Messiah's birth and know from the Mic 5:2 prophecy that he is born in Bethlehem, they are unwilling to travel a few miles to seek the infant Christ. However, the magi from the East, representatives of the pagan Gentile world, travel an enormous distance to worship Jesus and offer him their treasures (Matt 2:1–12).

John the Baptist attacks the notion that the coming Messiah provides salvation exclusively for Israelites by exclaiming, "Don't presume to say to yourselves, 'We have Abraham as our father.' For I tell you that God is able to raise up children for Abraham from these stones" (Matt 3:9). The implication is clear—if God can transform mere stones into members of the covenant people, he can surely incorporate repentant and believing Gentiles into his family as well.

The theme of Gentile inclusion in the people of God continues in Matt 4:15–16, which quotes the messianic prophecy found in Isa 9:1–2. Jesus intentionally chose to locate his ministry headquarters in "Galilee of the Gentiles" and near the major highway heavily trafficked by Gentile caravans to reach Gentiles with his miracles and his message. It was no accident that the news about him spread throughout Syria (Matt 4:24) and that people from the ten Gentile cities that composed the Decapolis (Matt 4:25) began to follow Jesus almost as soon as his ministry began.

In Matt 8:5–13, yet another representative of the nations approaches Jesus, a Roman centurion. Amazingly, Jesus offers to break a Jewish taboo by entering the Gentile's home (Matt 8:7; Acts 10:28). Jesus exclaimed that this Gentile had a faith stronger than any he had observed in any Israelite. He explained that this man was representative of many from among the nations who would enter his kingdom together with the Old Testament patriarchs: "Many will come from east and west to share in the banquet with Abraham, Isaac, and Jacob in the kingdom of heaven" (Matt 8:11). In Matt 11:20–24 Jesus indicts the people of Galilean cities and villages by insisting that if notoriously wicked Gentile cities like Tyre, Sidon, and even Sodom had witnessed Jesus's miracles, they would have repented eagerly and escaped divine judgment.

Matthew 12:17–21 identifies Jesus as the fulfillment of Isaiah's first Servant Song (Isa 42:1–4), which climaxes with the promise that "the nations will put their hope in his name." Matthew 12:41–42 identifies the people of Nineveh and Sheba as examples of these hopeful Gentiles for they will stand up in eschatological judgment to accuse and condemn the scribes and Pharisees who rejected Jesus.

In Matt 15:21–28 a Canaanite woman confesses Jesus as Messiah and as Lord in a manner that implies her recognition of Jesus's deity. Though the Canaanites were the most hated enemies of Israel in the Old Testament, Jesus praises the woman's faith: "Woman, your faith is great" (Matt 15:28). When Jesus goes on to describe the judgment of the nations, he assigns their destiny based on how these nations have treated his disciples, not based on their descent from Abraham (Matt 25:31–46). The implication is that people of any nation who accept Jesus's messengers and the gospel of the kingdom they bear will receive eternal life. But people of any nation who reject these messengers and their message, including Israelites, will "go away into eternal punishment" (Matt 25:46).

Finally, as Jesus suffers on the cross, the Israelite criminals crucified beside him, the chief priests, the scribes, and the elders all mock Jesus's claim to be the Son of God. But in the climactic confession of the Gospel of Matthew, the Roman centurion and other Roman soldiers who supervised Jesus's crucifixion affirm the very truth that the Israelites mocked: "Truly this man was the Son of God" (Matt 27:54). Just as representatives of the nations (the magi) are the first to worship Jesus in this Gospel, they (the Roman soldiers) are the last to confess his identity as God's Son, thus unwittingly agreeing with the confession that the Father himself made at Jesus's baptism and transfiguration.

The magi are examples of those who come from the East and the Romans are examples of those who come from the West who will sit down with the Old Testament patriarchs at the great messianic banquet (Matt 8:11).

Consequently, when Jesus commands his disciples to "Go and make disciples of all nations," neither they nor Matthew's readers should be surprised. God's love for the nations and his intention to save people from groups all over the world are writ large through this entire Gospel. The Great Commission is the great culmination of this redemptive theme.[4]

Luke–Acts

The Gospel of Luke and the book of Acts are separated from each other by the Gospel of John in our NT canon. However, they were originally two volumes of a single work by the same author. Both volumes stress God's intention to save people from all nations.

When Jesus preached his first sermon in the synagogue of his hometown of Nazareth, he strongly implied his plan to serve and save people of other nations. He pointed out that Elijah was sent to aid a widow in Zarephath in Sidon rather than the widows of Israel. Elisha was sent to cleanse a Syrian leper, rather than Israelite lepers. These statements indicated that his ministry was not primarily for the benefit of people in his hometown or even his home nation. The people responded with murderous outrage (Luke 4:24–30).

In a parable unique to Luke's Gospel (Luke 10:25–37), Jesus makes a non-Israelite, a despised Samaritan, the hero of the story. A

---

[4] For a more detailed treatment of this theme in Matthew, see Charles L. Quarles, *Matthew*, Evangelical Biblical Theology Commentary (Bellingham, WA: Lexham, 2023), 97–100; and *A Theology of Matthew: Jesus Revealed as Deliverer, King, and Incarnate Creator*, Explorations in Biblical Theology (Phillipsburg, NJ: P&R, 2013), 99–132.

Samaritan receives another positive reference in Luke 17:16. Of ten lepers healed by Jesus at once, only the Samaritan (apparently the others were Israelites) praised God, worshipped Jesus, and expressed sincere gratitude to him. Jesus replied, "Didn't any return to give glory to God except this foreigner?" (Luke 17:18).

Finally, Luke 24:46–47 contains a statement roughly parallel to the Great Commission in Matthew. Jesus says that the Old Testament Scriptures foretold that "repentance for forgiveness of sins would be proclaimed in his [the Messiah's] name to all the nations, beginning at Jerusalem." Jesus's disciples were responsible for this proclamation.

Luke elaborates further on Jesus's statement at the beginning of Acts. After being empowered for their ministry by the Holy Spirit, the eleven disciples "will be my witnesses in Jerusalem, in all Judea and Samaria, and to the ends of the earth" (Acts 1:8). This statement identifies the broad contours of the book of Acts. By Acts 5:28, the Sanhedrin charges the disciples with this indictment: "You have filled Jerusalem with your teaching." By Acts 8:25, Philip and the disciples had preached the gospel throughout Samaria. The remainder of the book of Acts is focused primarily on the missionary journeys of Paul, which carry the gospel to Cyprus, Syria, Asia Minor, Greece, and finally to Rome. From Rome, the capital of a worldwide empire, the gospel will quickly spread to the ends of the earth. Paul's final words in the book of Acts declare: "Let it be known to you that this salvation of God has been sent to the Gentiles; they will listen." Paul did not just insist that the offer of salvation would be proclaimed throughout the nations. He asserted confidently that it would receive a glad acceptance there. For the same prophecies that lamented Israel's hardness of heart promised that the nations would repent and worship the one true God and bow before his Messiah.

The book of Acts clearly identifies several of the Old Testament prophecies that foretell the salvation of the nations. In his sermon at Solomon's colonnade in the temple, Peter identified Jesus as the promised seed of Abraham through whom all the nations on earth will be blessed (Acts 3:25–26). After his rooftop vision taught him that no person is unclean (10:1–16), Peter was reminded that "all the prophets testify about him [Jesus] that through his name everyone [including people from other nations like the Roman centurion Cornelius] who believes in him receives forgiveness of sins" (10:43). The Jerusalem Conference, where the church affirmed the inclusion of Gentile believers and sought to remove barriers to their conversion and fellowship with Jewish Christians, was moved by personal testimony from Peter, Barnabas, and Paul. But the deciding factor seems to have been James's quotation of the Old Testament (15:15–18; see Amos 9:11–12; Isa 45:21), which promised that in the reign of the Messiah "the rest of humanity may seek the Lord—even all the Gentiles who are called by my name."

Paul's address to the Athenian philosophers of the Areopagus expresses this theme of Acts very well. God made "every nationality to live over the whole earth" and assigned them to various regions "so that they might seek God, and perhaps they might reach out and find him, though he is not far from each one of us" (Acts 17:26–27). Consequently, through the gospel, God now commands "all people everywhere to repent" (17:30). The command to be witnesses "to the ends of the earth" (1:8) is intended to send the gospel to all those who need to repent, the group Paul defines as "all people everywhere."

Paul

As we might expect, the passion for the nations that characterizes Paul's ministry in the book of Acts is prominent in Paul's letters as well. Paul, the great "apostle to the Gentiles," is well-known for his fervor in fulfilling the Great Commission. Through his missionary journeys, he, more than anyone else described in the New Testament, labored to make disciples of all nations. As Paul introduces himself to the church at Rome, he explains: "We have received grace and apostleship through Him to bring about the obedience of faith among all the nations, on behalf of his name" (Rom 1:5). He also concludes his letter with a reference to "the command of the eternal God to advance the obedience of faith among all the Gentiles" (Rom 16:26). It is this commission and command that compelled Paul to preach the gospel "from Jerusalem all the way around to Illyricum" and "to preach the gospel where Christ has not been named" (Rom 15:19–20).

In the final years of his ministry, Paul summarized the great "mystery of godliness" in only six short simple phrases (1 Tim 3:16). His passion for the Great Commission is apparent in the fact that two of the six phrases focus on humanity at large: Christ was "preached among the nations, believed on in the world."

Paul made no apologies for this focus on the nations. He recognized that worldwide mission required by the ancient promise that Abraham and his promised descendant, the Messiah, would bless "all the nations" (Gal 3:8). He appealed to numerous Old Testament passages to demonstrate Israel's responsibility to proclaim God among the nations and God's desire to save the nations. For example, Rom 15:9–12 cites 2 Sam 22:50; Ps 18:49; Deut 32:43; Ps 117:1; Isa 11:10. Romans 15:21 adds Isa 52:15 (see Rom 9:24–25 citing Hos 2:23) to argue that God's grace extends far beyond the nation of Israel to all the Gentile nations.

God's love for the nations was galvanizing for Paul. The gospel simply could not be hidden and hoarded by a few. The message had to be shouted from the rooftops. Missionary service was necessary because "in Christ, God was reconciling the world to himself" (2 Cor 5:19). Worldwide evangelization was essential because "the grace of God has appeared, bringing salvation for all people" (Titus 2:11). Carrying the gospel to the nations was mandatory since "God our Savior . . . wants everyone to be saved and to come to the knowledge of the truth" (1 Tim 2:3–4).

John

Although the Gospel and Letters of John do not use the term "nations," this does not imply his lack of concern for the many peoples of the earth. In John's writings, the term "world" sometimes functions as a close synonym to "nations." Although "world" sometimes refers to humanity standing in rebellion against God, "that which is hostile to God, i.e., lost in sin, wholly at odds with anything divine, ruined and depraved,"[5] it may also refer to humanity in general, people from all nations, cultures, and linguistic groups. This latter meaning is the clear sense in some of the most soaring descriptions of divine love and Christ's saving work in John's writings.

John 1:29 quotes the declaration of John the Baptist: "Here is the Lamb of God, who takes away the sin of the world!" (CEV). The declaration must have been startling to the "Jews from Jerusalem" and the "priests and Levites" who attended John's baptism (1:19). The Passover lamb (Exod 12:1–28), the lambs offered in the daily morning and twilight offerings (Exod 29:38–46), and the lambs presented as a sin offering (Lev 4:32) were presented for the benefit of Israelites specifically. However, John likely derived his description of the Messiah as a sacrificial "lamb" from Isa 52:13–53:12 and noticed that the messianic sacrificial lamb would "sprinkle many nations," i.e., the people of the world. Furthermore, John the Baptist is associated with Isa 40:3 in all four Gospels and John himself recognized that he was the "voice of one crying out in the wilderness" to prepare the way of the Lord (John 1:23). John had undoubtedly studied that prophecy with extreme care and noted that when "the glory of the Lord will appear," then "all humanity together will see it" (Isa 40:5). The LXX translated this last clause: "and everyone will see the salvation of God" (see Luke 3:6). Based on such

---

[5] "κόσμος," BDAG, 562.

prophecies, John knew well that God was extending salvation to all the peoples of the world.

John 3:16 describes the incarnation of Christ and the sacrifice of his Son as the supreme expression of God's love for the world, and he adds (3:17; see 12:47; 1 John 2:2) that God sent the Son "to save the world." Here the term "world" is inclusive of all humanity since the purpose of the Son's sacrifice was that "everyone who believes in him will not perish but have eternal life." Two texts strongly suggest that John uses the term "world" to demonstrate God's inclusion of peoples other than Israel in his plan for salvation. In John 4:1–42, Jesus showed kindness and offered the gift of the Spirit and eternal life to a sinful Samaritan woman even though "Jews do not associate with Samaritans" (John 4:9). After Jesus stayed in the homes of the Samaritans for two days, many of them believed and confessed that Jesus "really is the Savior of the world" (John 4:42). The confession apparently means that Jesus is not merely the Savior of sinners from within the nation of Israel, but even believing Samaritans as well.

Similarly, in John 12:19 the Pharisees complain: "Look—the world has gone after him!" (ESV). This seems to be an instance of Johannine irony in which John recognizes that the Pharisees spoke far more accurately than they realized.[6] Although the "world" to which the Pharisees intended to refer was merely the crowds of Jewish believers gathered in Jerusalem for Passover, the very next verse (12:20) records that "some Greeks" who were at the festival approached Philip and exclaimed, "Sir, we want to see Jesus" (12:21). John is signaling that the "world" that will follow Jesus includes Jews, Samaritans, and even Greeks.

Even though John does not use the term κόσμος (*kosmos*, "world") in the book of Revelation, the concept is pervasive throughout the book. John's use of "world" becomes even clearer when we examine the final

[6] J. Ramsey Michael, *The Gospel of John*, New International Commentary on the New Testament (Grand Rapids: Eerdmans, 2010), 683.

writing of John, the book of Revelation. Revelation not only describes Jesus's rule and authority over the nations (Rev 2:26; 12:5; 13:7) and his judgment of the nations (Rev 19:15), but it also confirms that the Lamb of God who takes away the sin of the world (John 1:29) will be slaughtered to redeem people for God "from every tribe and language and people and nation" (Rev 5:9). Revelation also insists that "a vast multitude from every nation, tribe, people, and language" will worship the Lamb (Rev 7:9; cf. 15:3–4). This redemption of the nations and worship by the nations is possible because the "eternal gospel" is announced "to the inhabitants of the earth—to every nation, tribe, language, and people" (Rev 14:6). The book of Revelation concludes with the nations walking by the glory of God and the lamp of the Lamb (Rev 21:23–24) and bringing their honor and glory into the new Jerusalem (Rev 21:26). The final chapter of Revelation, which is also the final chapter of the Christian Scriptures, promises a new tree of life, fed by the river of the water of life, whose leaves "are for the healing of the nations" (Rev 22:2).

This background informs the meaning of Jesus's description of his commission to his disciples in John 17:18: "As you sent me into the world, I also have sent them into the world." The "world" into which and for which Jesus sent his disciples consists of every nation, culture, and linguistic group in humanity. Thus, the worldwide mission of Jesus's disciples in John parallels the Great Commission in Matthew and the similar commissions in Luke–Acts.

Conclusion

This brief essay has merely skimmed over the Scriptures to highlight a few of the many references to God's desire to save the nations, which prompts believers to obey the Great Commission. We have seen that God's love for the nations and his desire to save the peoples of the world flows through the Books of Moses, the Prophets, the Psalms, the Synoptic Gospels and Acts, the letters of Paul, and John's writings, climaxing with the book of Revelation. Even this cursory treatment is sufficient to demonstrate that the priorities of the Great Commission are not relegated to a few isolated passages in the Bible. These themes are part of the warp and woof of the fabric of Scripture. To diminish the importance of the Great Commission is not merely to ignore a handful of texts but to eviscerate Scripture and reject a theme that permeates the Bible from its first book to its last. Thus, the mission of Southeastern Baptist Theological Seminary under Dr. Akin's leadership of equipping students to serve the church and fulfill the Great Commission is a legacy that all who love the Bible should respect and be thankful for—and a legacy that we should pray shall endure until Christ comes again.

CHAPTER TWO

EVANGELISM AND THE GREAT COMMISSION: ONE JOB

James Merritt

Introduction

I am grateful and honored that I was asked to contribute to a Festschrift for one of my dearest brothers in Christ, Dr. Danny Akin. I must begin with a background on how I got to know Dr. Akin. I had been invited to be the co-pastor at First Baptist Church of Dallas, Texas, with Dr. W. A. Criswell by the pastor search committee. For several reasons, I did not feel in my heart that it was the right thing to do and so I declined their gracious invitation.

Not long afterward I was invited to preach at Criswell College, where Dr. Akin was a professor. Before I got up to speak, this young (at the time) man walked up to me, stuck out his hand and said, "I want to meet the man who turned down the First Baptist Church of Dallas, Texas!" Little did I know that with this strange introduction I was meeting one of the very best friends I have on this planet. Little did I know that I would preach to the man who one day will preach my funeral, which presumes he will outlive me. I have told him, "Danny, if you don't come to my funeral, I will not come to yours!"

From that time, I have watched Dr. Akin rise through the academic ranks from right-hand man to another dear friend, Dr. Albert Mohler at Southern Seminary, to president of Southeastern Seminary, where he has done an outstanding job. I have had the honor and privilege of preaching in chapel there every year, which I do not take lightly. So, it is with both joy and enthusiasm that I am honored to contribute this chapter on Evangelism and the Great Commission. I join the others in giving honor to whom honor is due.

According to a recent survey, more than 15,000 leadership books have been published in the modern era.[1] Every so often a book comes along that offers something both so simple and so profound that it changes the way you think. One of those paradigm-shifters is Simon Sinek's 2009 book, *Start with Why: How Great Leaders Inspire Everyone to Take Action.*[2]

Sinek looked at the most innovative, influential, and profitable leaders of movements and companies in recent history. He found that people like Steve Jobs, Martin Luther King Jr., and the Wright Brothers all started by answering the question, "Why?" Why do we do what we do? Businesses would ask, "Why do people need this product, service, movement, or idea?" Sinek learned that you can influence human behavior in one of two ways: you can either manipulate it, or you can inspire it. The way to inspire it is to start with "Why?" and build everything else on that.

---

[1] "The Paradox of Leadership," Harvard Extension School, https://www.extension.harvard.edu/professional-developments/blog/paradox-leadership.

[2] Simon Sinek, *Start with Why: How Great Leaders Inspire Everyone to Take Action* (New York: Portfolio, 2009).

The twenty-first-century church needs to go back and answer the question, Why is there a church at all? Indeed, why did God come up with the idea of the church to begin with? Why is the church the central piece of God's plan for the world? We do not have to wonder what the answer to these questions is because it all goes back to one job that the founder of the church, the Lord Jesus Christ, has given to the church and therefore, every follower of Jesus. It is found in Matthew 28.

One of the many reasons I love Jesus is that he simplified the complicated where we tend to complicate the simple. He left planet Earth and ascended into heaven. He gathered eleven disciples who had spent three years of their lives with him and shared with them in basically two words what they needed to do with the rest of their lives and what their central focus must be. The raison d'être, if you will.

We are on top of a Galilean hillside. Jesus is giving his farewell address and saying his goodbyes when he gives his disciples one last commandment: "Go, therefore, and make disciples of all nations" (Matt 28:19). In two simple words, Jesus gave the church its marching orders. They are to make disciples. Calvin Coolidge once allegedly said, "The business of America is business." The business of the church is making disciples. It is the job of the church corporately and every follower of Jesus individually.

Jesus did not just give this job to pastors, preachers, professors, priests, or professionals. This one job is everyone's job. Jesus was talking to people of all stripes, all colors, all ethnicities, men, women, rich, and poor. We all have the same job, to make disciples. Yes, we are instructed to be salt and light in the world (Matt 5:13); we are to do all things for God's glory (1 Cor 10:31); and out of love for others, we are called to live for the good of our neighbors (1 Tim 6:17–19). In fulfilling these callings, we also acknowledge that we are not here to do good works and live honorable lives. We have been put here to make disciples. That is why the church is here. That is why, as followers of Jesus, you and I are here.

Now, this is a daunting task. This is the greatest assignment given to any organization or any individual in the planet's history. In fact, it never ceases to amaze me that Jesus did not give this job to angels or some supernatural spiritual beings. He gave it to us, his followers, and there is no plan B. In the Great Commission he also promised that we have three tools to enable us to carry out this job, and in such a way that though we will receive the blessing, God will get the glory.

We Have the Power of Jesus behind Us

All good leaders have something in common: they never assign responsibility without also enabling the power and the authority to do it. Jesus is not just a great leader—he is the perfect leader. He says to every one of his followers that we have the power and the authority to carry out this job. "Jesus came near and said to them, 'All authority has been given to me in heaven and on earth'" (Matt 28:18).

That word *all* is used three times in this passage. The first *all* tells why we can carry out the mission on which Jesus sends us. We go because the One who sends us has all authority. In Matthew's Gospel, Jesus is proclaimed as One with authority (Matt 9:6; 11:27; 20:22; 27:38), but Matthew 28:18 seems a definitive and distinct expression of his authority. Indeed, his resurrection less than two months before the Great Commission pronouncement ratified the authority he displayed in his earthly ministry. The claim to authority is illuminated by its connection to Dan 7:13–14, which states that the One who is like a son of man is given authority over all the nations. Through resurrection, God vindicated Jesus, who is now able to freshly affirm his authority in and over any and every circumstance "in heaven and on earth."[3]

---

[3] John Nolland, *The Gospel of Matthew: A Commentary on the Greek Text*, New International Greek Testament Commentary (Grand Rapids: Eerdmans, 2005), 1264–65.

We may have the power to do something, but without the authority, we cannot exercise the power. On the other hand, the authority to act, but not the power to do so means we cannot exercise the authority. Both the authority and the power are necessary. Jesus makes the incredible claim that he has all authority and all power in all the universe. His declaration in Matthew 28:18 is that he has the power and authority to complete his mission through his disciples. We go out on his mission knowing that we have been sent by the One with all authority and power. We share with a lost world that Christ is the only way to God; that people need to repent and believe in Jesus; and that forgiveness of sins and eternal life are available for those willing to take God's gift with confidence. The One who sends us is able to save those who believe in him.

The disciples must have been astounded at Jesus's claim. Without hesitation, he said he had all authority in heaven and earth. If he had said, "All authority in Jerusalem has been given to me," that would have been an extraordinary claim. Certainly, the chief priest, Pontius Pilate, and the Roman army would have a quite different opinion. He did not say "All power in Rome has been given to me," because certainly Caesar would have had a different idea. He went further than that. He said, "All authority from one end of the universe to the other belongs to me." Jesus is the CEO of the universe. He is in complete control of everything. He really does have the whole world in his hands!

He then vested in his followers the authority and power to do what he called us to do. Then, as any great leader should, he told them in detail about the job. For what, exactly, was this authority and this power given to us? The answer gives us the second tool we need to carry out the job.

We Have the Plan of Jesus before Us

Remember, Jesus was about to ascend into heaven, and he would not see his disciples physically again until his return. He was giving his final instructions to them then and to us now. As a church that seeks to follow Jesus's commands, we can decide *how* to pursue the mission Jesus gave us, but not *whether* to pursue the mission assigned to us. Jesus gave clear instructions for what the church is to do corporately and individually. The job description is expressed in one sentence and includes only one verb while describing three aspects of the job.

In the English translation, there appears to be more than one verb in the Great Commission, but in the Greek the only verb is the imperative "make disciples." But closely tied to this imperative are three participles, which break down this one job into three parts. First, we are commanded to be *going*: "Go, therefore . . ." (Matt 28:19). Whatever else we may do in life, we will never do our one job if we do not go. That word "go" is one of Jesus's favorite words, especially after the resurrection.

When the first women came to Jesus's tomb and saw it was empty, an angel told them Jesus was risen, then said, "Then go quickly and tell his disciples . . ." (Matt 28:7). They did not get far before they met Jesus himself. And what did he tell them? "Go and tell my brothers . . ." (Matt 28:10). When he met Mary Magdalene on the Road to Emmaus, he said, "Go to my brothers . . ." (John 20:17). Of the ten resurrection appearances Jesus made, five times the disciples are told to "go." Christianity is a faith on the go!

We followers of Jesus need to relearn that our primary job is not to gather at the church. Although we have a responsibility—a command—to assemble in church to worship the Lord together (Heb 10:24), the call is to challenge one another to live the life Jesus calls us to live. The mission of a follower of Jesus is to go out and to make disciples, bringing people into the church through baptism and teaching them to follow him (Matt 28:18–20). The only way we can obey this calling is to go out as the body of Christ and engage those who do not know Christ (see Acts 1:8).

The early church was not primarily concerned with church buildings. The contemporary church tends to think of the church's ministry activity as being in and around church buildings. This perspective can influence our thinking about the primary responsibilities of followers of Christ. We tend to think about "coming to church." So, I will say again: the primary responsibility of followers of Jesus is to go from the church to people outside the church who need the church! In Jesus's final marching orders to his disciples, he said, "Go therefore and make disciples of all nations" (Matt 28:19). We should not come to church to cool down. We should come to church to get fired up to go from the church and find people who do not go to church, then do all that we can to get them inside the church and make disciples of them.

Simply put, we come to church so we can go from church and be the church for people who do not even attend church.

That we "gather to go" is the point of the admonition in Hebrews. We assemble with the church so that we might be edified and equipped to go outside what the writer of Hebrews calls the "city's gates" (Heb 10:24–25; 13:12–16). This is why Jesus gifted the church with apostles, prophets, evangelists, pastors, and teachers (Eph 4:8–11), so they could invest in the lives of church members and equip them for the ministry (Eph 4:12). Jesus wants our feet to be covered with readiness for the gospel of peace so that we will share the good news (see Eph 6:15; Isa 52:7; Rom 10:15). We are compelled by this task because our Lord commissioned us for it and because those who do not know Christ cannot know him unless we tell them (see Matt 28:18–20; Rom 10:14–15).

Even as we go to church, we should be making disciples. We are first called to be a disciple, and then we are to be disciple-makers. Simply put, disciples are to make disciples. For those reading these words right now, one of two things is true about you: you either need to become a disciple or to become a disciple-maker. What Jesus spent the three years of his earthly ministry doing is the same thing we are to do while we are on earth.

The first step in making a disciple is getting a non-follower to follow Jesus. In other words, evangelism is the first part of our job of making disciples. Therefore, anybody who tries to separate evangelism from discipleship makes a false dichotomy. Evangelism and discipleship are Siamese twins, two sides of the same coin. Evangelism is the root of discipleship, but discipleship should be the fruit of all evangelism. That is why it is so important. Evangelism's goal is not making church attenders, or Baptists or Methodists or Presbyterians. It is not making good citizens or good people or well-behaved people. It is making disciples. The most common term used by both believers and unbelievers was "followers of Jesus." This way of life is exactly what Jesus called his disciples to (Matt 4:19), and it is the way of life that early Christians followed (Acts 9:1–2; 19:9, 23; 22:4; 24:14).

Everyone who is a true disciple, follower of Jesus, is a Christian, but not everyone who calls themselves a Christian in our day is a true disciple. We become disciples when we become followers of Jesus, and then our top job is to find non-followers of Jesus and turn them into followers of Jesus. Disciples make disciples who make disciples. But whom are we supposed to be making disciples of?

The answer is simple: "make disciples of all nations" (Matt 28:19). "All nations" means discrimination should have no place in the church. We should believe in amazing grace for every race. The word "nations" does not refer to countries or political states. It refers to ethnic, language, or cultural groups. In other words, the church is to be multicultural and multinational.[4] Everybody is a candidate to become a disciple, regardless of race, ethnicity, color, or nationality.

Sadly, only 16 percent of all congregations across all faith groups in America are multiethnic/multiracial, which is defined as "no one

---

[4] For a helpful overview of the use of *ethnos* in the Bible, see John Piper, *Let the Nations Be Glad!* (Grand Rapids: Baker, 2010), 177–224.

race making up more than eighty percent of the congregation."[5] Make no mistake: diversity is written into the job description that Jesus gave the church, and it is in the very DNA of the gospel.[6] It has been this way from the beginning. Now the good news is roughly 20 percent of Christians live in Africa; 20 percent in Asia; 20 percent in North America; and 20 percent in South America. Another major religion has 80 percent of its followers concentrated on one continent. Christianity is the most diverse faith moment in history. What is true globally needs to become truer of the local church. We are to be making disciples of all nations.

Becoming a faith follower of Jesus is only the beginning of a Christian life. The second participle in the Great Commission is "baptizing," which means the second part of our one job of making disciples is to baptize them. As we go and make disciples, we are to be "baptizing them in the name of the Father and of the Son and of the Holy Spirit" (Matt 28:19). Surprisingly this is really the first step a new disciple of Jesus is to take. Jesus's words "make disciples" are nearly next to "baptizing" in the same sentence.

Jesus clearly expected a follower to be baptized. In the Bible, when someone began following Jesus, he was immediately baptized, except for the thief on the cross. It is important to note the order Jesus gives for the steps to do the job. They are very specific and instructive. He did not say we are to baptize people, then teach them, and then make

---

[5] "Released! New 2020 Statistics on Multiracial Churches," Multiethnic Church, January 8, 2020, https://multiethnic.church/released-new-2020-statistics-on-multiracial-churches/.

[6] For a helpful recent treatment of this point, see Jarvis Williams's *Redemptive Kingdom Diversity: A Biblical Theology of the People of God* (Grand Rapids: Baker Academic 2021). In addition to demonstrating that multiethnicity is in the DNA of the gospel, Williams also clearly defines for us the categories ethnicity, race, and multi-ethnic. I am using the term "multiethnic" based on this helpful discussion.

disciples. He did not say we are to teach them, then baptize them, and then make disciples. He said we are to

Make Disciples → Baptize → Teach

Baptism is not just about water, and it is more than just getting wet, because Jesus goes on to say that we are to baptize people "in the name of the Father and of the Son and of the Holy Spirit" (Matt 28:19). Baptism is about one's identity becoming associated with the triune God, so that one's manner of life is transformed by following the teachings and the way of life that God requires of his people.

The baptized are baptized "into" the name of God. In short, they are identified by God himself as the "people of God" or the "body of Christ." Perhaps the best equivalent in Matthew's Gospel is found in Matt 18:20, where disciples come together in the name of Jesus, and in that process Jesus will be there with them. "In the name" communicates unity with Jesus in Matt 18:20 and unity with the triune God in Matt 28:19. These expressions in Matthew communicate the idea of solidarity with the one with authority. This implies a profound and unreserved allegiance, loyalty, submission, and willingness to follow.[7] Baptism is a picture of a disciple coming into the possession of God and entering his family. Baptism shows that we have entered the family of the *Father*, through the sacrifice of the *Son*, by the power of the *Holy Spirit* (see 1 Pet 1:2). And just like those who gather in a group of two or more in the name of Jesus have the promise that he will be present with them (Matt 18:20), those who are baptized in the name of the Father, Son, and Holy Spirit and are sent on his mission have the promise of his presence (Matt 28:20).

[7] Nolland, *The Gospel of Matthew*, 1268–69.

Jesus is letting us know that Christianity is not a Lone Ranger proposition. When you become a follower of Jesus, you agree to join his family; his family belongs in the church. That is why baptism is important. That is why baptism is crucial to the job. Our job is not in making disciples just to go after people outside the church, but to get people inside the church. And the point of entry is believer's baptism.

This brings us to the third participle in the Great Commission: teaching. We are not called to "dip them, dunk them, and drop them." After baptism is where the real work of discipleship truly begins because Jesus said of the baptized that we are to be "teaching them to observe everything I've commanded you . . ." (Matt 28:20). You might call the church the "graduate school" of Christianity because disciples are not just followers—they are learners. They are not just to learn truth, but they are to be taught to live truth.

We are to teach them to obey everything Jesus has commanded. Now that speaks pointedly to the church, not just of the twenty-first century, but of any century. Jesus never foresaw a time when anything he taught was irrelevant, superseded, outmoded, or untrue. Everything he taught then we are to teach now. What we learn, we are to live. Our belief is to determine our behavior.

It is a reminder that we are not just to preach and teach for information, but for transformation. Again, a disciple is not just someone who looks at truth or learns truth, but he lives truth. That is why Jesus was careful to say we are to teach everything *he commanded.* Today there is a lot of tiptoeing around truth and selective teaching. We talk about grace, but we will not talk about judgment. We talk about mercy, but we do not talk about justice. We want to talk about heaven, but not about hell.

The problem is that "lite" teaching and preaching produces "lite" disciples. Discipleship begins discipleship by faith in Jesus. One behaves like a disciple by following Jesus. Therefore, again, every disciple's job is to lead people to believe in Jesus and then to teach people to behave like Jesus. They go together. To summarize, we have one job broken into three different components. We are to get people to believe in Jesus (the first step to making disciples). Next, we are to get people to belong to Jesus (the second step, which is baptism). Then, we are to get people to be like Jesus (the third step, teaching them to obey his commands). To be clear, this is a difficult job. It is hard. It is frustrating and messy. It can be very discouraging. That is why we must remember we have one more tool at our disposal.

We Have the Presence of Jesus beside Us

Every time we *go*—whether it is going outside of our home, outside of our business, or outside of the church—we have this great promise of Jesus: "And remember, I am with you always, to the end of the age" (Matt 28:20). Jesus wanted those eleven men to know something that he wants us to know today. We are not on our own. We are not on an island. We are not by ourselves. We have not been thrown into the water without knowing how to swim or having a lifeguard right beside us in case we begin to sink. We have his presence. We have it particularly and prominently and personally when we are doing this one job.

In reflecting on my years of following Jesus, if you were to ask, "When have you most felt the presence of Jesus in your life?" I could honestly say I feel his presence most when I am sharing the gospel, when I am telling people about Jesus, when I am trying to get people to "trust and obey." I have never done it—ever—that I did not completely feel like Jesus was beside me.

Here is a great lesson I have learned. Jesus will be most real to you when you share that Jesus is most real with others. So, to every follower of Jesus and to every church that claims to be a New Testament church, we have but one job. It is for all places, for all time, and for all of us to carry out. The question is not, "How can we do this?" The question really is, "How can we not do this?" We must remember that we have his power behind us, his plan before us, and his presence beside us.

I will end with two stories, both from World War II. When America was strategizing with Great Britain on the best path to victory, there was a huge debate. Admiral Ernest King, being a navy man, argued that Japan was the primary enemy and the war effort should focus primarily on Japan. General George Marshall, who was the army man, was immovable in his conviction that the Allies should concentrate on Germany first. He refused to siphon off war materiel for the Pacific, instead prioritizing Germany. The reason was that Marshall was taught that the primary job of the commander was to select the main effort, the top job, and support that effort with every available resource. He was convinced the important effort was to defeat Germany, the country that started the war. The rest is history.

The second story is about a Japanese soldier. When Japan formally surrendered to the Allied powers on September 2, 1945, World War II was finally over for everyone on the planet except for Hiroo Onoda. He was a Japanese Army lieutenant stationed on the Philippine island of Lubang. Just two months before the surrender, he had been given clear orders from his superiors: stay and fight. He did just that for another twenty-nine years.

Onoda would raid villages for rice and meat and sometimes even kill people he still believed were enemy combatants. In 1974, he was finally persuaded to give up his guerrilla campaign only after his former commander was brought back to him to relieve him of his duty. When Onoda finally returned to Japan to a hero's welcome, reporters asked him what he had been thinking about for those twenty-nine years when he was the only one still fighting a war that was over. He simply replied, "Nothing but accomplishing my duty. All I thought about was carrying out my orders."[8]

---

[8] Robert D. McFadden, "Hiroo Onoda, Soldier Who Hid in Jungle for Decades, Dies at 91," *New York Times*, January 17, 2014, https://www.nytimes.com/2014/01/18/world/asia/hiroo-onoda-imperial-japanese-army-officer-dies-at-91.html.

We have much to learn from a general and an ordinary soldier. As Matt 28:19–20 has shown us, we have one job, and we need to support that job with every available resource we have until the job is done. Everything else is peripheral. Our one job is to make disciples. We have been given orders by our commander-in-chief, and they boil down to two words: "Make disciples." Unless and until those orders are changed—and they never will be—then until our commander returns, we are to devote ourselves to accomplishing our duty and carrying out our orders.

CHAPTER THREE

DISCIPLE MAKING AND THE GREAT COMMISSION

George G. Robinson

Introduction

My passion for disciple making is based, in part, on the fact that I was a beneficiary of it. Though I did not grow up in a Christian home, a student at the university I attended engaged me in a winsome conversation about the gospel. Soon after, I turned from my sin and trusted in Jesus. I was blessed to be discipled by a farmer who immediately taught me to follow Jesus and fish for men. He helped me to see that all of life, including my career as a public-school teacher, provided an opportunity to share the hope of the gospel. After teaching, coaching, and discipling high schoolers for nearly six years, I eventually felt called to serve cross-culturally.

My calling to the international mission field is what brought me to Southeastern Baptist Theological Seminary as a student in the summer of 1997. Dr. Danny Akin had recently left Southeastern to join the faculty of The Southern Baptist Theological Seminary. Though I did not meet him until he returned as president of Southeastern in 2004, his commitment to the Bible and to sound theology was well known throughout the Southern Baptist Convention. Not long after his return to serve as the president of Southeastern, God would inspire in him an unquenchable desire to transform Southeastern into a place where "every classroom would be a Great Commission classroom." Little did I know that a decade after attending Southeastern, I would be asked to return and join the faculty to help Dr. Akin build and expand that vision—a vision that continues to bear much fruit through current and former students serving all over the world.

Much has changed in the world over the past two decades. Skepticism regarding the Bible is as common in my backyard in Wake Forest now as it was in the cross-cultural settings I have worked in. The cross of Jesus, to much of the world, comes across as either a sentimental gesture with a sad ending or absolute foolishness. Skepticism regarding Jesus spans from the apathetic agnostic to the downright angry atheist. Much of the skepticism here in the West is rooted in the disparate and often incoherent messaging that Christians are sending. Our appalling cultural syncretism ties the gospel with secondary or even tertiary issues, leaving the message blurred. To be clear, the Bible addresses myriad issues, but we must not betray the foundational message of the Bible on the battlefield of our culture wars. My understanding the need for clarity only heightened when I was invited to serve under Akin's leadership. He helped me see that the world desperately needs to wrestle with the implications of the metanarrative of the Scriptures. God delivered the good news to the world, not merely in a few verses or even a small section of the Bible. He delivered it in context of that grandest of narratives that makes sense out of history broadly and of the significance of the cross specifically. Against this backdrop we see the good character of God displayed most profoundly in the cross of Christ.

As I began to interact with Dr. Akin and the faculty at Southeastern, I was challenged to explore how to faithfully proclaim the gospel in ways that might connect to those who do not have a biblical worldview. Akin's commitment to both systematic and biblical theology created an ethos that fueled my appreciation for the grand metanarrative and how the cross of Jesus is central to the entire story. According to Jesus in Luke 24, the cross was not a tragic accident where God had lost control of history. The resurrection made the cross "make sense" to those early disciples, so that their hearts were burning with understanding and passion. And their burning hearts led to burning lips that could not keep their serendipitous worldview shift to themselves. I believe that we communicate what we cherish. We will never communicate the gospel broadly until we cherish the gospel deeply. Luke documents how the disciples' familiarity with the person of Jesus had a seismic collision with the cosmic plan of redemption. Much to their surprise, redemption was not limited to social or political freedoms. The rescue experienced by the early disciples tore down the dividing wall between the secular and sacred, providing them entrance into a life of worship and obedience. The gospel still accomplishes that today, which should cause us to cherish and communicate.

At my first faculty workshop at Southeastern, Dr. Akin had us read Christopher Wright's *The Mission of God.* Wright's thesis states, "The Bible renders to us the story of God's mission through God's people in their engagement with God's world for the sake of the whole of God's creation."[1] As a new professor on the faculty of what was becoming a Great Commission seminary, I realized that the gospel saves us from sin, for God, into the church, and on to God's mission. I came to understand the gospel, evangelism, and disciple making in the light of the grand narrative under Dr. Akin's leadership. Therefore, the remainder of

---

[1] Christopher J. H. Wright, *The Mission of God: Unlocking the Bible's Grand Narrative* (Downers Grove, IL: IVP Academic, 2006), 22.

this chapter will survey the breathtaking true story of the whole world and make the connection to our call to make disciples of all nations.

There are four major plot movements in the Bible that address the four fundamental worldview questions. First, the Bible gives us the story of creation to answer the all-important question of how life began and where it finds its purpose. It also explains the story of the fall to show what went wrong in the world. Then, the story of the rescue is revealed as the answer to humanity's search for hope. And finally, the Bible tells the story of restoration to show what the future holds. G. K. Chesterton once mused, "I had always felt life first as a story; and if there is a story, then there's a storyteller."[2] God is the author and hero of the story. He who had no beginning was there in the beginning. We who were not there in the beginning desperately need to know him if we are ever to find meaning and purpose in life.

Creation

"In the beginning, God created" (Gen 1:1). God created all things with order, purpose, and direction. Genesis 1 presents the creation account as it might be viewed through a telescope—bringing the vastness of all that God made into view. Days one through three describe the realms God made: heavens, waters, earth/vegetation. Days four through six describe the inhabitants God made to fill those respective realms: sun, moon, and stars; fish, birds, animals, and humans. The crescendo of creation is humans, made "imago Dei." God made everything for his glory, but humans reflect God's goodness and glory in a unique way. He made humanity in his own image so that we could relate to him through worship and obedience.

If Genesis 1 provides a telescope view, then chapter 2 can be likened to a microscope—focusing on and magnifying God's relationship with

---

[2] G. K. Chesterton, *Orthodoxy* (Auckland: Floating Press, 2008), 90.

what he made, particularly our purpose as imagers. While the landscape of Genesis 1 is as vast as the universe, the landscape of Genesis 2 is a particular location known as Eden. It is there that God placed the first man and woman, establishing an ordered relationship between himself and them, and between them and the rest of creation. John Sailhamer, who taught at Southeastern years ago, noted that Gen 2:15 conveys the nature of our vertical and horizontal relationships: we were created to worship and obey God while cultivating what he entrusted to our care.[3] Perhaps this is partially why theologians like G. K. Beale believed that Eden was the original temple and Adam its priest.[4] But Adam was not to fulfill his purpose alone. He was given Eve, without whom he could not fulfill his broader purposes of spreading harmony and flourishing to the ends of the earth.

God's image bearers were to cultivate his created order toward flourishing by filling the entire earth with worshipers. In Genesis 1, after each creative act, God proclaimed his creation to be "good." But after entrusting the cultivation of it all to the first man and woman, he said the whole was "very good." The conditions for flourishing were in place, but humanity, as vice-regents, were meant to steward creation as an act of worship and obedience toward God. How? "God blessed them and said, 'Be fruitful and multiply and . . . subdue'" (Gen 1:28 ESV). They were to fill the earth with worship and obedience, bringing God's order and purpose to everything—the result of which would be flourishing or wholeness. And the creation account ends in a condition that, to a Hebrew in the days of Moses, would have seemed an unimaginable flourishing and harmony conveyed by the image of the first man and woman unclothed and yet unashamed.

---

[3] John Sailhamer, *Genesis Unbounded: A Provocative New Look at the Creation Account* (Colorado Springs: Dawson Media, 2011).

[4] G. K. Beale, *The Temple and the Church's Mission: A Biblical Theology of the Dwelling Place of God* (Downers Grove, IL: IVP Academic, 2004), 81–87.

While we are not told how long that Edenic harmony lasted, we are set up by the beauty of it all to ask, "If that's how good it was, then what went wrong?" To understand the answer to that question, we must step back to the pre-fall goodness of the garden in Genesis 2:16–17, where God gave Adam the parameters for his vice-regency, saying, "Eat [from these trees] . . . do not eat" from this one. The first couple were given unlimited possibilities for obedience, but only one possibility for disobedience. The Tree of Knowledge of Good and Evil mentioned in that passage had to be ontologically good because it was made to serve God's purposes. Everything God made was good, provided it remained in right relationship with him and subsequently functioned according to the purpose for which he made it. So if God made everything good, what went wrong?

Fall

In Gen 3:1, a new character in the story emerges as the plot moves from creation to fall. He enters the story as an antagonist described as "more crafty than any other beast of the field" (ESV). Notice that Moses does not explain where he came from. But the reader must assume that the serpent is indeed a created being. And if created, then he had to be good—at least initially. Much later in the Bible we learn that this embodiment of evil had once been an angel but had twisted God's wisdom centripetally, resulting in a spectacularly devastating fall. It is tragic that here, in Adam's realm and, by extension, under Adam's authority, the shrewd beast engages Eve in a manipulative dialogue. *"Did God really say . . . ?"* (Gen 3:1). The very question is frighteningly familiar to all humanity as this first couple's progeny. The antagonist we first met here would eventually use this same rhetorical device on our protagonist, Jesus, though not in a lush garden with unlimited possibilities for obedience. The temptation narrative recorded in Matthew 4 has the serpent's new dialogue partner emaciated after a forty-day fast in a barren wilderness. In that conversation the serpent challenged Jesus that if he is truly God's son, he should be feasting, not fasting. And, again, the serpent tried to pressure him into diverging from the will of his father.

In Genesis 3 and Matthew 4, what is at stake is the character of God. When God speaks, can he be trusted? He spoke the prohibition to Adam. He spoke the affirmation to Jesus. Yet the serpent tempted them both by insinuating God could not be trusted. The basis of all temptation is distrust of God's character. Character is displayed through trustworthiness and the keeping of promises. Thus, distrusting God's character leads to rejection of his Word, resulting in disobedience. Not so for Jesus. He would continue to trust and obey the Father.

Eve and Adam took the bait when the serpent promised in Gen 3:5 "you will be like God." In a tragic display of irony, they already were! They, not the serpent, bore the image of God. And yet, in Gen 3:6 "they ate." It should be strongly emphasized that the reason they ate must have originated in a newfound distrust of God's good character. Before the man and woman became lawbreakers, they chose to be lawmakers—deciding what is good and bad without reference to God or his word. Sin is not just transgressing God's commands; it is questioning his character behind those commands and usurping his authority. It is this nature that we have inherited from our first parents, and it is this disposition that we destructively cultivate by our own sinful choices. We become a law unto ourselves. We legislate our own morality as if our finitude could bear that weight.

The consequence of the fall is that humanity went from being awestruck worshipers to brazen idolaters. Once our first parents questioned the character of God and deemed his word to be irrelevant, they then acted on their unbelief. And the consequences could not have been more devastating. In seven short verses, Adam and Eve transitioned from the security of paradise to "naked and ashamed" in Gen 3:7. The shame is only the beginning of their tailspin. The fact that they immediately "sewed fig leaves" to cover their nakedness illustrates that they *knew* something was profoundly wrong. There is a problem with their solution. When you pull a leaf from the bush, you cut it off from its life source and it begins to die. Their solution only illustrated the problem—they were now cut off from their Life Source and, though still breathing, they were as good as dead. Perhaps the fig leaves are illustrative of our man-made religion, all of which is a futile, if not vain, attempt to fix ourselves—man's independent effort to return to right standing with God.

I find it interesting that the Gospels capture the fact that Jesus cursed a fig tree on his way up to Jerusalem, because it gave the appearance of fruitfulness but had no fruit. Once in Jerusalem, at the temple, Jesus runs out the money changers and confronts the fruitless religiosity he sees. When departing, his disciples find the fig tree withered from the root—reflecting the lifelessness of what they had just seen condemned in the Temple. And back in Genesis 3, it is not just the fig leaves that are dying. It is God's image bearers because their sin cuts them off from the Author of Life. Autonomy, the making of laws for oneself, is far different than they thought it would be. Their newfound freedom was about to swing the gates of the garden in an unanticipated direction—they would be trapped outside of its goodness.

Subsequently, the pursuit of human flourishing would be sweat-inducing, toilsome, painful, and ultimately, impossible. The Tree of Life, which had been theirs to enjoy, would now fade from their sight but never from their memory. Because we were made for life and a relationship with God characterized by worship, our human identity as worshipers was irrevocable. The problem is that our worship is misdirected. In our fallen nature, we distrust God's character and become brazen idolaters rather than God-directed worshippers. Paul describes this situation well in Romans 1. He says humans "exchanged the truth about God for a lie and worshiped and served the creature rather than the Creator" (Rom 1:25 ESV). Whether Allah or Vishnu, spirits or sprites, ancestors or ourselves, our insatiable propensity for worship spans from religious to academic institutions, from the philosopher's navel-gazing to the dictator's megalomania. Every human worships someone or something, if not themselves.

But God knew. And he entered this broken realm displaying his impeccably merciful character. The first couple had become rebels to God's cause, yet God would reveal to them the relational distance that now existed between them. In Gen 3:8 "they hid" when they heard God coming. Tragic! For the first time, they run *from* God, not *to* him. And it is tragic today that we do the same. God said, "Where are you?" not because he had lost track of them. The image bearers were facing away from the One they were created to reflect. God spoke to orient them to himself. His voice is terrifying when we are hiding from him. Perhaps that is why when we speak of God to those who are far from him, they often do not want to hear it. Regardless, all their relationships were broken—with God, themselves, and all creation. God spoke again. "Where are you?" (Gen 3:9). God pursued them (and us) by entering the brokenness. And that in itself is grace.

Yes, there are dire and devastating consequences for sin. But God, true to his character, did not abandon us to those consequences. Rather, he initiated a costly rescue mission that would prove his character to be unquestionably good! And that leads us to the next worldview question, and another plot transition: Is there any hope?

Rescue

God's response to man's sin was to promise a rescuer. No sooner had they fractured the foundations of creation order than God initiated his plan not only to set things right but to establish an irrevocable kingdom of flourishing. In Gen 3:15, as God explains the dire far-reaching consequences of their distrust, he makes a not-so-subtle promise to destroy the serpent. This promise is commonly referred to as the "protoevangelion," or beginning of the gospel. When God promises to send a rescuer through the offspring of the woman, he sacrificially commits to destroy the devil and all his works. Then, before graciously banning the first couple from the garden, in Gen 3:21 God removes their ineffective leaves and provides for them a "covering of skin." The consequence of sin was dying and death, but God provided an archetypal substitute.

Once they were out of the garden temple, the rest of the Old Testament is one long, indispensable, detailed answer to a very short but complex question, "Who is the Rescuer?" Between the last chapter of 2 Chronicles, which is the chronological ending to the Hebrew Old Testament, and the birth of John the baptizer, there were 400 years of silence. But we must never equate silence with inactivity. God was working to bring about the Lamb of God to take away the sins of the world long before John announced that the Old Testament sacrificial system predicted it. In fact, there has never been a time in human history when God was not working to accomplish his purpose and keep his promise.

The New Testament begins with Matt 1:1 "the Son of David, the Son of Abraham." The tax collector turned disciple-maker testifies that God kept that foundational promise. The rescuer had arrived in the person of Jesus. From there, Matthew and the other Gospels writers provide narrative encounters, profound didactic synopses, and documentation of Jesus's authority over anyone and everything. The result is a technicolor tour of the landscape of his life, leaving little doubt that he is the promised Rescuer. His character—impeccable! His works—inexplicably powerful! His words—profoundly simple, and yet simply profound!

As alluded to earlier, Jesus's public ministry began with the testimony of God himself declaring, "This is my Son" (Matt 3:17), followed by his being driven into a barren wilderness. There he encountered the serpent, with only God's word as his weapon. God's word was also sufficient to sustain him in his emaciated state following his fast. He did not have to throw himself from the temple, for he trusted the Father's character unreservedly. And as the daunting shadow of the cross loomed over him, Jesus refused to shrink back and take the shortcut that would have sealed our demise and left him with an empty kingdom. Instead, he emerged victorious from his temptation and for the next three years could not be dissuaded from fulfilling his purpose of rescuing sinners and reconciling us back to the Father.

Jesus did eventually find himself in a garden. And there, he began to feel the crushing weight of our sin as the Father went silent. Jesus accepted what lay ahead. That trust led Jesus from Gethsemane's garden to the judgment of Gabbatha, where Pilate thought he was sealing his fate. But no one could take Jesus's life from him. He had vowed to lay it down and take it back up himself. So, Gabbatha gave way to the tortuous journey up the Via Dolorosa to a hill called Golgotha. And finally, we see it . . . the greatest display of worship and obedience the world has ever or will ever know. Eviscerated. Naked. Despised. Rejected. He trusted the character of the Father who had formulated this rescue plan. Yes, God had orchestrated all human history to reach its pinnacle on the side of that hill. And there, Jesus maintained his trust to the moment of his death. "Father, into your hands I commit my spirit" (Luke 23:46 ESV). Do you see the profundity of that utterance? As he breathed his last, Jesus unflinchingly trusted the character of God. He was acting in unthinkable obedience to the word of God. Jesus, the Son of God crucified—worshiped and obeyed *through* his last breath.

We do not know everything that happened after the Author of life subjugated himself to death. But we do know that on the third day when his foot touched the floor of that dusty tomb, the serpent's head was beneath his heel! And ever since that day when we look at that Cross through the lens of the true story of the whole world, we see that "God demonstrates his love for us, in that while we were still sinners,

Christ died for us" (Rom 5:8 NASB1995). We see that "God made him who knew no sin to become sin for us, that in him, we might be made righteous" (2 Cor 5:21, author's translation). The "good news" is that God sent his Son to rescue us through his life of perfect worship and obedience, his atoning death, his triumphant resurrection, and his ascension. Jesus is God's promise kept!

I have experienced rapturous joy in my life. And I have endured devastating pain through waves of loss and mourning. But when those moments of pain and disillusionment come—when my mind cries out, "Why God!?"—those are the moments that I see most clearly through my tears. The message is the same to the skeptic without and the skeptic within: "He did not even spare his own Son, but freely gave him up for us all. How will he not also with him give us all?" (Rom 8:32, author's translation). The cross was not some tragic oversight on the part of God. It was not a vain attempt to inspire humanity to try harder. The cross of Jesus was not an unnecessary display of stubbornness on the part of a good yet misguided guru. The cross of Jesus is the vindication of the character of God before a skeptical world! The only fitting response to the cross of Jesus against the backdrop of history is to trust the character of God seen in his sacrificial rescue; obey the word of God by turning from sin and trusting in Jesus; and live out obedience as people saved from sin, for God, into the church and onto God's mission. This reality leads to our final worldview question and plot movement.

Restoration

Christians have portrayed heaven in uncompelling and, frankly, unbiblical ways for too long. From the Renaissance artists' naked cherubs floating on clouds to fictional apocalypses that emphasize the leaving rather than our great destination, I fear that the world yawns at the prospect of our future hope. Blaise Pascal once wrote that Christians need to talk in such a way as to "make good men wish it were true, and then show that it is."[5] Once again, the backstory is everything when talking about heaven. It should depict a destination in a way that makes people who are far from God wish it were true, even if they do not yet believe it.

What does the future hold? God has promised to restore all things to their original purpose and harmony. There will be flourishing to a degree that we simply cannot fathom. In the Bible's final chapters, we find (in the words of Tolkien), "Everything sad will become untrue."[6] In Revelation 21 we are told there will be a "new heaven and a new earth" and that "God's dwelling is with humanity . . . Death will be no more; grief, crying, and pain will be no more . . . [God is] making everything new." Then, in chapter 22 we read, "there will no longer be any curse. The throne of God and of the Lamb will be in the city, and his servants will worship him . . . and they will reign forever and ever."

Notice how the story ends with the character of God firmly and unquestionably established. The curse that our first parents brought upon the world through distrusting the character of God, rejecting his word, and acting in disobedience, we have reinforced through our own sin. The world we live in is broken, but not beyond hope as long as God is the author and hero of the story. God kept his promise with the removal of the curse. We are not going back to the garden, but God is "making everything new" (Rev 21:5). When that happens, all will acknowledge the goodness of God. On the Day of Judgment, those who did not trust God's good character will have their mouths stopped and confess that "Jesus is Lord!" to the glory of God the Father. Unlike in the garden, where God visited in the cool of the day, in this city, God takes up permanent residence and we will never lose sight of him.

---

[5] Blaise Pascal, *Pensées*, trans. A. J. Krailsheimer (New York: Penguin, 1995), frg. 12, p. 4.

[6] J. R. R. Tolkien, *The Return of the King*, The Lord of the Rings (Boston: Mariner Books, 2004), bk. 6, chap. 4.

The true story of the whole world begins in a garden and ends in a city! In our broken world, cities everywhere are filled with millions of sinful and selfish people living near one another. This manner of life is the antithesis of the greatest commandment and the second one that goes with it (Luke 10:25–28). But the heavenly city described in Revelation is brimming with life and diverse ethnicities, and its citizens are reigning with Christ and living out the golden rule. Think back to Gen 1:28, where God's first command was to "be fruitful, multiply and fill the earth with worshipers and reign over it" (author's translation). God's original purpose is fulfilled at the end of the story. Flourishing and creativity will have no end because the heavenly city will be filled with disciples of Jesus. Heaven will not be some static environment with only one song playing. Boredom is an absolute impossibility there. And the perfection that characterizes this city is immutable! Because all its citizens are in right relationship to God and to one another—made possible by the gospel of Jesus Christ.

Conclusion

One of the great mysteries of the gospel is that once we embrace it and center our trust in the character of God to keep that promise, the Holy Spirit of God then indwells in us, and we can begin to experience kingdom life here and now. Discipleship is critical to our understanding and application of this newfound worldview. When we invite people to surrender to Christ and then fail to disciple them in how to live out that relationship, our passivity dims their view of God *and* their hope of heaven. Disciple making is training people to live in worship and obedience to King Jesus on earth as it will be in heaven. Disciple making brings about the confluence of the gospel story and worldview in such a way as to grow our dependence upon the cross of Christ and our trust in the character of God. The gospel of Jesus Christ vindicates the character of God before a skeptical world and makes it possible for us to pray, "Your kingdom come. Your will be done on earth as it is in heaven" (Matt 6:10).

I first presented the content in this chapter as a faculty lecture at Southeastern Seminary. Afterward, Dr. Akin approached me with tears in his eyes and said, "That lecture led me to worship! It needs to be published." And now, appropriately I suppose, it will be an essay conveying my gratitude for the privilege of serving under his leadership. God used him to cultivate a deeper passion for the Great Commission in me. We communicate what we cherish. Serving alongside Danny Akin at an institution known for hot-hearted evangelism, disciple making, and missions has caused me to cherish the gospel all the more. And now it is my prayer that this chapter would help do the same for you, the reader.

CHAPTER FOUR

PREACHING, BIBLICAL AUTHORITY, AND THE GREAT COMMISSION

David L. Allen

This chapter is a revised and edited version of an earlier chapter, "Preaching for a Great Commission Resurgence," in Chuck Lawless and Adam Greenway, *Great Commission Resurgence: Fulfilling God's Mandate in Our Time* (Nashville: B&H Academic, 2010), 281–98. It has been included here with permission of the publisher.

Introduction

I have known Danny Akin since we were in college together in 1977. Throughout the years of his ministry, Dr. Akin has stood firm on three crucial issues: biblical authority, expositional preaching, and the Great Commission. One might say these are three defining characteristics of a lifetime of ministry, culminating in a twenty-year presidency (so far) at Southeastern Baptist Theological Seminary. Thinking through these three issues is the task of this chapter.

Biblical Authority

The Enlightenment, which some have called the modern period, is often described as the "age of reason." Many have attributed this shift to the philosophical influence of René Descartes, who was committed to autonomous scientific reasoning to arrive at certainty and determine what is true.[1] So one main issue during this period was how to know what is true. The question is really about authority. This development significantly impacted theological knowledge. Until the Enlightenment, theology traveled what could be called "Authority Avenue" because of the reliance upon divine revelation for knowledge about God.[2] But in the eighteenth century, "Reason Way" was constructed as a new road. This development replaced the authority of Scripture with the authority of the autonomous mind. The result was politically, socially, ethically, philosophically, and religiously momentous. The Enlightenment began the rise of religious liberalism, resulting in a growing denial of biblical authority.

With the death of Nietzsche in 1900 and the publication of Adolf von Harnack's "What Is Christianity?" that same year, old grandpa liberalism limped into the twentieth century already ailing from what would turn out to be a terminal disease. He had lived his life in the far country of subjectivism and had all but squandered his precious Reformation heritage through riotous historical-critical living.

---

[1] Cf. Craig G. Bartholomew and Michael Goheen, *Christian Philosophy: A Systematic and Narrative Introduction* (Grand Rapids: Baker Academic, 2013), 114–34, and James K. Dew Jr. and Paul M. Gould, *Philosophy: A Christian Introduction* (Grand Rapids; Baker Academic, 2019), 40–56.

[2] John M. Frame, *A History of Western Philosophy* (Phillipsburg, NJ: P&R, 2015), 214–50.

Among his progeny was a young man named Karl Barth, who came to his senses and sought to return to the Father's house. Oddly enough, it was Barth's experience in the pulpit that taught him the bankruptcy of theological liberalism. However, Barth got sidetracked and never quite made it completely back home. Barth's major theological faux pas, which had immense repercussions for theology and homiletics, was his assertion that the Bible, as a witness to revelation, is not itself revelation.[3] Barth's dichotomy of the Word of God and the words of Scripture is sinister for theology—and for preaching.[4]

When churches and denominations abandon biblical authority, the first casualty is the pulpit. Even evangelical denominations and churches have not escaped unscathed. Evidence suggests the need to rethink the importance of biblical authority and inerrancy, coupled with a strong commitment to the *sufficiency* of Scripture in our preaching. The inerrancy of Scripture is still affirmed among most evangelicals, but even here there has been significant erosion in the twenty-first century.[5] While the battle for the inerrancy of Scripture will go on, today evangelicals are engaged in a new battle: the *sufficiency* of Scripture in preaching. Is the Bible, and the Bible alone, sufficient to change hearts and grow a church?

The Scripture itself presents God as its ultimate author not only in such texts as 2 Tim 3:16 but in the fact that the biblical writers often viewed *God* and *Scripture* as interchangeable terms via metonymy when quoting the Old Testament. God is often viewed as the author of a

---

[3] Karl Barth, *Church Dogmatics* I/2, ed. G. W. Bromiley and T. F. Torrance, trans. G. T. Thomson and Harold Knight (Edinburgh: T & T Clark, 1956), 463. For Barth's view of Scripture as witness to revelation, see especially Klaas Runia, *Karl Barth's Doctrine of Holy Scripture* (Grand Rapids: Baker, 1962), 15–86.

[4] For an analysis of Barth's impact on preaching, see David L. Allen, "A Tale of Two Roads: Homiletics and Biblical Authority," *JETS* 43, no. 3 (2000): 489–515.

[5] See Greg Beale's *The Erosion of Inerrancy in Evangelicalism: Responding to New Challenges to Biblical Authority* (Wheaton, IL: Crossway, 2008).

scriptural citation when he is not, in fact, the speaker (Matt 19:4–5). Likewise, "Scripture says" is a phrase that is sometimes used when God is the direct speaker (Rom 9:17). God is seen by the biblical writers to be the author of all Scripture. What Scripture says is in fact the Word of God.

As the Word of God, Scripture is inspired, inerrant, and sufficient, according to 2 Timothy 3:16–17: "All Scripture is inspired by God and is profitable for teaching, for rebuking, for correcting, for training in righteousness so that the man of God may be complete, equipped for every good work." The authority of Scripture is the very authority of God. Our authority for preaching comes from God himself and from his Word, Scripture. As Haddon Robinson reminds us, "Ultimately the authority behind preaching resides not in the preacher but in the biblical text."[6]

Thus, to preach, *kerrusō*, is an authoritative public proclamation of Jesus the Word and of Scripture as the Word of God. First Thessalonians 2:13 makes clear that the source and authority for preaching is God himself: "This is why we constantly thank God, because when you received the word of God that you heard from us, you welcomed it not as a human message, but as it truly is, the word of God, which also works effectively in you who believe."

Peter Adam rightly stated, "Without God's words there can be no ministry of the word. . . . The first great theological foundation for preaching, then, is that God has spoken."[7] God has spoken to us in his Son (Heb 1:1–2), the living Word, and he has spoken to us in the Scriptures, his written Word. If, to use J. I. Packer's famous phrase, Scripture is "God preaching,"[8] then the best method of preaching must be expository preaching. A high view of biblical authority creates a solid

---

[6] Haddon Robinson, *Biblical Preaching: The Development and Delivery of Expository Messages*, 3rd ed. (Grand Rapids: Baker Academic, 2014), 7.

[7] Peter Adam, *Speaking God's Words: A Practical Theology of Preaching* (Vancouver, BC: Regent College Publishing, 2004), 25.

[8] J. I. Packer, *God Has Spoken* (Grand Rapids: Baker, 1979), 97.

foundation for expositional preaching. Biblical exposition week after week from the pulpit is the logical outcome of a high view of biblical authority and the most effective means of fulfilling Paul's mandate to "Preach the Word!"

Preaching and the Great Commission

If the mission of the church is to evangelize the lost and to equip the saved, then of all things the church does, preaching must be at the apex. A careful study of the Great Commission given by Jesus indicates precisely that. The Great Commission appears in all four Gospels in some form, as well as in the first chapter of the book of Acts.

> "Go, therefore and make disciples of all nations, baptizing them in the name of the father and of the son and of the Holy Spirit, teaching them to observe everything I have commanded you." (Matt 28:19–20)
>
> "Go into all the world and preach the gospel to the whole creation." (Mark 16:15 ESV)[9]
>
> "This is what is written: The Messiah will suffer and rise from the dead the third day, and repentance for forgiveness of sins would be proclaimed in His name to all the nations, beginning at Jerusalem." (Luke 24:46–47)
>
> "As the father has sent me, I also send you." (John 20:21)

From these accounts, we observe the following: (1) Jesus has been given all authority in heaven and on earth; (2) on this authority, the

---

[9] This is part of the longer ending of Mark, which most scholars doubt was a part of the original. See the succinct discussion of this complicated issue in Bruce Metzger, *A Textual Commentary on the Greek New Testament*, 2nd ed. (Stuttgart: German Bible Society, 1994), 102–6.

apostles, and by implication all Christians, are sent forth to make disciples; (3) the gospel message is to all the nations, hence a worldwide endeavor; (4) new believers are to be baptized and taught; (5) preaching is the primary means of making disciples; (6) this preaching is grounded in Scripture ("thus it is written," Luke 24:46 ESV). In the Greek text of Luke 24:47 (ESV), the aorist passive infinitive translated "should be proclaimed" stands first in the clause for emphasis.

If the mission of the church is the evangelism of the lost and the equipping of the saved, then of all things the church does, ought not preaching to be at its apex? It is interesting to compare how the Great Commission is expressed in Matthew and in Mark. Whereas Matthew 28:19 speaks of going into all the world and "making disciples," Mark 16:15 says, "Go into all the world and preach the gospel." Obviously preaching plays a paramount role in the church's mandate to fulfill the Great Commission.

Thus, it is not surprising to find preaching is at the heart of birth and growth of the church in the book of Acts. In fact, Acts is a book about preaching, since sermons make up 30 percent of the book. Preaching is the principal strategy for church growth in Acts. Note how the five summary statements that Luke places at key points in Acts exemplify the importance of preaching: Acts 6:7; 9:31; 12:24; 16:5; 19:20. We are told in Acts 6:4 that prayer and preaching were the priorities of the apostles. Acts 4:8 illustrates the role of the Holy Spirit and preaching in the early church. Throughout Acts, preaching is the seed of church planting and the tool for church growth.

The nature of the church requires that preaching be paramount in the fulfillment of her mission. The church was born in preaching, according to Acts 2. Paul says in Romans that "faith comes from what is heard, and what is heard comes through the message about Christ" (Rom 10:17). Evangelistic preaching grows the church. Biblical preaching edifies the church. The New Testament itself testifies to the foundational nature of preaching for the mission and purpose of the church. In his swan song, Paul tells young Timothy to "Preach the word" (2 Tim 4:2). You cannot have a church without preaching, and you cannot have church growth without preaching. Preaching is fundamental to New Testament ecclesiology. Preaching must be foundational in the mission of the church for theological reasons.

Preaching is the strategy for both evangelism and discipleship in the book of Acts. Key words used for preaching in Acts include *preach*, *speak*, *persuade*, *say*, *announce good news*, *herald*, *exhort*, *teach*, *publicly proclaim*, *reason/debate*, and *solemnly testify*. Notice the key places where preaching occurs in Acts: the temple, council chambers, a desert road, Cornelius's house, synagogues, marketplaces, jails, courtrooms, ships, schools, and lecture halls. Likewise, Satan's strategy is ever an attempt to silence the preaching of the apostles and early Christians primarily by means of persecution.

The primary content of preaching in Acts was the person and work of Christ (Acts 2:36), salvation in Christ alone (4:12), and the necessity of repentance and faith in Christ (2:38; 20:21). Eternity and judgment were frequent subjects as well (2:20; 17:30–31). Acts reveals the manner of preaching: constant appeal to the conscience about sin (2:23), admonishing people with warnings (2:40; 28:23–28), intensity and boldness (4:13, 31), and compassion and tears (20:19, 31). Preaching in Acts regularly called for a response from the hearers, as in Acts 2:38 and 16:31.

Finally, Acts informs us about the results of preaching: 3,000 were saved at Pentecost after Peter's sermon (2:41); Stephen the preacher was martyred after his sermon (7:54–60); and frequent references occur in Acts of people's response to preaching as either obedience or rejection (28:23–28). Jews and Gentiles alike heard the gospel, repented of sin, and believed in Jesus as a result of the preaching of the early church. According to Acts, the early church, with laser-like intensity, understood the Great Commission of Jesus and sought to carry the gospel to the ends of the earth. The early Christians' understanding, vision, and commitment to the Great Commission should be the pervasive pattern today.

Paul states that it is the "foolishness of the message preached" that God is pleased to use in the salvation of the lost (1 Cor 1:21). Paul's mandate to Timothy to "preach the Word" (2 Tim 4:2) makes it clear that preaching is God's program for the church.

In the New Testament epistles, preaching serves as the means to motivate and equip the church to fulfill the Great Commission. The epistles of Paul, Peter, and John, along with James, Jude, and Hebrews, are all examples of how these early Christian authors used preaching to fulfill the Great Commission mandate of teaching the church all things. Right doctrine is necessary for the health and growth of the church. All true evangelism and missions must be built on the foundation of sound doctrine. Many of the New Testament letters are essentially sermons and constitute what their authors believed the early church needed to learn to fulfill the Great Commission.

Paul's method of evangelistic preaching in Acts 17:2–3 is informative: "As usual, Paul went into the synagogue, and on three Sabbath days reasoned with them from the Scriptures, explaining and proving that it was necessary for the Messiah to suffer and rise from the dead." Paul's New Testament letters to the churches are mostly written sermons. They contain what Paul would have preached to them had he been with them in person. Hebrews is itself a written sermon that develops several Old Testament texts of Scripture, Psalm 110:1, 4 being primary.

The necessity of preaching for the mission of the church is illustrated in the history of the church. Many of the confessions of faith developed by the Anabaptists,[10] magisterial reformers, and other post-Reformation groups speak about the primacy of preaching for achieving

---

[10] See Abraham Friesen, *Erasmus, the Anabaptists, and the Great Commission* (Grand Rapids: Eerdmans, 1998), 98–99.

the mission of the church. The church cannot be the church unless she is the preaching church. The reformers show, by their own preaching and writing, they considered preaching critical to the establishment, growth, and health of the church.

Pastoral care illustrates the necessity of preaching in the church's mission. The classical definitions of pastoral care throughout church history identify preaching as the primary method of pastoral care.[11] For example, Luther said:

> If anybody wants to preach, let him suppress his own words and let them prevail in worldly and domestic affairs; here in the church he should speak nothing but the Word of this rich Householder; otherwise it is not the true church. This is why it must always be said that it is God who is speaking. . . . Therefore a preacher . . . dare not say anything different from what God says and commands. And even though there may be a lot of talk which is not the Word of God, the church is not in all this talk, even though they begin to yell like mad.[12]

Thomas Oden has contributed a significant body of work on the importance of pastoral care and the necessity of preaching as a primary

---

[11] See the classic work on this subject by Gregory the Great, *The Book of Pastoral Rule*, in *Nicene and Post-Nicene Fathers*, Second Series, ed. Philip Schaff and Henry Wace, vol. 12 (reprint; Grand Rapids: Eerdmans, 1977), 69, wherein Gregory argued that preaching must be used in pastoral care. This work is probably the single most influential book in the history of pastoral care. Lisa Kaaran Bailey's dissertation, "Preaching and Pastoral Care in Late Antique Gaul: The Eusebius Gallicanus Sermon Collection" (PhD diss., Princeton University, 2004), argues that preaching was a crucial aspect of pastoral care during this period and was one of the foundations for the success of the late Patristic church in integrating itself into Western European culture.

[12] Martin Luther, "Sermon Preached in Castle Pleissenburg on the Occasion of the Inauguration of the Reformation in Leipzig, John 14:23–31, May 24, 1539," in *Luther's Works*, vol. 51, *Sermons I*, ed. Jaroslav Jan Pelikan, Hilton C. Oswald, and Helmut T. Lehmann (Philadelphia: Fortress, 1999), 305.

means of doing pastoral care.[13] Preaching to the church plays a crucial role in preparing and maintaining Christians spiritually to fulfill the Great Commission.

In his swan song, Paul tells young Timothy to "preach the Word" (2 Tim 4:2). The centerpiece and climax of the discourse structure of the entire letter is this very passage. This is the only place in Scripture where *word* (*logos*) occurs as the direct object of the verb *to preach*. Preaching is God's method of heralding the gospel to a lost world. Preaching is God's method of teaching his church doctrinal and ethical truths. We refer to these two aspects as *kerygma* (heralding the gospel) and *didaché* (teaching). Both words occur in 2 Tim 4:2–5.

You cannot have a church without preaching. You cannot have church growth without preaching. You cannot have church revitalization without preaching. Preaching is fundamental to New Testament ecclesiology. Preaching must be foundational in the mission of the church for theological and pastoral reasons. The church cannot be the church unless she is the preaching church.

Two great English Baptist forefathers demonstrate this well: Andrew Fuller and William Carey. Both men stressed the necessity of the Great Commission as the foundation for their missionary endeavors. Each preached now-famous sermons that served as catalysts for the modern missions movement.

On April 27, 1791, Fuller preached at an association ministers meeting at Clipstone. His text was Haggai 1:2 and his title was "Instances, Evil, and Tendency of Delay, in the Concerns of Religion." This sermon, as first preached and later in its published form, proved important in the founding of the Baptist Missionary Society one year later. A key

---

[13] Thomas Oden, *Pastoral Theology: Essentials for Ministry* (San Francisco: Harper, 1983); Thomas Oden, *Care of Souls in the Classic Tradition* (Philadelphia: Fortress, 1984); Thomas Oden, *Ministry through Word and Sacrament*, Classical Pastoral Care 2 (Grand Rapids: Baker, 2000).

portion of the sermon concerns Fuller's direct challenge to his hearers to be involved in world missions based on the Great Commission in Matthew 28:19–20. Listen to these provocative words:

> When the Lord Jesus commissioned his apostles, he commanded them to go and teach "all nations," to preach the gospel to "every creature;" and that notwithstanding the difficulties and oppositions that would lie in the way. The apostles executed their commission with assiduity and fidelity; but since their days, we seem to sit down half-contented that the greater part of the world should still remain in ignorance and idolatry. Some noble efforts have indeed been made; but they are small in number, when compared with the magnitude of the object. And why is it so? Are the souls of men of less value than heretofore? No. Is Christianity less true or less important than in former ages? This will not be pretended. Are there no opportunities for societies, or individuals, in Christian nations, to convey the gospel to the heathens? This cannot be pleaded so long as opportunities are found to trade with them, yea, and (what is a disgrace to the name of Christians) to buy them, and sell them, and treat them with worse than savage barbarity! We have opportunities in abundance: the improvement of navigation, and the maritime and commercial turn of this country, furnish us with these; and it deserves to be considered whether this is not a circumstance that renders it a duty peculiarly binding on us. The truth is, if I am not mistaken, we wait for we know not what; we seem to think "the time is not come, the time for the Spirit to be poured down from on high." We pray for the conversion and salvation of the world, and yet neglect the ordinary means by which those ends have been used to be accomplished. It pleased God, heretofore, by the foolishness of preaching, to save them that believed; and there is reason

> to think it will still please God to work by that distinguished means. Ought we not then at least to try by some means to convey more of the good news of salvation to the world around us than has hitherto been conveyed? The encouragement to the heathen is still in force, "Whosoever shall call upon the name of the Lord shall be saved: but how shall they call on him in whom they have not believed? and how shall they believe in him of whom they have not heard? and how shall they hear without a preacher? and how shall they preach except they be sent?" . . . Were every true minister of the gospel to make a point of preaching as often as possible in the villages within his reach; and did those private Christians who are situated in such villages open their doors for preaching, and recommend the gospel by a holy and affectionate behaviour, might we not hope to see the wilderness become as a fruitful field? Surely, in these matters, we are too negligent.[14]

On May 30, 1792, William Carey preached his celebrated sermon "Expect Great Things; Attempt Great Things" at the annual Association Meeting at Nottingham. Isaiah 54:2–3 was the text, and Fuller was in attendance. Carey's sermon, a plea for the formation of a missionary society, was electrifying. But the following morning during the business meeting attended by only the pastors, it appeared nothing would be done. Deaville Walker relates the spine-tingling tale:

> The following morning the ministers met alone for their usual conference, and Carey's proposal to form a missionary society came up for discussion. But the enthusiasm kindled by the previous day's sermon had passed and the cold logic of practical

[14] Andrew Fuller, *The Complete Works of the Rev. Andrew Fuller, with a Memoir of His Life by the Rev. Andrew Gunton Fuller*, 3 vols., ed. A. G. Fuller, rev. J. Belcher (1845; Harrisonburg, VA: Sprinkle Publications, 1988), 1:147–48.

> difficulties seem overpowering. That little band of comparatively insignificant preachers felt the task to be beyond their strength. They came to the conclusion that Carey's proposal was for the time being impossible; they turned it down, and the gathering prepared to break up. In distress, Carey seized Fuller by the arms and asked whether they were once more to separate without doing something definite. Then a change came over the company, and after further discussion, and passionate exhortation from Carey, it was decided to place on their minutes a resolution that: "A plan be prepared against the next ministers' meeting for forming a Baptist Society for propagating the gospel among the heathens."[15]

Thus was born what was to be called the Baptist Missionary Society, with Carey serving as its first missionary and Fuller its secretary. From that time on, Baptists were firmly committed to missions.

Conclusion

The mission of the church to fulfill the Great Commission cannot be accomplished without preaching. Preaching that does not communicate the gospel clearly nor explain the meaning of Scripture to equip Christians to fulfill the church's mission will result in a spiritually dwarfed church and a truncated witness to the world. Preaching that does not inform and challenge believers to understand that the crux of being Christian is to be committed to the Great Commission will fail to build Great Commission Christians and Great Commission churches.

Samuel Pearce was an early English Baptist with a heart for both the Great Commission and preaching. The moving story of Pearce's 5:00

[15] F. Deaville Walker called the sermon "nothing short of epoch making," in *William Carey: Missionary Pioneer and Statesman* (Chicago: Moody, 1951), 78–79.

a.m. sermon to 200 farm laborers in Guilsborough, Northamptonshire, in May 1794, should give all of us pause to reflect on our preaching commitment and its relationship to the Great Commission. Here is the account as related by Cox in his two-volume *History of the Baptist Missionary Society*.

> Following the sermon, Pearce was seated at the breakfast table with a few people, including Andrew Fuller. Fuller remarked to Pearce, his dear friend, how pleased he was with the sermon. But he went on to add that it appeared Pearce's sermon was poorly structured in that it seemed Pearce did not close when he had finished, but he appeared to begin again at the end of the sermon. Pearce responded tersely, acknowledging the accuracy of the observation but stated he had his reason. In a "jocular manner," Fuller kept urging Pearce for the reason. When he finally responded, Pearce said:
>
> "Well, my brother, you shall have the secret, if it must be so. Just at the moment I was about to resume my seat, thinking I'd finished, the door opened, and I saw a poor man enter, of the working class; And from the sweat on his brow, and the symptoms of his fatigue, I conjectured that he had walked some miles to this early service, but that he had been unable to reach the place till the close. A momentary thought glanced through my mind—here may be a man who never heard the gospel, or it may be he is one that regards it as a feast of fat things; in either case the effort on his part demands one on mine. So with the hope of doing him good, I resolved at once to forget all else, and, in spite of criticism, and the apprehension of being thought tedious, to give him a quarter of an hour."[16]

[16] David L. Allen, "Preaching for a Great Commission Resurgence," in *The Great Commission Resurgence Fulfilling God's Mandate in Our Time*, ed. Chuck

The words of Cox following his relating this anecdote speak volumes to all of us today.

> It cannot be supposed that such a man could be lukewarm, while others were feeling for the distant heathen, and planning a missionary enterprise. No; he was just the individual to kindle at once. His reason, his heart, his conscious, his every power and passion, became consecrated to the cause; the materials for the sacred fire were already in his mind; it was only to apply the torch, and he blazed forth, until his zeal consumed him.[17]

May God deliver us all from our lukewarmness, and may the Holy Spirit "apply the torch" and empower us to fulfill conjointly our Lord's Great Commission and Paul's admonition to "Preach the word!" Let us join with the very heart of God and our Lord Jesus himself, who as Paul says, through us pleads with all people to be saved based on Christ's shed blood for all people:

> Everything is from God, who reconciled us to himself through Christ and gave us the ministry of reconciliation: that is, in Christ, God was reconciling the world to himself, not counting their trespasses against them, and he has committed the message of reconciliation to us. Therefore, we are ambassadors for Christ, since God is making his appeal through us. We plead on Christ's behalf, "Be reconciled to God." (2 Cor 5:18–20)

Lawless and Adam W. Greenway (Nashville: B&H, 2010), 297, quoting F. A. Cox, *History of the Baptist Missionary Society, from 1792–1842*, 2 vols. (London: T. Ward and G. and J. Dyer, 1842), 1:52–53.

[17] Cox, *History of the Baptist Missionary Society*, 53.

CHAPTER FIVE

WORSHIP AND THE GREAT COMMISSION

Mark Liederbach

Introduction

The purpose of this chapter is to demonstrate the connection between worship and the Great Commission. I begin with a discussion of Genesis 1:1 to establish a theocentric ordering of creation and thereby argue that the universe itself is designed by God as a "grand symphony hall of worship." Next, I interact with Genesis 1:27–28 to show that God designed and created his image bearers as *missional worshippers* tasked to *go* into the created order and fill it with *peoples and nations* who glorify God. Following this, I briefly discuss the impact of sin and the fall on both the worship and mission of image bearers followed by an equally brief discussion on how the gospel restores us not only to a right relationship with God, but also to our created purpose as missional worshippers. Finally, by way of conclusion, I suggest two conclusions. First, that the "worship mandate" given to Adam and Eve in Genesis 1:27–28 is best understood as a precursor for, and even the first iteration of, the Great Commission Jesus gave to his Church in Matthew 28:18–20. Second, that Christian missions exist because *proper worship* does not.[1]

God and the Grand Symphony Hall of Worship

The opening words of the Bible, "In the beginning God created the heavens and the earth," are crucial for a proper understanding of both worship and mission. They provide the theocentric anchor point of all existence as well as the context for, and missional purpose of, the image bearers God created as his stewards.

In the Beginning God

The first four words of the English Bible, "In the beginning God" (Gen 1:1), reveal that the universe is not self-created, self-existent, or self-sustaining. Rather, its existence depends upon the One who created it and by his power causes it to remain. By beginning with these four words, the Bible focuses the reader on the glorious nature of the One who created the wonder. These words prompt us to ask, "*Who* is this God that exists 'in the beginning?' and what does his existence demand of us?"

Regarding *who* this God is, the Scriptures teach that God is an eternal being. As Ps 90:2 states, "Before the mountains were born or You gave birth to the earth and the world, even from everlasting to everlasting, You are God." God has always been and will always be. He does not depend upon anything for his existence. In Exod 3:14, God identifies himself to Moses as "I AM WHO I AM" (YHWH)—a phrase that indicates that his existence does not depend on anything

[1] This theme is at the heart of John Piper, *Let the Nations Be Glad! The Supremacy of God in Missions*, 30th anniversary ed. (Grand Rapids: Baker Academic, 2022).

else except himself. He is the one *non-contingent* being upon whom everything else that exists depends for its existence. All other things that exist do so because God created them and gave them being—only in this God do we "live and move and have our being" (Acts 17:28).

We also learn from the phrase "in the beginning God" that God is the center of the story of the universe and all existence. To highlight this, consider the remaining words of Gen 1:1 as well as the message of the first two chapters of Genesis. In Gen 1:1, the word "created" is the verb, and the subject of that verb is God. And we are told that he created the "heavens and earth." As the Creator, he is the center of the story; the story is about his acts and his purposes. More than thirty times in Genesis 1, a direct reference is made to God and how he is crafting the world.[2] Almost every verse draws attention to God with phrases like "then God said," "and God saw," "God separated," "God called," "God made." It is as if Moses is shouting through the ages to us from the very first words of the Bible: "If the *creation* is incredible . . . how much more stunning is the *Creator*?" That which is created has been created to give testimony to the greatness of the Creator.

If we do not grasp the centrality of God in the creation narrative, we will read the story with what's created as the central point. We will read as if the story revolves around us. However, when we see God as eternally preexistent and Creator of all things, then we will acknowledge that he *is* the Lord of all things and that he *ought to be recognized as such* by all that exists (Rev 4:11). As the psalmist puts it, "The earth and everything in it,the world and its inhabitants, belong to the Lord" (Ps 24:1). It is right that we would worship him because he is God.

Scripture also reveals that God is good and glorious (Ps 86:5) and merciful, gracious, and kind (Pss 33:4–7;103:8; 121; 145:8; Eph 2:4–9).

---

[2] Gen 1:1, 2, 3, 4 (twice), 5, 6, 7, 8, 9, 10 (twice), 11, 12, 14, 16, 17, 18, 20, 21 (twice), 22, 24, 25 (twice), 26, 27 (twice), 28 (twice), 29, 31.

It also teaches that he is a holy God who has all knowledge and is wise in all he does (Isa 6:3; Ps 139:1; 1 Cor 1:20–26).[3] His justice, therefore, is always perfect in both its assessment and application (Ps 96). In addition to these (and the many other splendid attributes not mentioned here), the Bible also emphasizes that God is a God who is defined by love (1 John 4:8).

The reality of *who* God is calls us to worship God and obey him. God is worthy of our awe-filled worship because of his great power and majesty. His infinite goodness and splendid moral attributes also summon us to an awe-filled wonder and affection. The very first words of the Bible compel us to recognize that the One who is at the center of the story of creation must be understood to be both the anchor and focal point of eternal worship.

The Purpose and Telos of All Creation Is Worship

God designed and ordered the entirety of creation toward an ultimate end. He fashioned the universe to display his own greatness to all who observe or participate in it, and he created it so it would resound his glory and majesty. As Col 1:16 states, "For everything was created by him in heaven and on earth, the visible and the invisible, whether thrones or dominions or rulers or authorities—all things have been created through him and *for* him." Or as Rom 11:36 (ESV) puts it, "For from him and through him and to him are all things. *To him be the glory forever.* Amen" (emphasis added). The glory of God, then, is the purpose of all creation. Noel Due captures the importance of this idea when he says, "God's decision to create the universe is the effective

[3] For a great devotional read and study of the attributes of God, see A. W. Tozer, *The Knowledge of the Holy* (New York: HarperOne, 2009). Another classic study of the nature of God that is accessible for the lay person is J. I. Packer, *Knowing God* (Downers Grove, IL: InterVarsity, 1973).

cause of worship. He creates and that which springs into being through his Word and Spirit as a result of his creative will worships."[4]

Metaphorically, we could say that creation serves as the grand symphony hall built for worship, in which the whole of creation is meant to sing a song of worship to the great and loving God who created it and fashioned it to display his wonder. Indeed, John Calvin used a similar image to portray the role of creation. He called it the *theatrum gloriae Dei.*[5] For contemporary theologian Jonathan Edwards, the glory of God is the chief end of all of God's works.[6] Nineteenth-century Reformed Presbyterian theologian Charles Hodge summarized it well: "The final cause of all God's purposes is his own glory."[7] Creation, because it occurred *by*, *through*, and *for* God (Col 1:16–17), was designed to reflect the glory of God.

No surprise, then, that Scripture says the "heavens are telling of the glory of God; and their expanse is declaring the work of His hands" (Ps 19:1 NASB1995). Or as Psalm 148 indicates, it is the right and proper ,the creation of humankind, God wove the very fabric of creation with the thread of praise and worship. Reality itself is a tapestry of worship with God as the centerpiece because he is the fountain of all life, love, and joy. He is the one being who is wholly worthy of all worship.

The first point in understanding the connection of worship and the Great Commission is the realization that the universe was created and

---

[4] Noel Due, *Created for Worship* (Ross-shire, UK: Mentor, 2005), 35.

[5] John Calvin, *Institutes of the Christian Religion,* ed. John T. McNeil, trans. Ford Lewis Battles (Philadelphia: Westminster, 1960), I.5.8, I.11.12, I.14.20, and II.6.1.

[6] Jonathan Edwards, *A Treatise Concerning Religious Affections*, available online at https://www.jonathan-edwards.org/ReligiousAffections.pdf (accessed May 8, 2020). See sections 2.3.142; 2.4.221; 5.10. 238–39; 7.264–85.

[7] Charles Hodge, *Systematic Theology*, 3 vols. (Grand Rapids: Hendrickson, 2003), 1:535.

designed by God, and his creation exists by and for him who was *in the beginning*. When God created humanity, Adam and Eve "came into a worship-filled creation. By implication, their existence was also to be taken up in worship."[8] For this reason, any discussion of the missional purpose of human existence must be pursued from within the framework and context of the greater purpose for which all creation exists: the worship and glory of God.

God's Design and Purpose for Image Bearers as Missional Worshippers

God's Design for Humans

Having considered the theocentric nature and purpose of creation, we now consider the place that human beings have in the grand symphony hall of worship we call the universe. Genesis 1:26–28 indicates human beings are unique and set apart from all the rest of the created order because they alone are created in the image and likeness of God.

> Then God said, "Let us make man in our image, according to our likeness. They will rule the fish of the sea, the birds of the sky, the livestock, the whole earth, and the creatures that crawl on the earth." So God created man in his own image; he created him in the image of God; he created them male and female.
>
> God blessed them, and God said to them, "Be fruitful, multiply, fill the earth, and subdue it. Rule the fish of the sea, the birds of the sky, and every creature that crawls on the earth."

A look at the grammatical structure of these verses can again help us understand what God intends for us to learn from them. Note the ordering of ideas in verses 26 and 27:

---

[8] Due, *Created for Worship*, 37.

a. God creates human beings in his image and likeness.

b. God creates human beings as male and female.

Then in verse 28:

b'. He instructs humans to be fruitful and multiply and fill the earth.

a'. God instructs humans to subdue and rule.

This chiastic ordering (a, b, b', a') highlights the essential functions humans are to carry out related to the nature of what they are. That is, because humans are made in the image and likeness of God (a), they are tasked with the function to subdue and rule (a'). Similarly, because humans are created male and female (b), the corresponding function is to be fruitful and multiply and fill the earth (b').

Exactly what it means to be an "image bearer" has long been debated. Several scholars suggest that understanding the term is related to ancient Near Eastern monarchs' use of statues to represent their authority. By placing a statue or "image" of themselves in a region, a king established his authority and right to rule in that part of the kingdom. Thus, when God declared human beings to be his "image bearers," he established that we are to be his visible representatives to rule and reign over the created world. As such, we were both designed and tasked to function with a derived authority to act as God would act and rule over the created order as God himself would rule.[9] Because humans are made in the image and likeness of God, they are also specifically designed and uniquely qualified to play a dual role in the created order. As image bearers, they carry an authority over the rest of creation. In this role, they are supposed to use their authority to rally and guide the created order to be God directed. They are set apart to govern creation,

[9] Gordon J. Wenham, *Story as Torah* (Grand Rapids: Baker Academic, 2000), 25–26. See also William J. Dumbrell, *Covenant and Creation: A Theology of the Old Testament Covenants* (Carlisle, UK: Paternoster, 1984), 31–34.

care for it, shape it, use it, and make it to flourish in a manner that represents it as an act of worship.

Humanity, as image bearers, are like God in that we have a position of authority over the rest of created order. Humans are created and designed to be God's representatives and carry out his wishes and commands to the rest of creation. We could say that humans are "over" creation and tasked to act as God's representatives to creation. In this role, we are to "go" into the created order to communicate and fulfill God's design for the world. God commissioned humans to "teach the created order to obey" so that the entire created realm and all the humans that would eventually dwell in it would worship him as he designed and intended in the beginning.

Understanding this unique position of humans gives context to appreciate the instructions God gave Adam and Eve when he commanded them to "subdue" and "rule" over the earth. The Hebrew word translated into English as "subdue" is the word *kabash*. The word connotes the use of strength or force to control or subjugate. The Hebrew word *radah* translates into English as "rule." *Radah* also strongly connotes a ruler with dominion over a kingdom. The implication is that those made in the image of God are designed as part of the created order and use their authority and strength to shape or subdue the earth in a manner in keeping with the nature and moral character of God.[10] They are stewards of the great King who care for all the things of God to return them to him for his honor and glory.

Likewise, those who go out in the likeness of God should *rule* over earth so that their governance rightly represents the wishes of God regarding the created order. They are champions of God going forth in his name to herald his good cause to all the earth. The image bearer's mediation between God and the rest of creation should result in all

---

[10] For an example of how this might look, consider Psalm 104.

glory, honor, praise, and worship for God from every aspect of the created realm.[11]

Two direct and crucial implications emerge in the discussion of worship and the Great Commission. The first is that humans are missional by definition. Because God created humanity as image bearers with dominion over creation, humanity represents God to the world and represents the world to God. Humankind was created to cultivate a flourishing world full of praise and glory to God. Therefore, a "mission" is not merely something we "do." Rather, it is a part of who we are. God created humans to be missional by nature. We express the fundamental nature of humanness by going forth from God and in the name of God to champion the things of God in the world.

Second, human beings are worshippers by nature as well as image bearers. As missional beings embedded in the created order, humans go forth into creation as God's champions, acting in his name to lead creation as if God himself were leading and nurturing it. In so doing, they are loving God, honoring God, and returning to him what he is due. Thus, human beings are not merely created *to* worship, nor are they created simply *for* worship. Describing them in either of these ways suggests that worship can be separated from their nature. Instead, humans are best understood as worshipers by the very nature of their constitution. Humans were created as worshipers who are "continuously outpouring" worship because we are dependent creatures and because we are creatures made to represent our Creator.[12]

---

[11] For further investigation of these ideas, see J. I. Packer, *Concise Theology* (Carol Stream, IL: Tyndale House, 1993), 71–76. See also Francis Schaeffer's discussion of this dual mediatorial role of human beings in *Pollution and the Death of Man* (Wheaton, IL: Crossway, 1970), 48.

[12] Harold Best, *Unceasing Worship: Biblical Perspectives on Worship and the Arts* (Downers Grove, IL: IVP, 2003), 23. For a fuller discussion of the nature of humans, see Mark Liederbach and Evan Lenow, *Ethics as Worship* (Phillipsburg, NJ: P&R, 2021), 38–54.

The Mission of Filling the Earth with Worship

When God placed Adam into the garden to worship and obey, he did not intend for Adam to be alone. God's grand design included the creation of Eve, a partner with Adam in accomplishing the great goal for which all creation was formed. In the chiastic structure of the Genesis 1:26–28 passage, we have already seen that being made in the image and likeness of God, Adam and Eve were created to "subdue the earth and rule over it." Their work in the garden made it flourish, worshipping God. The second part of the chiasm is this: in being made as "male and female," Adam and Eve were created to "be fruitful and multiply and fill the earth."

The reason it was "not good" for Adam to be "alone" (Gen 1:27–28) becomes clear in Gen 2:18–20: it would be difficult for Adam to be fruitful and multiply by himself. God perfectly designed the male–female binary and the husband–wife relationship to be a means for accomplishing his purposes for the world. The procreative element is one purpose of marriage. But we must be careful not to limit God's special depiction of Eve as a "helper suitable" merely to help Adam populate the earth. Being a wife and mother are beautiful and praiseworthy aspects of womanhood, but these qualities, alone or together, do not capture the fullness of God's design and intent for Eve.[13]

So why did God point out that it was not good for Adam to be alone, then create a helper for him? God desired their relationship

---

[13] It is important to point out that if we reversed the flow of the conversation, we would come to the same conclusion for men. That is, if Eve had been created first, we would say the same thing for her: "How could she be fruitful and multiply without Adam?" Likewise, we would point out that certainly Adam's role would not be simply understood as a seed producer to make babies. Finally, while we would certainly want to honor the high and glorious calling for the man to be a husband and father, we would likewise say that neither by themselves nor both together would they capture the fullness of God's design or intent for Adam.

and fruitfulness to result in a world full of worshipers to maximize the glory of God made manifest throughout all creation. A fundamental purpose of marriage is to perpetuate the mission of God. The children born of Adam and Eve were to take up the mission of God and champion the things of God to manifest the glory of God and give marvelous testimony to the Creator's awesome glory. In short, through their complementary roles, Adam and Eve were designed to lead worship.

If Adam and Eve had not sinned, if they had obeyed God and fulfilled the task God created them for, they would have filled the earth with sinless worshipers who lived in joyful, flourishing obedience. People, cultures, and nations would have been united in one purpose: to fill the grand universal symphony hall of worship with his praise.

God designed human beings as missional worshipers and embedded them in the created order to maximize his praise and glory throughout the earth. The first parents were designed and instructed to seed and shape the world and the various cultures as societies of worship. Therefore, it is proper to describe Genesis 1:27–28 as a worship mandate and not merely as a cultural mandate. Indeed, because it involves God's instruction to his image bearers, we can even describe it as the great missional mandate (or commission) God gave his people in the beginning.

Sin, the Gospel, and the Restored Mission

Sin

The immense tragedy of the fall is amplified by the God-centered nature of all reality, the function of the created order as a symphony of worship and mission. As Scripture indicates, Adam and Eve's sin plunged not only themselves but the entire human race into a disordering of both worship and mission (Genesis 3, Romans 5). In fact, Scripture poignantly shows us that not long after the initial sin, those God designed as his champions to fill the earth with cultures of rightly ordered worship instead find themselves killing one another and creating cultures of depravity. Rather than causing life and flourishing, they are in immediate need of instruction and warning not to shed one another's blood (Gen 4:1–16; 9:6). Instead of "ruling" and "subduing" the earth such that God's glory is maximized, sinful humans more often introduce forms and patterns of oppression and domination such that creation itself groans and longs for redemption (Rom 8:22–24).

The missional worship of people created in the image of God has not ceased. Worship and missional energies continue. But these key and central purposes (ruling and subduing creation to maximize God's glory) are now fundamentally disordered, as image bearers exchange the glory of the immortal God for puny gods and inanimate things. Their worship, too, is toward false ends and their mission to counterfeit purposes (Rom 1:19–23). As John Calvin once so poignantly put it, sin has turned human hearts into "idol factories."[14]

Those whom God created to maximally worship him do not do so and have rightly become objects of God's wrath (Rom 1:18; Eph 2:1–3). As Romans so clearly indicates, all have sinned and fallen short of the glory of God; the wages of these sins for each human, created to maximize the worship of God, is death (Rom 3:23; 6:23).

But far more tragic than the eternal punishment humans rightly now receive—without question, the single greatest injustice of all time—is that the infinitely majestic, good, and holy God does not receive the worship he is due. God himself is robbed of the maximal praise, honor, and worship that every element of creation was designed to render unto him.

---

[14] Calvin, *Institutes of the Christian Religion,* I.11.8.

The Gospel

But thanks be to God! Because of Jesus Christ's penal substitutionary death on Calvary and his resurrection on Easter Sunday, humans have hope. Through the gospel, humans can once again be restored to right relationship with God by grace alone, through faith alone, in Christ alone (Eph 2:4–9). The gospel is also the way humanity can be restored to the right pursuit of good works and the original purpose God designed us to walk in (Eph 2:10). Through the gospel, God's image bearers can again pursue the original task: going into the created order and championing the maximal worship of God to fill the great symphony hall of the universe with worship.

The Restored Mission

This, then, is the precise point where we see the vital link between worship and the Great Commission. Jesus commissioned his followers, saying, "All authority has been given to Me in heaven and on earth. Go therefore and make disciples of all nations, baptizing them in the name of the Father and the Son and the Holy Spirit, teaching them to observe all that I commanded you; and lo, I am with you always, even to the end of the age" (Matt 28:18–20 NASB1995).

His instruction to make disciples of all nations follows the pattern of the original instructions he gave to Adam and Eve in the Garden of Eden. Christ's followers are tasked to maximize the worship and praise of God by making disciples who will likewise live lives of worshipful obedience and be on mission to reach others as well.

Conclusion

Having explored the theocentric nature of the universe and God's design for it to be a "grand symphony hall of worship"; having considered God's design of humans as missional worshippers tasked to go into the created order and fill it with peoples, cultures, and nations who maximally worship God; and having touched on both the redemptive and restorative nature of the gospel, there are at least two conclusions.

First, given the similarities between God's instructions to Adam and Eve to be on mission to fill the earth with worshippers and Jesus's instructions to his disciples to fill the earth with his disciples, it is right to conclude that the "missional worship mandate" given to Adam and Eve in Gen 1:27–28 is at least a precursor to, if not a first iteration of, the Great Commission Jesus gave to his church in Matt 28:18–20. If space allowed further development of the argument, one could conclude that the gospel is the ground and means to a full restoration of the original mission of God given to humans to fill the earth with worship, and therefore, Jesus's Great Commission would properly be understood as a recapitulation of the missional worship mandate of Gen 1:27–28.

Second, by exploring the connection between God's creation order design for worship and the Great Commission, we see that human sin does not end human worship nor does it stop human missional energies. Rather, sin distorts and derails the right ordering of both worship and mission. This means that even after sin, humans remain missional worshippers. The great tragedy of human existence is that missional worship is now ordered to, and champions, lesser things. Again, had space allowed for further development of the argument, one conclusion could be that the very reason for Christ giving his Great Commission marching orders to his disciples—indeed, the very purpose of Christian missionary task—is to see worship once again rightly ordered to its proper end. That is, the very reason that Christian missions exist is because proper worship does.[15]

---

[15] This theme is at the heart of Piper, *Let the Nations Be Glad!*

CHAPTER SIX

APOLOGETICS AND THE GREAT COMMISSION

James K. Dew Jr.

Introduction

It is a unique honor to contribute to this volume honoring Dr. Danny Akin, and before turning to the topic for this essay, I must start with a few words of gratitude for him. For the past twenty years in his post as president at Southeastern Baptist Theological Seminary, Dr. Akin has served the churches of the SBC with integrity and passion, impacting tens of thousands of people. Under his leadership, a generation of missionaries and pastors has been trained and commissioned to take the gospel to the nations and to our own country.

Like most of the students and faculty at Southeastern, I knew little about him when he arrived on campus in the summer of 2004. I was a PhD student at the time, and distinctly remember the encouraging changes that began to take place on campus when he arrived. From then until June 2019, when I left to become the president of New Orleans Baptist Theological Seminary, I grew to know him and love him as my president, my friend, and my brother in Christ.

For a multitude of reasons, I am indebted to Danny Akin. There are three reasons for my gratitude that I should mention here. First, professionally speaking, Danny Akin gave me my first teaching job in higher education. Like other PhD students, I was aware of how difficult it would be to land a teaching post after completing my degree. After years of hard work and prayer on my part, Dr. Akin invited me to join the faculty in the summer of 2011. I am as grateful for that opportunity today as I was when he hired me.

Second, in addition to hiring me at Southeastern, he invited me to join his cabinet a little over a year later. It was the opportunity of a lifetime. For the next six and a half years, I sat at his table "learning the ropes" of running a seminary. That role as dean gave me the ability to do more than mere administrivia. He empowered me and trusted me to lead. He gave me the ability to build programs, hire faculty, raise funds, lead departments, and cast vision for our direction as a school. As I would learn in the years to come, these are not normally things that deans get to do. These are things that presidents do. And providentially, given what my next ministry responsibility would be at NOBTS, I was prepared to be a president by sitting with him and the cabinet at SEBTS for almost seven years. The word "gratitude" does not begin to capture my heart when I think about the gift Dr. Akin gave me.

Third, it was in my time at Southeastern under Dr. Akin's leadership that the Great Commission took deep root in my own heart. A philosopher by training, I once cared deeply about becoming a serious academic. By God's grace and in His providence, I was able to earn the degrees, teach the classes, present the papers, and write the books. And it was all as fun and joyful as I had hoped it would be. But the whole time I was at Southeastern with Dr. Akin, there was a constant drumbeat that compelled us and shaped the work we did. That was the drumbeat of the Great Commission. As time went by under his leadership, I found myself caring less and less about my academic accomplishments and more and more about getting the gospel to the nations. Who cares if I ever get to publish another book? But I do care that my life should be spent equipping and empowering the saints to take the gospel into the darkness. That change in my heart came through Dr. Akin's impact on my life.

But of course, there is much more. I am grateful, not just for the wonderful opportunities he gave me, but also for what I saw in him as a president during that time. As a member of the cabinet, I got to see how Dr. Akin treated people and handled difficult situations. Presidents are often required to do hard things or have difficult conversations. In Dr. Akin, I observed a pastoral heart of compassion and grace. He always treated people well, no matter how tough a situation might have been in the moment. For all these reasons I will be forever grateful for my friend, brother, and colleague.

Dr. Akin, Tara and I love you and we are grateful for you and Mrs. Charlotte. Thank you for taking a chance on us, and for your constant love, encouragement, and support. This volume in your honor is well deserved!

And now to the assigned topic!

The Nature of Apologetics and the Task of the Great Commission

The relationship between the Great Commission and apologetics should be straightforward and natural, but I fear that it is often ignored. Academically speaking, apologists and missiologists seldom collaborate, treating their respective fields as isolated disciplines with little to say to each other. We may, from time to time, collaborate on topics in world religions or comparative religions, but even with that, there is not as much interaction and collaboration as there should be. For what it is worth, I have found missiologists to be some of the smartest people that I have ever encountered. As such, in what follows, I want to suggest that the two disciplines, and the scholars who work in each discipline, should collaborate more often. I can see at least three major reasons for this collaboration: (1) missiologists and apologists must both be jacks-of-all-trades; (2) they both regularly face intense resistance to the gospel; and (3) they both should attempt to show the beauty of Christianity.

Jack-of-All-Trades

First, scholars in both disciplines are required to engage a diverse range of topics to do their work well. Metaphorically speaking, missiologists and apologists are like farmers—a farmer must be able to do more than mere "farming." A good farmer must also be able to do carpentry work, mechanical work, veterinary work, agricultural work, and much more. He truly is a jack-of-all-trades. In the same way, a good missiologist or a good apologist must be skilled and proficient in many disciplines and able to apply those skills and disciplines to many different contexts.

Consider the skills a missionary needs. For starters, the missionary must be able to do sound biblical exegesis. Central to sharing the message of the cross is a proper reading of the sacred scriptures. If this is done incorrectly, the message itself is lost. Because of this, the missionary needs many of the same skills that our colleagues in biblical studies possess. But of course, this is just the beginning. The missionary must also be able to do the work of a theologian. He must be able to "put it all together" as doctrinal formulation in a way that accurately reflects the teachings of Christianity. An improper theological method will result in missiological catastrophe. With this, the missionary must also be able to recognize, analyze, and critique the philosophical and sociological worldview motifs within the surrounding culture. And, perhaps most difficult of all, he must have the skill of contextualizing so the teaching is rightly heard among the nations. In other words, to do his work well, a missionary must be able to do biblical exegesis, theological construction, philosophical evaluation, sociological analysis, and contextualization. That is a tremendous burden for scholars in the classical theological disciplines. Contextualizing and properly applying our theological message requires missiologists to have a truly diverse skill set.

Years ago, I saw firsthand just how difficult all this must be for the missionary. I had been asked to go to Vietnam to teach an ethics class to pastors training in a seminary there. As it turned out, they really wanted me to help these pastors (all of whom were rice farmers) understand the morality taught by Christianity. In preparation, I figured the best way to do this was to teach through the Ten Commandments. I must admit that I was woefully naïve about just how difficult it would be for me to properly communicate the teachings of Christianity to these dear brothers. As we touched on the very first two commandments, I quickly saw the terrible difficulty of the linguistic, cultural, educational, and spiritual barriers that lay between us. As I attempted to convey and apply the teaching "no graven images" to their context, I created a theological mess, cluttering more than I clarified. Simply put, the work of translation and contextualization was far harder than I anticipated, and I simply was not ready. In that moment, I came to appreciate the incredibly difficult job that missiologists have in their work. Again, this difficulty arises from the diversity of tasks that a missionary must be good at doing.

In many ways, this is also true for apologists. Apologetics is a "discipline" that spans all the other disciplines. Objections to our faith come from almost every corner. Sometimes the objection may be philosophical in nature (existence of God, problem of evil, etc.). In these cases, we are required to delve into the philosophical issues. But we dare not do that haphazardly or casually, lest we create more of a problem from the poor work we do. I must admit, I see this mistake quite often, and it is deeply frustrating. For many apologists, their grasp of the philosophical issues they speak of is minimal. And because of this, their defenses are either weak or downright problematic. But the same is also true for the other disciplines. By contrast, however, when an apologist is well versed in philosophical discourse, the work is the better for it. Sometimes the objection is scientific, requiring the same level of investment to respond. And so on for all types of objections that might arise. An objection to the faith may be philosophical, scientific, historical, textual, or any number of things. As a result, much like the missiologist, an apologist needs to be a jack-of-all-trades.

Gospel Resistance and the Hope of Conversion

Second, both the missiologist and the apologist encounter unique resistance to the gospel in their work, and both seek the same goal for their work—the conversion of souls. To be clear, resistance to the gospel is a human issue, not an "American" issue. Consider, for example, how the apostle Paul recognized this and responded in the book of Romans (1:18–23). Speaking about the rebellious disposition of our hearts, Paul noted the human tendency to suppress the truth of God and his holiness. He says:

> For God's wrath is revealed from heaven against all godlessness and unrighteousness of people who by their unrighteousness suppress the truth, since what can be known about God is evident among them, because God has shown it to them. For his invisible attributes, that is, his eternal power and divine nature, have been clearly seen since the creation of the world, being understood through what he has made. As a result, people are without excuse. For though they knew God, they did not glorify him as God or show gratitude. Instead, their thinking became worthless, and their senseless hearts were darkened. Claiming to be wise, they became fools and exchanged the glory of the

> immortal God for images resembling mortal man, birds, four-footed animals, and reptiles.

Here in Romans 1, Paul shows us that the human heart is, after the fall, naturally inclined to suppress truth, deny God's revelation, refuse to give him honor, and worship the creation instead of the creator. Once again, this is what all people do, whether they live in North or South America, Europe, Asia, Africa, or Australia.

In Romans 3, Paul goes a bit further by noting how all men, "both Jew and Greeks," are guilty before God. In vv. 9–18, he says:

> What then? Are we any better off? Not at all! For we have already charged that both Jews and Greeks are all under sin, as it is written: There is no one righteous, not even one. There is no one who understands; there is no one who seeks God. All have turned away; all alike have become worthless. There is no one who does what is good, not even one. Their throat is an open grave; they deceive with their tongues. Vipers' venom is under their lips. Their mouth is full of cursing and bitterness. Their feet are swift to shed blood; ruin and wretchedness are in their paths, and the path of peace they have not known. There is no fear of God before their eyes.

Paul's point here about our natural dispositions is quite alarming. He shows not just that we are all guilty as sinners before God, but that we are all also naturally opposed to God before our conversion. Notice here that Paul says no one is righteous. In fact, he even says that we "deceive with [our] tongues," and that our "mouth is full of cursing and bitterness."

Similarly, in Ephesians 2, Paul reminds us of our natural state before conversion. In vv. 1–3 he says:

> And you were dead in your trespasses and sins in which you previously walked according to the ways of this world, according

> to the ruler of the power of the air, the spirit now working in the disobedient. We too all previously lived among them in our fleshly desires, carrying out the inclinations of our flesh and thoughts, and we were by nature children under wrath as the others were also.

In this passage, Paul elaborates further upon our natural hostilities toward God before conversion. He reminds us that we were dead in our sins, controlled by satanic influence, carnal in our desires, and were children of wrath against God. In all these passages, and many more, Paul helps us understand how, apart from Christ, our hearts are turned against God and are naturally hostile to him. This is true of all people, in all places, and at all times. Yet in many cases, the hostility may not manifest in overt displays of aggression. It can be subtle or concealed.

There are also plenty of times when this hostility takes an outward expression of overt resistance. These are moments that apologists and missiologists tend to experience in unique ways. Missiologists, for example, take the gospel to people whose worldview is radically different from ours. Their beliefs, customs, values, and rhythms of life arise from non-Christian worldviews that are completely different. As such, missiologists often encounter significant resistance when they preach the gospel among the nations. Likewise, apologists are primarily engaged with people who are hostile to Christianity and all it teaches. The critics and skeptics that the apologist speaks to are often actively engaged in opposing the gospel, and their attacks can be vitriolic and antagonistic. Evidentially, they reject the propositional and supernatural claims of the Bible. Morally, they also reject commands regarding the Christian lifestyle. The apologist deals with all sorts of objections and experiences the strongest forms of opposition to faith.

Apologists and missiologists experience similar kinds of resistance in their work. But it is also true that they share the same goal for their work. The goal is not just to present the claims of Christianity to the nonbeliever but to see them come to faith in Christ. This work requires significant time and patience with non-believers. It requires forming and cultivating meaningful relationships and may take years of investment. But in each case, for the apologist and the missiologist, their work requires them to break through the natural resistance they face and seek the salvation of the people they minister to.

Showing the Beauty of Christianity

Third, apologists and missiologists also share the work of showing the beauty and desirability of the Christian faith. Our work, in both enterprises, is not just to disseminate the propositional facts of Christianity to the nonbeliever. If this is all we do, then Christianity is seen as nothing more than a collection of facts and is stripped of its natural aesthetic. Rather, our job is to help the nonbeliever see that Christianity is true *and* that following Jesus is life-giving, fulfilling, redemptive, and joyful. For the missionary, this is certainly central to their work. When they go to the nations, expounding on the biblical and theological content of Christianity is obviously essential. But they must also labor to show Christianity in all its aesthetic beauty. They do this in the way they teach, share life, build friendships, and showcase their faith in the whole of life itself.

For much of recent history in apologetics, most objections against the faith have been evidential in nature. Whether the nonbeliever objects to the existence of God, the resurrection of Jesus, the possibility of miracles, the existence of the soul and life after death, or the reliability of the scriptures, the accusation underlying these objections has been irrationality. In other words, whatever the specific kind of objection, the common theme is that believers are irrational for believing, given the lack of evidence and data to support our claims. And to make matters worse, the modernity and the Enlightenment that inform

Western culture insist that just two types of evidence "count" when it comes to epistemic support for faith: empirical data and rational argument. Personal stories of redeemed and changed lives are not evidence. Neither are religious experiences that motivate a believer's life. For a believer to show that Christianity is true, he must provide empirical data or some kind of philosophical argument that supports it. Otherwise, Christian faith would always be inferior to science and philosophy. As a result, in past decades, evidentialist apologetics was important and popular in evangelical circles. And during this period, Christians did fantastic work of marshalling evidence, constructing sound arguments, and defending the faith against these accusations of irrationality by showing the intellectual strength of the faith.

Yet, I am not at all convinced that this approach to apologetics is what is most critical now for at least two reasons. First, this approach tends to strip our presentation of the faith of all the existential aspects that make it desirable in the first place. By doing so, this approach reduces Christianity to a mere intellectual belief system. Again, I want to be careful here. Surely our faith is intellectually robust, and it has held up well against the strongest intellectual attacks over the past 2,000 years. But Christianity is so much more than just an intellectual belief system. It is a faith that brings redemption, hope, love, and deep communion with the God of the universe. Most people who come to faith in Christ do so because of the encounters they have with Christians who embody the beauty of Christianity in our lives (though our evidentialist approach to apologetics would cause us to deny it). As such, we should reject the arrogant demands of the Enlightenment. Sure, empirical data and rational argument are a part of our case, but they are not the only kinds of evidence that count. And if we labor only to provide the evidence that Christianity is true, and do not labor to show them the actual love of Jesus Christ and the beauty of a life that is grounded in him, then we should not be surprised when the nonbeliever is unmoved toward belief.

Second, I fear that an "evidentialist only" approach fails to appreciate the cultural shifts that have happened around us. Today, most of the major objections to our faith are not about Christianity's rationality or a lack of evidence to support it. Most objections today suggest something much different. Where nonbelievers once said we were irrational for believing what we do, now they say we are bad people for believing as we do. Author Sam Harris, for example, says, "That religion may have served some necessary function for us in the past does not preclude the possibility that it is now the greatest impediment to our building a global civilization."[1] This sentiment is not new with Harris. In 1971, for example, John Lennon was already singing this idea—literally—in his song "Imagine," in which he urged his fans to imagine that there is no heaven, no hell, no religion whatsoever, equating such a scenario with a life of peace where all the people of the world live as one.[2]

Well before Harris, cultural influencers like Lennon suggested that religion was the major problem in human culture and dreamed of its full removal from society. This was also one of the central ideas in Marx's communism. What is different now is that these are no longer the voices of a few. This kind of disposition has become mainstream. Increasingly, nonbelievers see the content of our faith not merely as irrational but as morally problematic. Consider the way you might hear it said:

> "Who do you think you are to tell people what they can or can't do with their bodies?"
>
> "How dare you tell people who they can or cannot love and marry?"
>
> "How dare you tell me what my gender is?"

---

[1] Sam Harris, *Letter to a Christian Nation* (New York: Vintage, 2006), 91.

[2] John Lennon and Yoko Ono, "Imagine," in *Imagine* (Apple Records, 1971), studio album.

How do we respond to all of this? Rational argument and empirical data may have a part to play but are not enough. An additional part of our response must be to simply show them Christianity and all that makes it beautiful. We invite them into our homes, our churches, our lives, and into friendship. We show them how Christians worship, live, care, and love. We must let them see God at work in our lives, the way he's changed us, and the hope that is ours. By doing this, we help them see that they may want Christianity to be true in the first place.

Blaise Pascal is helpful for us here. He reminds us that before we can show people that the Christian faith is true, we must get them to the place where they would want it to be true. He says, "Men despise religion. They hate it and are afraid it may be true. The cure for this is (1) to show that religion is not contrary to reason . . . (2) make it attractive, make good men wish it were true, (3) show that it is true."[3]

It is important to note that when he says "make it attractive," Pascal was not suggesting some form of cultural compromise that makes Christianity more palatable for the nonbeliever. Rather, what he envisions here is showing Christianity for all that it is, not just its intellectual foundations. In other words, he wanted us to show the beauty of Christianity, not just evidence to support Christianity. Then and only then, for Pascal, will the hostile nonbeliever be willing to consider it properly.

I think Pascal is right and is timely in this cultural moment. As we seek to persuade the nonbeliever, we will labor to show that Christianity is true, but we must also labor to show the nonbeliever why they might want it to be true. I suspect this is once again a shared burden between missiologists and apologists. And the more we collaborate, the better our work for the kingdom will be.

---

[3] Blaise Pascal, in *Christianity for Modern Pagans*, ed. Peter Kreeft (London: Ignatius, 1993), 28.

Conclusion

Danny Akin's heart for the nations is obvious to anyone who spends time with him or hears him preach. As a young philosopher/apologist, I was deeply shaped by his voice while serving with him at Southeastern. As I've suggested here, there is far too little dialogue and collaboration between the two disciplines, and each is the poorer for it. With greater dialogue and collaboration, each discipline would be strengthened. As I've tried to argue here, scholars in both disciplines regularly face resistance to the gospel. Both must be jacks-of-all-trades, and both should focus on showing the full beauty of Christianity.

CHAPTER SEVEN

PASTORAL MINISTRY AND THE GREAT COMMISSION

R. Scott Pace

Introduction

When I first met Danny Akin in August 2004, I was a second-year PhD student struggling with my place in the degree program as a young, married pastor with a newborn. Research languages, colloquiums, and academic pursuits did not seem to fit with my calling, and I was wrestling with the decision to continue or not. Dr. Akin, as Southeastern's new president, was invited to introduce himself and address all the PhD students at the beginning of the academic year. In that meeting, he cast his vision for a pastor–theologian model, one that would thoroughly equip students with the necessary tools to serve the local church and fulfill the Great Commission. Specifically, I remember him describing the worthlessness of ivory tower theology that was not equipped to share the gospel and minister to hurting people in complicated, real-life scenarios. This resonated deeply with me and renewed my heart for ministry and academic training. It was refreshing to hear someone so committed to rigorous theological education also express a passion for pastors and people. I was overwhelmed when I learned I would have the honor of studying under him as my mentoring professor!

Since that fateful day, I have had the privilege of learning from him in a variety of capacities. I have walked through church struggles and sought his counsel. I have navigated new ministry assignments and benefited from his wisdom and support. I also transitioned into full-time ministry training, serving and equipping ministry leaders while learning how to balance my calling in the local church. I have coauthored multiple books with him and am privileged to serve on his administrative team and on the Southeastern faculty. I continue to learn from his leadership and through his personal investment in my life.

One of the most inspiring aspects of his ministry is that he weds his love for pastors to his passion for the Great Commission. Interestingly, these concepts—pastoral ministry and the Great Commission—are often discussed in isolation from one another. Typically, the field of pastoral ministry is approached from a pragmatic perspective that focuses on the requirements, the role, and the responsibilities of the office. The Great Commission, on the other hand, is commonly relegated to discussions about missions or evangelism. But in many ways, these two aspects of kingdom service are mutually dependent. In honor of Danny Akin, who has faithfully embodied their complementary nature, it is my privilege to consider three interlocking characteristics of the relationship between pastoral ministry and the Great Commission.

The Pastor's Work Must Be Defined by the Great Commission

The church's mission and the pastor's ministry are inextricably linked, and their mutual relationship hinges on the Great Commission.

The pastor's role and responsibilities are determined by the church's expected obedience to King Jesus's final marching orders, to "make disciples" (Matt 28:18–20). The symbiosis of the church's mission and the pastor's ministry is readily identifiable, and reinforced by foundational truths that confirm and clarify the pastor's work.

Our understanding of the pastor's work begins by recognizing that the Great Commission defines the mission of the church. Jesus's guiding mandate for the church was evident before his final instructions at his ascension. For instance, Jesus asked the penetrating question, "Who do you say that I am?" and Peter professed, "You are the Messiah, the Son of the living God!" (Matt 16:15–16). Jesus affirmed Peter's reply and made a promise founded on the eternal truth of his identity, "I will build my church" (Matt 16:18). His expressed intention reveals several important truths that define the new covenant people of God and their purpose. His definitive declaration "I will" asserted his divine supremacy over all creation and, more specifically, the church (see Col 1:15, 18). The possessive pronoun "his" was used in Titus 2:14 to express his ultimate authority over and personal affection for his redeemed people, "his own possession." Also, by designating his people as the "church," he identified his followers as called to be a spiritual community of believers (see 1 Pet 2:9).

In addition to identifying the church's essential nature, his declaration revealed its mission. Jesus's intention to "build" his church established him as the foundation and cornerstone of his spiritual household (see 1 Cor 3:11; 1 Pet 2:6–7). But this characterization of the church and its construction also implies growth and expansion, which are "built" by continually adding new members to the covenant community. In other words, Jesus's original design and intention for the church included its missional expanse by proclaiming the good news that he is the Savior of the world. The blueprint and instructions for our participation in the Great Commission are grounded in Jesus's original declaration, which established the church.

The church's mission to "make disciples" of all nations is also demonstrated through the uncompromised focus and advance of the early church. Through the promise of the Holy Spirit, Jesus commanded and empowered his disciples to be his "witnesses . . . to the ends of the earth" (Acts 1:8). Following 3,000 conversions at Pentecost (Acts 2:41), the expansion of the church continued—"every day the Lord added to their number those who were being saved" (Acts 2:47). By their communal witness, ministry efforts, and bold proclamation of the gospel, "the churches were strengthened in the faith and grew daily in numbers" (Acts 16:5).

The faithful testimony of the church and its continued growth throughout history affirm God's desire for the gospel message to be a global message delivered by his people (Rom 10:13–15; Col 1:5–6). The church's mission is confirmed by the fulfillment of the Great Commission, when we will witness "a vast multitude from every nation, tribe, people, and language" worshipping King Jesus as the risen Lamb of God (Rev 7:9–10)!

Since it so clearly defines the mission of the church, we can also recognize that *the Great Commission defines the ministry of the pastor.* This is consequential to the governing and guiding influence of Jesus's missional command to his disciples. As the prevailing instruction for his people, the Great Commission should determine the pastor's service to the church. However, defining the ministry of the pastor goes beyond simply deriving pastoral implications from the church's mission.

The Bible defines the pastoral office and functions through a list of qualifications and corresponding exhortations (1 Tim 3:1–7; Titus 1:5–9; 1 Pet 5:1–5). These biblical standards are typically understood as character traits and ministry skills required for the role. While the qualifications and exhortations preserve the dignity and integrity of the office and present a Christlike example to the flock, they are also directly related to the Great Commission.

The interchangeable terms for the pastoral office imply various aspects of "making disciples," including guidance and leadership ("overseer"), wisdom and counsel ("elder"), and care and spiritual nourishment ("shepherd") (see Acts 20:17, 28; 1 Pet 5:1–2). In addition, the supporting participles in the Great Commission, "going," "baptizing," and "teaching," also correspond to required elements of the pastoral office.

"Making disciples" begins with living the mission and sharing the gospel as we "go." This is particularly true for pastors who are called to "do the work of an evangelist" (2 Tim 4:5). While we are responsible to serve God's people, we must also maintain a "good reputation among outsiders" through a life consistent with the gospel (1 Tim 3:7). Many character attributes required for the office involve public testimony on the pastor's disposition and lifestyle, which must be "above reproach" (1 Tim 3:2–3). This means pastoral qualifications are directly related to his responsibility to fulfill the Great Commission.

The "baptizing" component of the Great Commission also helps define the ministry of the pastor. The physical immersion of a professing believer reflects the spiritual reality of their new life in Christ and their adoption into God's family. Ministerially speaking, it involves the assimilation of converts into the local church. Pastors typically baptize to welcome new believers into the covenant community through their public profession of faith. Performing baptisms is not restricted to pastors, but the responsibility as "overseer" certainly would include facilitating believer's baptism and leading the congregation in affirming those who profess Christ. This crucial aspect of "making disciples" is a pastor's essential responsibility as a designated "under-shepherd" who assimilates new sheep into the flock.

The most obvious aspect of a pastor's work that is reflected in the Great Commission is "teaching." Shepherds must be "able to teach" (1 Tim 3:2) and must be grounded in the truth of Scripture so they can "encourage" God's people with "sound teaching" and to "refute those who contradict" the Scriptures (Titus 1:9). As pastors, we are accountable before God for our diligence and faithfulness in the handling of his Word (2 Tim 2:15). This most certainly includes the "teaching" elements of our pulpit ministry (2 Tim 4:2). It also involves the mentoring and modeling aspects of our responsibilities (1 Thess 2:8; 1 Cor 11:1). Those who teach in the church are held to a higher standard because of the sacred nature of our task and the spiritual influence we have (Jas 3:1). A primary responsibility of the pastoral office, the "teaching" aspect of "making disciples," along with "going" and "baptizing," clearly defines the ministry of the pastor.

By defining the mission of the church and the ministry of the pastor, the Great Commission ultimately defines our work. This does not mean as pastors we are solely responsible for fulfilling the Great Commission. But it does mean that every aspect of our leadership, from caring for those in need to providing administrative oversight to preaching God's Word, should be evaluated through the lens of "making disciples." The success of our ministry is determined by our faithfulness and our fulfillment of this singular Great Commission goal.

The Pastor's Heart Must Be Devoted to the Great Commission

While our role and responsibilities are defined by the Great Commission, Jesus's command to "make disciples" is not intended as an obligation we perform. Obedience to the Great Commission must be a heartfelt response to the Great Commandments, to "love God" with our entire being and to "love [our] neighbor" as ourselves (Matt 22:37–40). Obedience to our Savior must always flow from a heart of reciprocated love for the undeserved kindness which he mercifully extends to us in Christ (1 John 4:10–11, 19). This is especially true when it comes to obeying the Great Commission. As we become captivated by his love for us (and the rest of humanity!), we begin to reflect his heart for our neighbors and the nations.

To cultivate a heart devoted to the Great Commission, *we must share God's heart for our neighbors.* It is easy for pastors to feel we live in the spotlight of public ministry and under a microscope of constant scrutiny. As a result, in our personal lives we may tend to isolate ourselves from the community. Add the intensity of the culture wars and the increasingly sinful world around us, and we are even more prone to distance ourselves from nonbelievers. Our daily immersion in the church, our members and ministries results in our being mostly insulated from the rest of the world.

While Jesus calls us to keep our virtues and values separate from the world, he also sent us to engage the world with the gospel so that "the world may believe" (John 17:15–18, 21). The natural drift toward separation requires intentional effort to resist and to reach our communities for Christ. This includes being committed to preaching the gospel from the pulpit and providing opportunities for hearers to respond. But it also requires us to go beyond simply hosting church outreach events and issuing invitations at the end of services. After all, the Great Commission is more about "go and tell" than "come and see."

As pastors, we are called to set the tone for our people as we model personal evangelism. Each of us bears a personal responsibility to be "hospitable," to be "a lover of strangers," and to demonstrate a heart for the lost around him (Titus 3:2). This begins by conditioning our hearts to love, not resent, the lost in our communities. Jesus expressed a heartfelt compassion for lost people, and as he recognized the magnitude of the potential harvest, he urged his disciples to pray for laborers who would engage the world with the gospel (Matt 9:36–38).

We can foster this same compassion for our neighbors, showing kindness and "gentleness to all people," by reminding ourselves that "we too were once" enslaved to sin and hopeless apart from Christ

(Titus 3:2–3). Instead of criticizing and condemning others, we must make the most of every opportunity by seasoning our conversations with grace as we wisely and strategically consider how to engage "outsiders" with the love of Christ (Col 4:5–6). Like Jesus, we cannot view others as obstacles or interruptions, but as opportunities and individuals who are desperate to be rescued by a Savior who loves them.

In addition to sharing God's heart for our neighbors, *we must share God's heart for the nations.* It is easy for our perspective to be skewed by our own circumstances and contexts. Often we operate as though the world consists of our community and our country. But the global emphasis of the Great Commission must expand the horizons of our hearts and ministries to consider those around the world who need the gospel.

This global perspective is evident in its consistent emphasis in the various New Testament accounts of Jesus's missional admonition and its culmination in universal praise to the King (emphasis added in each):

- "Go, therefore, and make disciples of *all nations*" (Matt 28:19).
- "Go into *all the world* and proclaim the gospel to the *whole creation*" (Mark 16:15 ESV).
- "Repentance for forgiveness of sins will be proclaimed in his name to *all the nations*" (Luke 24:47).
- "As you sent me into the world, I have also sent them *into the world*. . . . As the Father has sent me, I also send you" (John 17:18; 20:21).
- "You will be my witnesses in Jerusalem, in all Judea and Samaria, and *to the ends of the earth*" (Acts 1:8).
- "There was a vast multitude from *every nation, tribe, people, and language*, which no one could number, standing before the throne and before the Lamb" (Rev 7:9).

The global emphasis of the Great Commission reveals several important truths about God's heart for the nations. First, it demonstrates the universal availability of salvation in Christ that does not discriminate against or exclude anyone (John 3:16). It reveals the global heart of God "who wants everyone to be saved" and is "not wanting any to perish but all to come to repentance" (1 Tim 2:4; 2 Pet 3:9). Furthermore, the global emphasis highlights the exclusivity of Jesus as the only way of salvation since the gospel is not ethnically or culturally limited and Jesus is the "one mediator between God and mankind" (1 Tim 2:5; cf. John 14:6). It also affirms the sufficiency of salvation through Christ, who is "the atoning sacrifice for our sins, and not only for ours, but for those of the whole world" (1 John 2:2).

Collectively, these truths that reflect God's heart for the nations make our privilege and obligation to participate in his worldwide mission abundantly clear. The greatest missionary in human history, the apostle Paul, explains this undeniable rationale in his letter to the Romans. The universal reality that "everyone who calls on the name of the Lord will be saved" (Rom 10:13) immediately translates into our global responsibility. "How, then, can they call on him they have not believed in? And how can they believe without hearing about him? And how can they hear without a preacher? And how can they preach unless they are sent? As it is written: 'How beautiful are the feet of those who bring good news'" (Rom 10:14–15).

The vast number of unreached people groups with little to no access to the gospel should compel us to go to the nations. But the magnitude of the need is intensified by God's heart for the nations and the compelling truths of salvation. The urgency of the mission is ultimately determined by the brevity of life, the certainty of death, the reality of hell, the exclusivity of the gospel, the sufficiency of Christ, and the glory of his name. These truths are the impetus of Jesus's command to go to the nations, and they must captivate our heart as pastors. When our passions begin to reflect God's heart, we will lead our people, both by example and exhortation, to fulfill the Great Commission by reaching our neighbors and the nations.

The Pastor's Vision Must Be Determined by the Great Commission

To fulfill our role that is defined as "making disciples," and as our hearts are compelled by God's love for the nations, we must lead our churches to be consumed with a passion to fulfill the Great Commission. A pastor's leadership includes caring for the sheep, feeding the flock, and leading them to follow God's will for the congregation. On a practical level, this involves managing the ongoing operations of the church and providing direction for the various programs and ministries. These administrative details, including budgets and calendars, are often viewed as limiting factors or "necessary evils" in ministry. Instead, they reflect the priorities of the church and the vision of its leadership.

A primary responsibility in shepherding our congregation is the reality that we are called to motivate God's people for the mission. As pastors, we can be guilty of using a variety of tactics to challenge our people to evangelize. Most of them are well-intended, but when we attempt to guilt people into sharing their faith by manipulating their emotions, our message becomes more like an advertisement for abandoned pets than genuine compassion for the lost. Sometimes we can unintentionally incentivize our people through public recognition or competitive challenges, which leads to self-serving motives that disregard the people we are trying to reach. It can also short-circuit the mission by pursuing a goal that is more about making decisions than making disciples.

While Paul chose to rejoice in the proclamation of the gospel regardless of the messenger's motive (Phil 1:15–18), he certainly was not endorsing misguided intentions. Paul repeatedly emphasized the urgent truths of the gospel and the glory of Christ as the ultimate motivation for spreading the gospel. His passionate defense of the exclusivity of Christ and salvation by grace alone challenged the church to preach the gospel (Gal 1:6–9). His personal compassion and brokenness for the lost was so deep that he expressed an impossible willingness to give up his own salvation for their sake (Rom 9:3). And his supreme passion for the glory of Christ motivated him to devote his life to the mission of the gospel (Acts 20:24).

In the same way, we are called to motivate God's people for the mission by celebrating his extravagant love extended to us in Christ, the glorious riches of his grace, and the unrivaled majesty of our Savior. When we behold the beauty of the gospel, it motivates our hearts with gratitude, stimulates a deeper affection for Jesus, and compels sincere compassion for the lost. The urgent reality of their impending eternity separated from Christ combined with his worthiness to receive their worship serves as divine inspiration to obey the Great Commission.

As pastors, our passion for "making disciples," fueled by the proper motivation, can stimulate our people to fulfill the mission. Our personal commitment must also be combined with a consistent challenge for our people to reach the lost for Christ. It must be prioritized as we cast vision for our congregation and the direction of our church. It must become a primary standard for evaluating our ministries and budgets. The Great Commission must permeate every aspect of our church as we establish a missional culture of members who are motivated to fulfill God's mission.

In addition to motivating our congregations, we are also called to mobilize God's people for the mission. Nothing is more disheartening and frustrating than being inspired to do something but not being given the opportunity or resources to accomplish it. Often, we can be guilty of challenging our people to reach their neighbors and the nations without equipping them or providing them with avenues for missional engagement. To lead our churches to become Great Commission congregations, we must establish clear pathways for them to pray, give, and go.

Prayer is essential for fulfilling the Great Commission. Paul regularly interceded for churches and their missional efforts, and solicited prayers for his own evangelistic opportunities, "Pray also for us that

God may open a door to us for the word" (Col 4:3). While some people may be limited in their ability to give or go, everyone can participate in the mission through prayer. Interceding for the lost, petitioning God for witnessing encounters, praying for boldness to share the gospel and divine wisdom as they engage others—all are ways God's people can participate in the Great Commission through prayer. It is important for pastors to affirm the significance of prayer in fulfilling the mission and challenge our people to pray accordingly.

Giving is another important way to mobilize our people for the mission. Scripture clearly teaches that those with means should invest in the eternal kingdom (1 Tim 6:17–19). Paul rejoiced in the Philippians' "partnership in the gospel" (Phil 1:5) and affirmed their financial support of his missionary efforts as a sacrificial offering that was pleasing to God (Phil 4:15–18). In collecting the relief offering for the Jerusalem church, he also commended the generosity of the Macedonian churches, who "begged us earnestly for the privilege of sharing in the ministry to the saints" in order that the gospel may continue to go forward (2 Cor 8:4). Participating in the mission includes helping support missionaries and sending agencies, providing scholarships and supplies for trips, contributing to local mission efforts, and funding outreach events and evangelistic ministries. These are examples of how our people can be inspired by the grace of the gospel to participate in missions through sacrificial giving (2 Cor 8:9).

"Going" is how we are called to fulfill the Great Commission. Encouraging our people to "go" begins with teaching them to "live on mission" in their daily lives and circles of influence, to be "salt" and "light" in a dark and decaying world (Matt 5:13–16). But we must also challenge people to expand their spiritual horizons by participating in local, national, and international efforts. We must point out areas of our country and the world that have little or no access to the gospel. Paul traveled to strategic areas to share Christ (Macedonia, Acts 16; Corinth, Acts 18; Ephesus, Acts 19) and expressed the desire to "preach the gospel where Christ has not been named" (Rom 15:20). Jesus himself left heaven to come to earth (Phil 2:6–8), and he commissioned his disciples to "make disciples of all nations" (Matt 28:19) by expanding their missional influence from "Jerusalem . . . to the ends of the earth" (Acts 1:8).

When we experience God's work in a different context, it inspires us to be more faithful in our own. Changing our perspective opens our eyes to see how the Lord is working around us by reminding us that our lives are part of a bigger plan and by showing us that God is moving in the hearts and lives of people everywhere. A missional mindset is often cultivated through exposure to areas of desperate need and unfamiliar contexts. God also can use these experiences to call people to serve him in a full-time missional capacity or to replant their lives as part of a missionary effort. Leading our congregations to "go" requires us to plan, participate, and partner for missional opportunities as we motivate and mobilize them to fulfill the Great Commission.

Conclusion

The guiding mandate for the church is clear: Jesus commanded us to "make disciples of all nations" (Matt 28:19). As the church's mission, the Great Commission necessarily defines the work of the pastor. When we consider that the qualifications for pastoral office also directly correspond with Jesus's instructions to go, baptize, and teach, it becomes obvious that our leadership role and daily responsibilities must be filtered and funneled through the Great Commission.

While these marching orders prescribe the pastor's duties, God finally desires that the words consume our hearts. His love for our neighbors and the nations must become our passion as we reach the lost for Christ and challenge our people to do the same. As pastors, we must model community engagement, personal evangelism, a compassionate heart, and a global perspective. Each of these characteristics reflects the heart of Jesus epitomized in his incarnation, his earthly ministry, his willing sacrifice, and his unconditional love for everyone. May we be captivated by the heart of the Savior who cleansed and captured ours!

A pastor whose heart is consumed with the gospel will motivate and mobilize the congregation to become a Great Commission church. The mission of "making disciples of all nations" must permeate every aspect of our leadership vision as we consistently challenge our people to live missionally. We must also integrate opportunities to pray, give, and go into every ministry of the church. God's redemptive plan is built on local churches actively engaging the world for Christ to fulfill his mission. As pastors, we have the humbling and heavy responsibility to equip them accordingly.

Our personal faithfulness to our calling and the missional faithfulness of our churches will depend on a proper understanding of the mutual relationship between pastoral ministry and the Great Commission. To preserve our commitment to their essential connection, perhaps we can adopt Jesus's statement on marriage, "What God has joined together, let no one separate" (Matt 19:6). Pastoral ministry and the Great Commission have certainly been inseparable in Danny Akin's ministry—may they not be divorced in ours.

CHAPTER EIGHT

LEADERSHIP AND THE GREAT COMMISSION

Ryan R. Hutchinson

Introduction

Aside from a brief meeting on a downtown Atlanta street corner during the annual meeting of the Evangelical Theological Society, my first real interaction with Danny Akin was in a corner booth at Applebee's in Wake Forest, North Carolina, on January 14, 2004. The next day, Dr. Akin was to meet with the full Board of Trustees to be considered for Southeastern Baptist Theological Seminary's (SEBTS) sixth president. Before this time, Dr. Akin was only a name I had heard, albeit many times. His first years of service at SEBTS ended just before I started my time there. When leadership changes at an educational institution, everyone wonders what direction the new leader will take and how he will lead differently than the previous president. SEBTS had built a reputation for emphasizing preaching and missions, but would the new president share those same commitments?

In that corner booth, Dr. Akin said two things that settled my heart. He felt a commitment to continue building SEBTS on the major themes it had become known for, and he asked me to stay and be a part of the new administration. This led to a twenty-year working relationship and friendship in which I have had the joy of helping advance the Great Commission vision for SEBTS.

"Last words are meant to be lasting words." I have heard this statement from Dr. Akin more times than I can count as he communicates why SEBTS is a Great Commission seminary. Jesus's last words, recorded by Matthew, were, "Jesus came near and said to them, 'All authority has been given to me in heaven and on earth. Go, therefore, and make disciples of all nations, baptizing them in the name of the Father and of the Son and of the Holy Spirit, teaching them to observe everything I have commanded you. And remember, I am with you always, to the end of the age'" (Matt 28:18–20). The Great Commission Seminary trajectory on which Dr. Akin has led the school can be summed up in one of Christ's words, "Go."

Without Dr. Akin's leadership toward a Great Commission vision, SEBTS might have found herself in many different places. In setting priorities, it is not always the best things that can consume an academic institution. Leadership is necessary to make sure that the Great Commission imprint remains at SEBTS. How does one lead with a Great Commission emphasis? This chapter answers that question through two tracks: the leader's personal life and his or her professional life.

The Leader's Personal Life

A leader's personal life is the starting point because those who follow leaders want to know they are authentic. In kingdom work, Scripture puts great emphasis on the person's qualification to lead.

In Deut 17:14–20, God laid out for Moses the kind of man who should serve as King over Israel:

> When you enter the land the Lord your God is giving you, take possession of it, live in it, and say, "I will set a king over me like all the nations around me," you are to appoint over you the king the Lord your God chooses. Appoint a king from your brothers. You are not to set a foreigner over you, or one who is not of your people. However, he must not acquire many horses for himself or send the people back to Egypt to acquire many horses, for the Lord has told you, "You are never to go back that way again." He must not acquire many wives for himself so that his heart won't go astray. He must not acquire very large amounts of silver and gold for himself. When he is seated on his royal throne, he is to write a copy of this instruction for himself on a scroll in the presence of the Levitical priests. It is to remain with him, and he is to read from it all the days of his life, so that he may learn to fear the Lord his God, to observe all the words of this instruction, and to do these statutes. Then his heart will not be exalted above his countrymen, he will not turn from this command to the right or the left, and he and his sons will continue reigning many years in Israel.

While these words concern kings of Israel, the principles show God's heart for the man who is to lead his people. God specifies the qualities for a leader of people, but his first desire is to see the focus of the leader's heart on him.

Many temptations can draw a leader's heart away from the Lord. This Deuteronomy passage specifies two: horses and wives. While not a comprehensive list of things that could turn the king's heart from God, it is representative. Usually those in leadership have money, influence, power, and resources. All of these are temptations that can turn the heart of the leader away from God. The leader must protect his heart by neither trusting in himself nor succumbing to the ways of the world. Proverbs 29:2 says, "When the righteous flourish, the people rejoice, but when the wicked rule, people groan." These words in Proverbs tie the righteousness of the leader to the health of the people he leads.

Protecting the leader's heart includes protecting the pursuit of God's Word as well as protection from worldly temptations. The Word of God was central to the role of king. He was not only to write out his own copy of God's law but was to consult it and adhere to the path of fearing the Lord. For any leader called to kingdom work, love for Scripture is fundamental to the leader knowing and loving the Lord and his mission. The Great Commission is the mission left to us by our Lord. Without a commitment to the inspired, inerrant, infallible, and all-sufficient Word of God, a leader's heart can be drawn away, resulting in a leader who will struggle to lead others to see the Great Commission fulfilled.

A leader's personal life should reflect a commitment to stay tethered to the Scriptures and not be tempted by the world. While a leader provides strength and resolve, the leader doing kingdom work should be marked by humility. When leading the charge to see the Great Commission fulfilled, the leader should always remember that he is a man just like those he is leading and seek to remain humble while he bears the weight of the responsibility that accompanies his role.

The importance of the leader's personal life is likewise seen in the New Testament as Paul lays out the qualifications for elders in 1 Tim 3:1–7 and Titus 1:6–9. Not everyone leading in kingdom work serves as an elder, but these qualifications emphasize the importance of the personal qualities in those God calls to lead his people. None of the qualifications speak to the leader's grand vision for an organization, ability to persuade people, or administrative prowess. These qualifications prioritize the leader's spiritual character over specific leadership functions, as important as those may be. The qualifications speak to the heart of the leader, namely his personal life before the Lord.

They can be divided into eight categories: (1) maintains a good reputation among people;[1] (2) leads his family well and is devoted to them;[2] (3) controls one's desires, temptations and impulses;[3] (4) relates well with other people;[4] (5) maintains an openness towards others;[5] (6) practices integrity in all areas of life;[6] (7) knows God's Word;[7] and (8) teaches effectively and defends faithfully God's Word.[8] Of these eight categories, only two deal with competency for leadership: leading a family well and ability to teach the Scriptures. The reason these qualifications are set forth for elders is to ensure that leaders of the church will effectively lead and care for the church (1 Pet 5:2; 1 Tim 3:5; Jas 5:14–15); be a faithful example to the church (1 Pet 5:3); and protect the church from false teaching (Acts 20:28; Titus 1:9). For these same reasons, we also should prize character first when it comes to Great Commission leadership.

---

[1] "above reproach" (1 Tim 3:2; Titus 1:6), "respectable" (1 Tim 3:2), and "have a good reputation among outsiders" (1 Tim 3:7).

[2] "husband of one wife" (1 Tim 3:2; Titus 1:6), "must manage his own household competently" (1 Tim 3:4), and "with faithful children who are not accused of wildness or rebellion" (Titus 1:6).

[3] "self-controlled" (1 Tim 3:2; Titus 1:8), "not greedy for money" (Titus 1:7), "not hot-tempered" (Titus 1:7), "not quarrelsome" (1 Tim 3:3), "not an excessive drinker" (1 Tim 3:3), and "not be a new convert, or he might become conceited and incur the same condemnation as the devil" (1 Tim 3:6).

[4] "sensible" (1 Tim 3:3), "righteous" (Titus 1:8), "not hot-tempered" (Titus 1:7), "not quarrelsome" (1 Tim 3:3), and "not arrogant" (Titus 1:7).

[5] "hospitable" (1 Tim 3:2; Titus 1:8) and "loving what is good" (Titus 1:8).

[6] "above reproach" (1 Tim 3:2; Titus 1:6), "not greedy for money" (Titus 1:7), "righteous" (Titus 1:8), "holding to the faithful message as taught" (Titus 1:9), and "holy" (Titus 1:8).

[7] "holding to the faithful message as taught, so that he will be able both to encourage with sound teaching and to refute those who contradict it" (Titus 1:9).

[8] "holding to the faithful message as taught, so that he will be able both to encourage with sound teaching and to refute those who contradict it" (Titus 1:9), and "able to teach" (1 Tim 3:2).

The personal life of the leader should start with a focus on his heart before the Lord and his love for God's Word. In Matt 22:37–38, Christ said, "Love the Lord your God with all your heart, with all your soul, and with all your mind. This is the greatest and most important command." Since this is the greatest commandment for all children of the King, it is also the chief aim of the leader.

Wisdom is one of the most significant benefits that can result from a leader's personal life centered on a love for God's Word. Psalm 111:10 says, "The fear of the Lord is the beginning of wisdom; all who follow his instructions have good insight. His praise endures forever." The psalmist makes the connection between a person's submission to the Word of God, the fear of the Lord, and wisdom. As King Solomon succeeded King David, it was Solomon's request for wisdom above all else that pleased the Lord. God asked Solomon what he should give him to lead his people. First Kings 3:9–10 records the answer from Solomon: "'So give your servant a receptive heart to judge your people and to discern between good and evil. For who is able to judge this great people of yours?' Now it pleased the Lord that Solomon had requested this." A leader desiring wisdom is pleasing to God, and God promises in Jas 1:5 to give wisdom liberally to all who ask for it in faith.

Leaders must make important decisions, and they are also often hard decisions. Therefore, it is imperative that a leader have God's wisdom in his life to lead well. Proverbs 8:15–16 says, "It is by [wisdom] that kings reign and rulers enact just law; by [wisdom], princes lead, as do nobles and all righteous judges."

In the twenty years I have had the pleasure of serving under Dr. Akin, I have found that one reason I am able to follow his Great Commission-focused leadership is that I see his heart for the Lord revealed in his personal life. Leadership style is important to a leader's success, but a leader in kingdom work must foremost show a love for the Lord and his Great Commission. His commitment to protecting his heart, loving God's Word, obeying God's Word, remaining humble, and seeking wisdom demonstrates this love. May God raise up more and more such leaders so that God's people can follow them into the Great Commission work our Lord and Savior Jesus Christ calls us to fulfill.

The Leader's Professional Life

Lists of leadership principles abound these days, and many are helpful. For kingdom work, I submit that three leadership traits are crucial: people, purpose, and priorities.

People

In professional life, a leader is known by the people with whom he surrounds himself. Sometimes we are given the people; sometimes we must recruit the people; often, both are true. The work of the Great Commission is mobilizing people who desire to obey that command and are willing to follow the leadership toward that end. Proverbs 25:4–5 states, "Remove impurities from silver, and material will be produced for a silversmith. Remove the wicked from the king's presence, and his throne will be established in righteousness." These verses convey one way that the people around a leader influence his ability to lead.

Leading people toward a goal is asking them to follow when the details are not completely clear, and to keep following even when there are mistaken decisions. There must be mutual trust between a leader and followers. The leader must build that mutual trust. Building mutual trust starts broadly but begins to narrow as a leader focuses on those closest to him. These are the people who will represent him and his goals to others. If the leader surrounds himself with people who are untrustworthy and self-seeking, they will fail to represent him well and fail to accomplish the leader's goals. The leader should carefully select his closest team and lead that team to carefully select the people on their teams. When leaders select people who align with their style and goals, it is much easier to build trust. Since building mutual trust is the leader's responsibility, he sets the tone for the culture of trust by extending trust to his team.

Mutual trust is necessary between a leader and his people because some days the path is not clear and some days the leader will make missteps. No amount of planning can cover every scenario. Difficult days will come. It is during those difficult days that mutual trust will promote working together rather than produce a culture of suspicion that derails progress and destroys a team. Difficult times will often produce ambiguity, and if the leader has surrounded himself with the right people, those difficult days of ambiguity will help lead an organization to brighter days.

Having the right team is also important because no leader is perfect. Leaders, no matter how good they are, will make missteps. If a leader surrounds himself with the right people, they will serve him well by graciously pointing out his missteps in a manner that shows their love and respect for him. In a culture of trust, a leader can correct his team for the benefit of each other and the organization.

Dr. Akin regularly quotes Adrian Rogers, who said that "A" leaders surround themselves with "A" people and "B" people surround themselves with "C" people. Therefore, a leader focused on seeing the Great Commission fulfilled must work hard to surround himself with the right people to accomplish the task that the Lord has laid before us.

The apostle Paul learned the importance of surrounding himself with the right people. In 2 Tim 4:9–15, Paul speaks of the right people and the wrong people he has had around him. Demas deserted him, and Alexander the coppersmith did him much harm. Others mentioned in the verses served Paul well but were sent out to other areas of ministry. Paul wanted Timothy to come to him and to bring Mark with him because of his usefulness. This section of 2 Timothy is an example of how a leader is helped or harmed by the right or wrong people around him.

The right people make a leader successful. The wrong people will make a leader fail. It is the leader's responsibility to surround himself with the right people, or else his purpose and priorities will never succeed.

Purpose

When Dr. Akin took the helm, the seminary already had a focus on the Great Commission, though a certain sharpness was missing regarding the effort. The seminary had a multi-paragraph purpose statement and a multi-paragraph vision statement that no one at the seminary could recite. At a 2006 cabinet retreat, under Dr. Akin's leadership, the seminary began operating under a new mission statement that clarified the institution's purpose: "Southeastern Baptist Theological Seminary seeks to glorify the Lord Jesus Christ by equipping students to serve the church and fulfill the Great Commission." Eighteen years later, this mission statement is readily recalled by many who work at the seminary, continues to guide our purpose, and has significantly contributed to the seminary's success.

The mission statement makes it clear that the seminary exists to serve the local church and to help see the Great Commission fulfilled. Christ set forth his Great Commission in Matthew 28 and established the church, his bride, as the means to accomplish his purposes in Matthew 16.

Leaders bring clarity to an organization's purpose, and that purpose fuels the people around him to move forward toward the goal with clarity and passion. But first, the leader must seek clarity in his own mind. If the leader's mind is not clear, confusion will spill over into the team, and the outcome of the work will never move an organization forward.

Second, after a leader has clarity of purpose, he must communicate that clarity to his team. A leader can have clarity of purpose but never communicate it to the people with whom he has surrounded himself. There are a variety of reasons why this can happen. I like to say that 96 percent (a percentage for emphasis rather than from research) of all organizational issues are communication problems. Ideas that are never spoken aloud. Assumptions that are rarely the case. Expressions spoken out loud but not fully received by the listeners. A leader must continually communicate until there is clarity among those around him.

The new simplified and clarified mission statement was received as marching orders to make "every classroom a Great Commission classroom." The clarity was strong enough that everyone latched onto the purpose. So much so that during one of the seminary's accreditation reaffirmation visits, one of the outside team members noted that no matter who they talked with, from the faculty down to the custodians, everyone could communicate the seminary's mission and was bought into it.

At times, a leader might experience frustration when his ideas for the future seem not to get any traction. That is when the leader must look within rather than at the followers. He must go back to the purpose. Is the purpose clear in his mind? He should express the purpose to those closest to him and ask if it seems clear. If it is clear to those closest to him, then he should determine whether it is clear to the rest of the organization.

Purpose is what gives people something to drive toward. With the right purpose and the right people, any organization is set to thrive.

Priorities

People and purpose are essential, but priorities address the ever-changing environment that an organization faces. A leader is helping the organization set the right priorities from a laundry list of possibilities. If a leader is unable to help the organization sort out its priorities, the organization will begin to move away from its purpose. Not all things are the right things to do, and not all right things are the best things to do at a given point in time.

Leaders can make the mistake of establishing priorities and then forgetting about them. The wheels are set in motion when the initial set of priorities is established. However, environments change and personnel change. The leader is in the mode of constantly assessing the environment. What new challenges are on the horizon? What was the situation before, and how is it different now? Personnel changes result in workers who were not around the last time priorities were set and the purpose was made clear. This necessitates repeated communication of the leader's goals and current priorities.

When Dr. Akin arrived at the seminary in 2004, there was a then-new method of delivering education, called "online education." It did not utilize synchronous in-person learning but rather asynchronous remote learning. Some thought online education was a fad, and others were certain it was the end of education. However, Dr. Akin led the institution to make it a priority. Now online education is a critical component of the seminary's fulfillment of the Great Commission vision that Dr. Akin has laid out. Online education has allowed the seminary to reach students beyond our normal regional reach and beyond the borders of our country. It is not unusual these days for a student's first visit to campus to be graduation day. Online education allowed the institution to quickly pivot during the COVID-19 pandemic when, in March 2020, all learning was forced to go online.

Online education is only one example of how important it is for a leader to ensure the organization's current priorities are on target. Over the years, Southeastern has operated under a shifting set of priorities to fulfill its mission of being a Great Commission seminary. Along with hiring the right people, a leader's job is to help the organization see what is more important when, while still driving toward the same goal.

With time, there will be periods when the wrong priorities are in place, or where, in a list of right things an organization could do, the best things don't rise to the top. When the leader recognizes these miscues, he must find a way to guide the organization back towards the right focus, where the organization is pursuing the right priorities to see the purpose fulfilled.

In Haggai, the prophet was coming to those who had returned from exile but with misplaced priorities. Instead of working on rebuilding the temple, they caved in to the pressure to build and beautify their own houses. The Lord said to his people through Haggai in Haggai 1:2–4, "'The Lord of Armies says this: These people say: The time has not come for the house of the Lord to be rebuilt.' The word of the Lord came through the prophet Haggai: 'Is it a time for you yourselves to live in your paneled houses, while [the temple] lies in ruins?'" People will naturally drift, and priorities will become misplaced over time. It takes a leader to remind the people what is most important and why we must focus on the hard but better priorities to fulfill the purpose set before us.

In 2017, Dr. Akin led the Cabinet and then the rest of the seminary to focus the institution's attention on the four marks of a Great Commission seminary: (1) consumed with a global focus; (2) certain in our doctrinal convictions; (3) committed to provide expansive ministerial preparation; and (4) characterized by spiritual vibrancy. These marks of a Great Commission seminary are examples of the leader's call to establish present-day priorities.

While the focus of the Great Commission remains from the clarified purpose established in 2006, priorities for seeing that mission fulfilled have shifted. It is the role of the leader to lead his team to keep the organization on track and to adjust where needed.

Conclusion

The Great Commission is large in both scope and importance. It represents the expansion of God's kingdom and the command of King Jesus for us to carry out. Every church and organization that supports the church has a clarion call to work toward the fulfillment of the Great Commission in the roles to which they are called. For churches and para-church ministries, like Southeastern Seminary, to fulfill their roles in helping to see the Great Commission fulfilled, leaders must rise to the occasion. These leaders must first be ones whose personal lives are tethered to the Word of God because of their unwavering love of God. The leader must be a man of wisdom to make the important and hard decisions that will be set before him. If the personal life of the leader is in order, the leader can then focus on his professional life. The professional life of the leader will emphasize people, purpose, and priorities.

I am thankful that God has raised up men like Dr. Akin. May God continue to raise up men like him to lead with the love of God in their hearts and obedience to the Great Commission as their goal.

CHAPTER NINE

SENDING CHURCHES AND THE GREAT COMMISSION: FOUR HINDRANCES TO SENDING

J. D. Greear

Introduction

The church I pastor—The Summit Church in Raleigh-Durham, North Carolina—has been blessed with a lot of college students. Duke University, the University of North Carolina at Chapel Hill, North Carolina State, The College at Southeastern, Meredith College, William Peace University, North Carolina Central, Shaw University—we have a lot of colleges. And that means *a lot* of college students.

College students "discovered" our church in 2003. If I remember right, it went something like this: one week about five college students visited. They liked the service, and because college students travel in herds, the next week they brought back 250 of their friends. They came in three cars.

In less than a month, our attendance doubled. Also during that time, our weekly average giving increased by $13.48. (College students bring a lot of great things to our church, but money is not one of them.)

One morning an usher came to me after the first service with a bacon, egg, and cheese biscuit from Bojangles. One of the college students had placed it in the offering plate with a little note on it that read (charitably misquoting Acts 3:6), "Silver and gold have I none, but such as I have, give I unto you."

We realized early on that God had given us a unique opportunity. With so many college students, we might never become the wealthiest church. But we would always have a large pool of potential missionaries.

So, we responded by mobilizing them. We made an outrageous goal of planting 1,000 churches by 2050. We began challenging all our students to give the first two years after graduation to the mission of God. Some people jokingly called it the "Mormonization Strategy." That's cheeky . . . but not terribly far from the truth. We tell these students often, "Give us two years and we'll change the world."

The Myth of Calling

What is true of our college students, it turns out, is also true for every believer. "Calling" is not a sacred experience for a select few conveyed only through a mystical experience. The question is not *if* we are called; the question is merely *how* (see Matt 4:19; John 20:21).

This "myth of calling" usually happens something like this: we believe that when God wants to call someone into ministry, he employs some odd kind of supernatural sign. He spells it out in their Cheerios—"pastor" or "foster parent" or "go to Nepal" or whatever. The problem is that most of us have asked God for guidance and never had this kind of experience. I know—I prayed for God to show me his will, but the more I looked at my Cheerios, the only thing I read was, "Oooooooo."

Here's the truth: the call to leverage your life for the Great Commission was included in the call to follow Jesus. When Jesus called the first disciples, he said, "Follow me . . . and I will make you fish for people" (Matt 4:19). Translation: when you accepted Jesus, you accepted the call to missions.

Which is why we tell our people, "Start by putting your 'yes' on the table. Then let God put it on the map."

Extraordinary "Ordinary" People

The moment people in our churches catch this vision of calling, incredible things begin to happen.

Luke, the writer of Acts, goes out of his way to show us that the gospel travels faster around the world in the mouths of "ordinary" Christians than it does through full-time, vocational Christian workers. Luke notes, for example, that the first time the gospel left Jerusalem, it was not in the mouths of the apostles. Regular people "went their own way preaching the word," while the apostles stayed in Jerusalem (Acts 8:1–4). The first time the gospel went out into the world, not a single apostle was involved.

Fast forward to the planting of the church at Antioch. Antioch, for context, would soon become the hub for missionary activity for the last half of the book of Acts. It was the first great church planting center. And who planted this great church? As Luke puts it, "those who had been scattered" there (Acts 11:19). Luke uses no personal names, only that the Lord's hand "was with them" (Acts 11:21) as they established the church.

"Them." "Those."

That is Luke's way of saying "a bunch of dudes whose names I won't mention because you wouldn't recognize them and won't hear anything about them again anyway."

This pattern continued as the early church grew. As Stephen Neill notes in his classic *History of Christian Missions*, "Nothing is more notable than the anonymity of these early missionaries. . . . Luke does not turn aside to mention the name of a single one of those pioneers who laid the foundation. Few, if any, of the great Churches were really founded by apostles. Peter and Paul may have organized the Church in Rome. They certainly did not found it."[1] Neill points to the existence of three primary Christian "centers" by the end of the first century: Antioch, Alexandria, and Rome. The most remarkable thing about those centers, he says, is that we have no idea who brought the movement there, or who planted the first churches in these cities.

Pretty extraordinary work for such "ordinary" people, isn't it?

The future of the Great Commission lies in the hands of "ordinary" people. I thank God for all the pastors and missionaries laboring around the world. (And I believe we need even more of each!) But the greatest work, historically, has come through the work of those who are not on the church payroll. Ordinary Christians have always been the tip of the gospel spear. They always will be.

Four Hindrances to Sending

The question, then, that presents itself to those of us in ministry is as simple as it is piercing: Why aren't we equipping our people to become the multiplying, called, commissioned, sent leaders that they are?

I have been doing this long enough to recognize four key hindrances that prevent our churches from being "sending" churches. Four hindrances that keep us from mobilizing God's people the way God

[1] Stephen Neill, *A History of Christian Missions* (Harmondsworth, UK: Penguin Books, 1986), 22.

intended. Four hindrances that stymie and stifle the movement God wants to do in our cities.

Sending people out to plant churches sounds exciting. But every time we commission people on a new church plant, I second-guess myself, and that is because the kinds of people who respond to calls for church planting teams are not usually "sideline" people whom you won't miss. They are heavily involved, giving generously, and usually leading ministries. Sending them out is painful.

And it is joyful. To date, we have sent out 1,200 members on church planting teams. I miss every single one of them. But those members have planted 502 new churches. Each weekend, while our church gathers, more than double our number gather in these church plants. For every one member we have sent out, there are twenty now worshipping in these churches. That is multiplication. It is bittersweet to send our best, but worth it.

I had to learn to overcome these hurdles the hard way. There's no "easy" way to learn to sacrifice. You will need to walk some of that road yourself. But my hope here is that knowing each of these hindrances can help you work through them when the time comes.

The future belongs to churches that send, and to churches that prioritize sending capacity over seating capacity. Let's look at the hindrances to that goal and—by the power of the Spirit—blast through them for the sake of the gospel.

Hindrance #1: A Failure to Take Seriously Jesus's Promises about the Holy Spirit

Jesus's promises about the greatness of the church always concerned the power of the Spirit multiplied on new leaders, *not* one person's ministry growing larger and larger. Consider his words in John 16: "Nevertheless, I am telling you the truth. It is for your benefit that I go away, because if I don't go away the Counselor will not come to you. If I go, I will send him to you" (v. 7).

"For your benefit" must have sounded absurd to those first disciples. Just imagine what it would be like to walk with Jesus for three years? To witness his miracles? To hear his teaching firsthand? To share meals with him where you can ask him every question you have? And then Jesus says, "It's actually better for you if I go"? What?

We balk at Jesus's claim because we undervalue the power of the Spirit. According to Jesus, the power of the Spirit through his disciples would be greater than the power of the Spirit through one person, even if that one person is Jesus himself.

The way Jesus said it in John 14 corroborates this: "Truly I tell you, the one who believes in me will also do the works that I do. And he will do even greater works than these, because I am going to the Father" (v. 12). Wow. Greater works than Jesus! Even if you take out the miracles, that is an astounding claim. Who has ever preached with greater power than Jesus? Who has ever offered greater spiritual counsel? Prayed with greater clarity? Loved others with more compassion? But apparently, the Spirit's work through a multitude of his followers would exceed even the ministry of Jesus.

The way we celebrate success in our churches turns this principle on its head. We measure churches by how many they can gather to bask in the anointing of one man. But Jesus's promises about the Spirit mean that the real power is released, not through one hyper-anointed person, but through the masses.

Jesus's vision of the church—the kind of church that would besiege the gates of hell—did not consist of a group of people gathered around one anointed leader, but multiple leaders going out in the power of the Spirit.

In Acts, the biggest advances of the gospel in the New Testament happened through ordinary people. Of the forty miracles in Acts, thirty-nine were done outside of the church. We need to expect that kind of ratio today, too. Which brings up the second hindrance to sending.

Hindrance #2: A Failure to Understand How Most People in Our Culture Must Be Reached Today

Each year in our country, the number of people checking the "none" box for religious affiliation on surveys increases at an astounding rate.[2] "Nones," as they are called, no longer casually make their way into churches, really, for any reason.

A recent Barna study in the United States found that non-Christians are not just skeptical of Christianity; they are increasingly suspicious of the church itself. More than half of the non-Christians surveyed said the church was not relevant to the world today. And one in five said the very existence of churches was harmful to the surrounding community.[3]

If half of your neighbors are convinced the church is an irrelevant relic (and much of that group thinks your church is inherently toxic), they aren't going to casually make their way through your doors. Not at Easter. Not on Christmas Eve. Probably not even for a marriage or a funeral. It is not necessarily that they are all angry at the church and boycotting it. Most simply do not see any place for church in their lives. What this means is that if we keep relying on the quality of our church "product" to win people, it will become increasingly ineffective. None of the people we want to win will even be there to experience it.

Increasingly, we need to operate as if we are engaging people of a completely different religion. "Nones" are notoriously resistant to religious labels, so they aren't all flocking to some other religion—at least

---

[2] Albert Mohler, "Life in Post-Denominational America," Albert Mohler website, September 22, 2009, https://www.albertmohler.com/2009/09/22/life-in-post-denominational-america/.

[3] Barna: State of the Church, "Five Trends Defining Americans' Relationship to Churches," February 19, 2020, https://www.barna.com/research/current-perceptions/.

not a formal one. They are thinking in ways that are so distinct, we must recalibrate how we attempt to reach them.

An example of a cross-cultural experience of my own may help here. When I lived in a Muslim country for a few years, at no point did I consider going to the mosque for religious guidance. I wouldn't have gone if I had been sad. Or lonely. I wouldn't have gone if the imam were doing a helpful series on relationships. I wouldn't have gone if they had added a rockin' drum loop to the prayer chant. I wouldn't have gone if the guest services were Disney-esque. Islam was a completely foreign world, and one in which I knew I clearly did not belong.

If we do not equip people to carry the gospel outside the church, we will lose all audience with those who need so desperately to hear the gospel. We will look around at our church buildings and wonder, "Why isn't this working?" Meanwhile all the people we want to reach will be asking their important questions somewhere else.

I believe the future of the American church will see many megachurches putting all their focus into weekend ministries, fighting each other for a larger piece of a rapidly shrinking pie of bored Christians. We are already beginning to see this trend.

For those of us who want to reach the rest of the culture, we need to think about growing the pie. And that means equipping people to carry the gospel outside the church—to be effective soul winners to people in their neighborhoods, schools, and workplaces.

Interestingly, this is where the gap between large and small churches begins to disappear. Sure, the church of 10,000 can afford to have incredible special effects on stage. But any church—whether 50 or 50,000—can teach its people to become disciple-making disciples, speaking the truth of the gospel and demonstrating the beauty of the gospel.

If our people do this well, the impact can be as miraculous as it is surprising.

Early in my ministry, I remember preaching through the book of Acts, and in Acts 8 we came to the story of Philip's revival in Samaria. As a result of Philip's ministry, Luke said, there was "great joy" in the city (Acts 8:8). Sadly, our ministry did not seem to be having the effect on our communities that the early Christians had on theirs.

I had just gotten back from a short-term mission trip to Southeast Asia, where I had spent time in the small city in the Islamic country where I lived for two years as a church planter. The city has a big gate marking entry into it, and as I passed through it, all these old emotions I had felt about that city during my time there flooded into my heart. That had been my city—I was the only church planter within 100 miles, and I had felt like God had made me responsible for it. During the time that I lived there, I had prayer-walked that city repeatedly; I felt that its schools were my schools; its problems, my problems; its lostness, my lostness. As I felt all those old emotions, a question popped into my head: Why don't you feel that way about your current city?

That piercing question marked the beginning of a new period of community engagement. I told the church that I needed to repent. No longer would our focus simply be on growing the church, I said. Instead, we would seek to reach and bless the city.

So we began to ask ourselves: "Where can we bring 'great joy' to our city as a demonstration of the gospel?" I met with the mayor and asked him to list out the five most underserved parts of our city so we could get involved there. The recurring answer: schools. We jumped in.

The beginnings were modest. Through one teacher, we found out about a family in need of temporary housing. One of our church members, who was about to get married, asked his guests to redirect any wedding presents to this family to stock their house. That led to another teacher inviting us to come pray for the students during their "end of grade" (EOG) exams. When their test scores were the highest on record, we were allowed in to paint classrooms, scrub floors, and bring the teachers breakfast.

By God's grace, our local outreach ministry has just kept expanding. Years after that first visit, I was invited to speak at our city's annual Martin Luther King Jr. rally. Durham is almost half African American, so this event is important. I agreed, but not being the typical candidate to keynote an MLK rally, I was a nervous wreck. The county manager, sensing my anxiety, said, "J. D., do you know why you were asked to speak today?"

"No sir," I said.

"It's because of how your church has blessed our city." Another city official shared with me later that afternoon, "It seems that everywhere in our city we find a need, we also find people from The Summit Church meeting that need. And we couldn't think of anyone to better embody the spirit of brotherly love we want to honor on this day than you all at the Summit."

When people in the streets see and hear and feel the power of gospel healing, they take note. This was the secret of the church in the book of Acts. And God's power to do it has not lessened a single iota since then.

Hindrance #3: My Own Idolatry

Ironic as it may seem, one of the biggest hindrances to our church becoming a sending church was the guy preaching sermons each week. That is, me.

Some years ago, I remember praying for a massive revival in our city—the kind that would lead to thousands of people getting saved; the kind that would rewrite the story of our entire city; the kind they would write about one day in history books. It seemed like a good request, but as I was praying, the Spirit of God impressed something on my heart that left me speechless: "And what if I answer this prayer, sending a revival into Raleigh-Durham beyond all you've asked or imagined, one that will reshape the city for centuries—but I choose a different church in this city to accomplish that? What if that church grows, and that pastor gets famous, and your church stays the same, and you do not? And what if one day when they write the history of the movement, they never even mention you or your church?"

I knew the right answer to that question. I was supposed to say, "Oh, yes, Lord! You must increase and I must decrease!" But while that may have been the right answer, it would not have been the real answer. I did not just want the kingdom of God to grow—I wanted the kingdom of J. D. to grow, too. I realized that somewhere along the way, "thy kingdom come" had gotten jumbled up with "my kingdom come."

Sending is not good for the "bottom line" of a church. It does not build up a pastor's kingdom. But when has that been the point? I had to decide that day: Was I in this to build my own legacy? Or to participate in God's? Did I want my church to multiply itself in new leaders and new churches and new believers around the world? Or did I want to feel better about myself?

I doubt I am alone in this struggle. We all need to grapple honestly with our idolatry, but those of us in ministry must always keep our sights on *ministry* idolatry. These aren't *our* churches. They're Jesus's. Shame on us if we commandeer Jesus's bride for our own benefit.

Early in the ministry of Jesus, John the Baptist described his role—and that of all preachers—as being like the best man at a wedding (John 3:29). Traditionally, the best man serves the groom and supports him. He is there as the right-hand man, helping everything go smoothly. But he is not the point. When the wedding starts, the focus is not on him. It is all about the bride and groom. Can you imagine how inappropriate it would be if, when the bride begins walking up the aisle, the best man nudged the groom out of the way and started making eyes at the bride? That would be a disgusting betrayal of his role.

And yet, when it comes to ministry, far too many of us try elbowing Jesus and his bride out of the way so the focus can be on us instead.

The pulpit is not a platform for us as preachers to prop ourselves up in front of others; the pulpit is a place to pour ourselves out for Jesus and his bride.

Planting, investing, sending, and sacrificing are costly. It hurts. But the trajectory of discipleship is toward giving away, not taking in. As Dietrich Bonhoeffer famously said, "When Christ bids a man to follow, he bids him come and die." Jesus did not say, "Come and grow," but "Come and die." And he showed us what that means by his own example.

Why would it surprise us that God wants to use the same process in our ministries? It is not through our success that God saves the world, but through our sacrifice. He calls us first to an altar, not a platform.

We live by losing. We gain by giving away. What we achieve by building our personal platform will never be as great as what God achieves through what we give away in faith.

But the biggest hindrance remains.

Hindrance #4: Fear

In the end, nothing threatens a culture of sending more than fear. I know that God calls me to give extravagantly, joyfully, freely. But I'm afraid to open my hands.

A few years ago, I sat around a table with four of our church planting residents, listening to the lists of those they had recruited from our church to go on their plants. As these four men shared their lists of commitments with me, I heard the names of elders. Worship leaders. Staff members. Key volunteers. Friends.

I had a sick feeling in my stomach. What were we doing? Had we thought this through? How on earth could we survive without these people?

It was then the Spirit of God gently nudged me again, "Whose church is this?" This time I knew the answer. I reached my hands under the table and stretched them open before God. Quietly I prayed, "God, this is your church, not mine. If you want us to grow large to reach this city, so be it. But if you want to take out the best of our people and our resources to start churches elsewhere, that's okay too. It's your church. Do with it what you will."

I had to force my hands open that day. It took all the willpower I had. But it was a liberating moment. Yet every morning, when I wake up, I find myself, once again, with closed fists. I have had to commit myself to releasing control, again and again and again and again. Choosing faith over fear. Choosing Jesus's path over my own preferences.

God only multiplies what we sow. In John 12, when Jesus spoke to his disciples about their future ministry, he used an odd analogy: "Truly I tell you, unless a grain of wheat falls to the ground and dies, it remains by itself. But if it dies, it produces much fruit" (v. 24).

I typically don't think of a seed planted into the dirt as dying. I think of it, in fact, as just beginning to live.

But in one sense it is dying. Its life as a seed is over. Its outer shell crumbles, and it can no longer be consumed as food.

But from that seed's death comes the potential of new life. And not just a single life, but life multiplied from generation to generation. Each seed might yield ten times, a hundred times, even a thousand times more than its original capacity. In the right conditions, it will replicate forever.

This principle is not always fun to live out, at least in the short run. But it is the truth, a growth principle God has woven not only into the earth's natural harvest, but into his spiritual harvest, too. Life in the world comes only through death in the church. God only multiplies what we sow. What you hang onto, you lose. What you give away, you keep for eternity.

We pastors are often fond of saying, "You can't outgive God." I believe it. I have seen it. I have preached it. But for me, it is much easier to practice when it comes to money than when it comes to leaders. And yet, through the years, I have seen God's faithfulness here as well. When we give God the first and best of our leaders, he responds in kind.

More Than One Way to Be Wicked

This is a matter of survival for the American church. If we shrink back from or ignore these hindrances, not only will we find ourselves increasingly ineffective; we might also find ourselves chastised and disciplined by God himself.

Consider, for instance, one of Jesus's most famous parables, the "parable of the talents." A rich boss left behind various sums of money for his servants to invest. To one he gave five "talents"; to another, two; to another, one.

A talent was a huge sum of money—about twenty years' salary for the average day laborer. So, you could translate that to $10 million, $5 million, and $1 million. Then, "the man who had received five talents went, put them to work, and earned five more. In the same way the man with two earned two more. But the man who had received one talent went off, dug a hole in the ground, and hid his master's money" (Matt 25:16–18).

The guy with $10 million turned it into $20 million. The guy with $5 million into $10 million. Not too shabby. Unsurprisingly, when the boss returned, he commended them for their wise investment of his resources.

But to the one that sat on his $1 million, Jesus responded much differently:

> His master replied to him, "You evil, lazy servant! If you knew that I reap where I have not sown and gather where I have not scattered, then you should have deposited my money with the bankers, and I would have received my money back with

> interest when I returned. So take the talent from him and give it to the one who has ten talents. For to everyone who has, more will be given, and he will have more than enough. But from the one who does not have, even what he has will be taken away from him. And throw this good-for-nothing servant into the outer darkness, where there will be weeping and gnashing of teeth." (Matt 25:26–30)

"Wicked?"

Unfruitful, ineffective, unfaithful—all these I understand. But wicked?

What wicked thing had he done? He had not stolen the master's money or spent it on prostitutes, wild parties, gambling, or lavish living. In fact, he returned every penny he had been given back to his boss.

So where lies the wickedness? Simply here: he had failed to risk what the Master had given him. He didn't sow any seed. He didn't take the risk. The Master had given him something in order to give it away, and he simply hung on to it.

There is more than one way to be wicked.

Is it possible that Jesus might consider some of our largest, richest, fastest-growing churches wicked because they have turned all their blessings back on themselves, failed to open up their hands, and refused to plant those blessings out in the harvest fields of God's kingdom?

The Good Old Days Are Now

I do not want to end this discourse negatively, because there is so much about this principle that is exhilarating and liberating. As I look to the future, I am brimming with profound gospel hope. I believe you should be, too. Do not think about the sacrifices. Do not dwell on the fear. Simply imagine the incredible opportunities we have—and the staggering promises Jesus has given us. The power of God's Spirit is still mightily available for all who are willing to follow Jesus in his mission. It is a wild journey, but it is also a fruitful one.

One of my favorite TV shows is *The Office.* Toward the end of the show, one character, Andy Bernard, has a rare moment of insight. He says, "I wish there was a way to know you're in the good old days before you've actually left them." That is not a word from Scripture. But I believe it is a word for the church today.

We tend to think of the "good old days" as the church back in the early centuries of church history. Peter preaches and thousands come to faith. Apostles heal people just with their hankies. In city after city, the movement of the gospel was so momentous that it felt unstoppable.

Except that if we had lived then, it would not have felt that way at all.

Church historian Rodney Stark notes that at the end of the first century, the number of Christians is estimated at around 7,500. That's it. There are hundreds of churches today with larger congregations. Seven thousand five hundred people spread over the entire Roman Empire would not have felt unstoppable and momentous. It might have felt fragile.

Yet by AD 300, that 7,500 had multiplied so dramatically that nearly half the population of the empire had confessed faith in Jesus. It did not happen through massive events. It happened through multiplication.

And it can happen again.

The prophet Amos had a word or two to say about our "good old days" theology, too. Listen to his command to the people of Israel: "For the Lord says to the house of Israel: Seek me and live! Do not seek Bethel or go to Gilgal or journey to Beer-sheba, for Gilgal will certainly go into exile, and Bethel will come to nothing" (Amos 5:4–6).

Bethel, Gilgal, Beersheba. Those place names might just wash over us without meaning. But Israel would have immediately understood the implications. These were not just cities; they were cities of profound spiritual power.

Bethel was where Jacob had his life-changing encounter with God, a place that symbolized for Israelites awakening and renewal.

Gilgal was where the children of Israel finally emerged from their forty-year wandering in the wilderness, believed God, and took possession of the Promised Land. When God miraculously parted the Jordan at Gilgal, he "rolled away the disgrace of Egypt" (Josh 5:9).

At Beersheba, God delivered Abraham by giving him a treaty with Abimelech that became instrumental in his possession of the new land. His son Isaac would make an altar there.

Bethel, Gilgal, Beersheba—the places representing the "good old days" of Israel's past. That is where Israel had consigned God and his mighty movements. So, God says to them, "Do not seek me there. Do not seek me in the past. Seek me *now.* Seek me *here*. And live." In other words, "Do not look back to the days of old. My saving acts are not simply a thing of the past; seek them in the present."[4]

It is time for us to stop peering backwards at "Bethel, Gilgal, and Beersheba." Whatever golden age of church history we idealize, that's not where God wants our focus. He wants our eyes on today. Today, there are more Southern Baptist churches in the United States than Starbucks, McDonald's, and Subways combined. What if we relearned how to multiply?

This has always been a north star for the Summit, but recently we have put it in ink. We say that we desire to be the most multiplying church in America. Not the biggest church. Not the church with the best preaching. Or the biggest budget. Or the most published authors. Or the most podcast downloads. But the most multiplying church. If there's one thing we excel at, we want it to be multiplication.

---

[4] I owe this insight to Mark Batterson, who connected these dots for me in *All In: You Are One Decision Away from a Totally Different Life* (Grand Rapids: Zondervan: 2013).

But here's the thing: I don't believe this is just something for the Summit. Every church is animated by the Spirit of God. Every church has been given the Great Commission. Every church is filled with God's saints, prepared for God's purposes.

So, I must ask . . . Might these be the good old days?

The Spirit of God is still available for those churches ready to devote themselves to the Great Commission. He is ready to move. The best days are not behind us, but before us. That is not rhetoric, either: When we think about history through the lens of the promises of Scripture, the church's best days must lie ahead! There are still more than 6,000 unreached people groups in the world, and history cannot end until they have been given a gospel witness. God will move through someone to get the job done. The only question is, "Will it be us?"

CHAPTER TEN

SOUTHERN BAPTIST IDENTITY AND THE GREAT COMMISSION

Nathan A. Finn

Introduction

The late church historian William Estep has argued that "the Southern Baptist historical experience can best be understood as a search for identity."[1] I am sympathetic to Estep's argument. Southern Baptist historians, theologians, and pastors have published dozens of books that address Baptist identity, distinctives, and other related themes. These writings are part of a larger corpus of such works written by Baptists since the early 1600s. Stan Norman has studied these writings

[1] William R. Estep, "Southern Baptists in Search of an Identity," in *The Lord's Free People in a Free Land: Essays in Baptist History in Honor of Robert A. Baker*, ed. William R. Estep (Fort Worth: Evans, 1976), 145.

extensively and asserts they represent a type of "confessional theology" among Baptists.[2]

In this short essay, I want to contribute to this uniquely Baptist form of confessional theology by considering the relationship between Southern Baptist identity and the Great Commission. Since the late 1700s, a desire to fulfill the Great Commission has been an important priority among most Baptists. From the beginning of the Southern Baptist Convention, Great Commission faithfulness has been part of our denominational ethos and shaped every facet of our history.[3] Though missionary commitment is not a traditional Baptist distinctive, it functions as a guiding principle among Southern Baptists, impacting how we think about the Christian life, the mission of the church, and our cooperative work as a convention of local churches.

Great Commission Denominationalism

Baptist Missionary Awakening

If we were to travel back to 1750, we would find that Baptists cared little for missionary advance. Baptists in North America were still a small and oft-persecuted sect, though some were beginning to experience spiritual awakening through the ministries of Jonathan Edwards and especially George Whitfield. Baptists in England were stronger numerically, yet they were hardly flourishing. Many General Baptists were drifting into Unitarian views, influenced by a form of

---

[2] R. Stanton Norman, *More Than Just a Name: Preserving Our Baptist Identity* (Nashville: B&H Academic, 2001), 24.

[3] I address this topic in an earlier essay, "Southern Baptist History: A Great Commission Reading," in *The Great Commission Resurgence: Fulfilling God's Mandate in Our Time*, ed. Chuck Lawless and Adam Greenway (Nashville: B&H Academic, 2010), 51–76. The present essay is in many ways a companion to this earlier piece.

rationalism that was common among British Arminians of the era. Many Particular Baptists were captive to a cold-hearted orthodoxy, influenced by the High Calvinism that was prevalent among British Calvinists at the time.

Though there were always pockets of faithfulness among the Baptists, it was Andrew Fuller and William Carey who played a catalytic role in a missionary awakening that would spread to evangelicals all over the English-speaking world.[4] In 1785, Fuller published an important treatise titled "The Gospel Worthy of All Acceptation." Though he was a committed Calvinist, Fuller argued that God's sovereignty in salvation does not negate the need to urgently call all sinners to repent and believe in Jesus Christ. Carey agreed with Fuller and applied his views to the question of global evangelism. In his 1792 treatise, "An Enquiry into the Obligations of Christians to Use Means for the Conversion of the Heathens," Carey argued that the Great Commission is a binding command on every generation of Christians. The two men and some friends formed the Baptist Missionary Society (BMS), which in 1793 sent Carey to India as one of its first missionaries. Fuller was the first secretary of the BMS.

In America, the first foreign missionary was George Leile, a former slave turned Baptist preacher. Leile was forced to flee to Jamaica in 1782, where he became an evangelist and church planter. Leile's work predated the BMS by a decade. The first Americans who felt called to relocate to another culture as missionaries were Adoniram and Ann Judson, who in 1812 were sent to India by the Congregationalists. The Judsons converted to Baptist views while en route, leading them to break with the Congregationalists. The Judsons relocated to Burma, where they were soon joined by other American Baptist missionaries. Luther Rice, a colleague of the Judsons, was instrumental in founding a

[4] An excellent starting place to learn about the missionaries discussed in this section is Daniel L. Akin, *Ten Who Changed the World* (Nashville: B&H, 2012).

Baptist foreign mission society in America in 1814, popularly called the Triennial Convention because it met every three years.

The missionary awakening among Baptists between about 1780 and 1820 led to the first real denominational structures beyond local associations. Baptists were eager to cooperate for the sake of evangelism, church planting, and other ministries that helped facilitate global gospel advance. In England, the Baptist Union was formed in 1812 to unite mission-minded Particular Baptists into a national group. In America, Baptists founded other societies modeled after the Triennial Convention, most notably the American Baptist Home Mission Society (est. 1832). Baptists also began forming state conventions, beginning with South Carolina in 1821. These evolving structures led to debates about the best way to fund missions, where best to focus missionary efforts (both domestic and foreign), and how other ministry priorities such as education and publications related to missions.

The Southern Baptist Convention

The Southern Baptist Convention (SBC) was founded in 1845. Many factors led to the new organization, including the aforementioned debates about funding and priorities. But another key factor, far more tragic, in the formation of the SBC was the relationship between slavery and missions. Simply put, Southern Baptists held to the racist notion that whether someone owned slaves or not should not impact his fitness for missionary service. They took this position despite the Great Commission command that believers share the gospel with people from every ethnic group. At the same time, growing numbers of Northern Baptists were arguing that slavery was a grave moral evil and that owning slaves should disqualify someone from missionary service. The differences proved irreconcilable.

It is important that we not minimize the seminal role that racism played in the formation of the Southern Baptist Convention. Racism is our denominational "original sin," and it has left a lasting stain on Southern Baptist life. Southern Baptists in general affirmed white supremacy for well over a century before a combination of courageous leaders, changing laws, and key biblical arguments persuaded most to reject racism as incompatible with authentic Christianity.[5] This culminated symbolically in a 1995 resolution that apologized for the role racism played in the formation of the SBC and much of our subsequent history. In recent years, we have further distanced ourselves from our white supremacist past, as evidenced in a variety of adopted resolutions and strategic initiatives. We still have a long way to go, and at this writing America is as divided by race as it has been at any point since the Civil Rights era. But I remain hopeful that God will continue the good work he has begun among Southern Baptists when it comes to overcoming racism and increasingly embodying what the Baptist minister and civil rights activist Martin Luther King Jr. called the beloved community.[6]

Even as we speak honestly about our racist past, Southern Baptists should not hesitate to argue that the founders of the SBC were

---

[5] See Mark Newman, *Getting Right with God: Southern Baptists and Desegregation, 1945–1995* (Tuscaloosa: University of Alabama Press, 2001); Alan Scot Willis, *All according to God's Plan: Southern Baptist Missions and Race, 1945–1970* (Lexington: University Press of Kentucky, 2004); David Roach, *The Southern Baptist Convention & Civil Rights, 1954–1995: Conservative Theology, Segregation, and Change* (Eugene, OR: Pickwick, 2021).

[6] In recent years, numerous African American Southern Baptist scholars and pastors have written helpful works about racism and racial reconciliation. See Isaac Adams, *Talking about Race: Gospel Hope for Hard Conversations* (Grand Rapids: Zondervan, 2022); Kevin M. Jones and Jarvis J. Williams, eds., *Removing the Stain of Racism from the Southern Baptist Convention: Diverse African American and White Perspectives* (Nashville: B&H Academic, 2017); Jarvis J. Williams, *Redemptive Kingdom Diversity: A Biblical Theology of the People of God* (Grand Rapids: Baker Academic, 2021); and George A. Yancey, *Beyond Racial Division: A Unifying Alternative to Colorblindness and Antiracism* (Downers Grove, IL: IVP, 2022).

animated by a desire to obey the Great Commission. In the preamble to the Convention's original constitution, the founding delegates declared their commitment to "eliciting, combining, and directing the energies of the whole denomination in one sacred effort, for the propagation of the Gospel."[7] Their first major actions were establishing mission boards for both foreign and domestic work. Between 1845 and 1925, Southern Baptists founded several denominational entities, including Southern Baptist Theological Seminary (1859), the Baptist Sunday School Board (1891), the Brotherhood Commission (1907), Southwestern Baptist Theological Seminary (1908), and New Orleans Baptist Theological Seminary (1917). They also established two strategic standing committees: the Social Service Committee (1913), focused on social ethics, and the Executive Committee (1917), which represented the Convention between annual meetings. All of these initiatives were an outgrowth of the Southern Baptist commitment to proclaiming the gospel and teaching its implications to all people.

Arguably more important than official Southern Baptist agencies and committees was the Woman's Missionary Union (WMU), which was founded as an auxiliary to the SBC in 1888. In 1885, the Convention decided that women could not serve as messengers. However, women were already meeting informally during the annual meeting for fellowship and to promote missions. The two key figures in the formation of the WMU were Lottie Moon, a highly respected missionary in China, and Annie Armstrong, who was involved in several mission initiatives in Baltimore. Moon wrote letters advocating for a Baptist missionary society for women, while Armstrong served as the WMU's first corresponding secretary. WMU began an annual Christmas offering to support the work of the Foreign Mission Board (FMB) in 1888, and by 1906, the year Armstrong stepped down, the FMB's annual receipts

[7] *Proceedings of the Southern Baptist Convention* (Richmond: H. K. Ellyson, 1845), 3.

had increased almost fourfold from around $86,000 to over $315,000. Today, the annual Southern Baptist Christmas offering for global missions is named for Moon, while our annual Easter offering for North American missions is named for Armstrong. For more than 130 years, WMU has remained a significant partner in promoting missions, especially among young women.[8]

In 1925, Southern Baptists took two important steps that mutually reinforced our commitment to cooperative mission for the sake of the Great Commission. The first was the adoption of the Baptist Faith and Message in response to the influence of Darwinism and other modernist ideas. While Southern Baptists had always enjoyed a consensus in matters of doctrine, the Baptist Faith and Message became a Convention-approved standard for summarizing that consensus and clarifying its boundaries. Subsequent revisions and amendments in 1963, 1998, and 2000 addressed additional threats to the consensus as they developed. By the early twenty-first century, all seminary professors, missionaries, and curricula writers were required to affirm the Baptist Faith and Message. There was also a strong expectation, though not always an official requirement, that all elected Convention officers and appointed trustees also affirm the confession. In terms of the wider SBC, the Southern Baptist form of confessionalism was not a "strict subscriptionism" like that found in some Reformed traditions, but rather was a "cooperative consensus" meant to facilitate like-minded churches cooperating for the sake of Great Commission faithfulness.[9]

---

[8] For more on WMU and its numerous contributions to Southern Baptist missions, see Catherine B. Allen, *A Century to Celebrate: History of Woman's Missionary Union* (Birmingham: WMU, 1987), and Rosalie Hall Hunt, *We've a Story to Tell: 125 Years of WMU* (Birmingham: WMU, 2013).

[9] For more on this cooperative consensus, see David S. Dockery, *Southern Baptist Consensus and Renewal: A Biblical, Historical, and Theological Proposal* (Nashville: B&H Books, 2008), and D. Scott Hildreth, *Together on God's Mission: How Southern Baptists Cooperate to Fulfill the Great Commission* (Nashville: B&H Academic, 2018).

The second key event in 1925 was the establishment of the Cooperative Program, which was a unified budget for denominational ministries. Before 1925, every SBC entity, as well as state-level institutions such as colleges, orphanages, and retirement homes, solicited money directly from local churches. This meant that these ministries competed for a finite number of resources from the same pool of churches. The Cooperative Program established a plan whereby churches would forward a percentage of their own budget money to their respective state convention. The state would keep a portion of that money, to be divided among state-level ministry partners, while forwarding the rest to the Executive Committee. The latter was responsible for developing a budget that would determine the percentages to be allocated for each SBC entity. By mid-century, most Southern Baptist churches had bought in to the Cooperative Program as the most strategic way to fund our shared ministry priorities. At the time of writing, over half the national budget is allocated to the International Mission Board, just over 20 percent goes to the Home Mission Board, and the rest is distributed to the other entities. If the Baptist Faith and Message provides the cooperative consensus, the Cooperative Program provides the cooperative mechanism for Great Commission faithfulness.[10]

Great Commission Distinctives

From the very beginning of the Baptist movement, we have been characterized by a variety of distinctives that shape our identity.[11]

---

[10] For more on the Cooperative Program, see Robert J. Matz and John Mark Yeats, *Better Together: You, Your Church, and the Cooperative Program* (Nashville: Rainer, 2019).

[11] For more on Baptist distinctives, see Anthony L. Chute, Nathan A. Finn, and Michael A. G. Haykin, *The Baptist Story: From English Sect to Global Movement* (Nashville: B&H, 2015), 325–45, and R. Stanton Norman, *The Baptist Way: Distinctives of a Baptist Church* (Nashville: B&H Academic, 2005).

The eighteenth-century missionary awakening did not change any of those distinctives. However, the increased commitment to Great Commission faithfulness did introduce some healthy "mutations" into the "DNA" of traditional Baptist distinctives. While not all Baptists "evolved" in their self-understanding because of the Great Commission, the above section demonstrates that the missionary Baptists in the South that became the Southern Baptist Convention were deeply influenced by their commitment to cooperative missions. Southern Baptist identity is characterized by a view of Baptist distinctives that overlaps with, and is informed by, our commitment to Great Commission faithfulness.

Southern Baptists are committed to the principle of soul freedom or liberty of conscience. As the Baptist Faith and Message (2000) says, "God alone is Lord of the conscience, and He has left it free from the doctrines and commandments of men which are contrary to His Word or not contained in it."[12] Advocacy for soul freedom does not entail an affirmation of unfettered freedom to embrace false doctrine or sinful practices, though in a fallen world many choose the latter route. Rather, soul freedom contends that individuals must decide to follow Jesus, by grace through faith. Individuals must decide to follow and obey his commands, with open Scriptures and calloused knees. Individuals must decide to share the good news with others, with confidence in God's promises and soft hearts toward the spiritually lost. The Great Commission assumes liberty of conscience because individuals must obey the command to make disciples and individuals must respond to the gospel by becoming disciples.

---

[12] The Baptist Faith and Message (2000), Article XVII: Religious Liberty, available online at https://bfm.sbc.net/bfm2000/#xvii (accessed September 10, 2022). In many Baptist writings, the concepts of liberty of conscience and religious liberty are closely intertwined, with the latter serving as a corollary of the former. While I affirm this approach in principle, for the purposes of this section I have divided them into two distinct principles.

Southern Baptists are not hyper-individualists; rather, we affirm the importance of the individual-in-community. Followers of Jesus should be members of local churches. In fact, church membership should comprise only individuals who are professing Christians. This principle is called "regenerate church membership," and many Baptists argue it is our foundational distinctive.[13] The sixteenth-century evangelical Anabaptists championed regenerate church membership, and the principle was subsequently embraced by the early Baptists that emerged out of English Separatism in the seventeenth century. For Southern Baptists, key evidence of our obedience to God's command for global disciple making is the formation of local communities of disciples who covenant to walk together as a local congregation. Further, these communities are embassies[14] of Christ's kingdom that proclaim his rule through their corporate witness, further advancing the gospel. The local church is "ground zero" for Great Commission faithfulness.

The Baptist tradition takes its name from our conviction that only professing believers should be baptized. Southern Baptists reject infant baptism and any other practice that applies this ordinance to an individual who cannot give credible evidence that he has responded in faith to the gospel and is now following King Jesus. Historically, Baptists have understood that when a new Christian is immersed in water, it constitutes his public profession of faith, marks his identification with the wider body of Christ, and represents the initial pathway into the membership of a particular local church. Baptism is included as a component of the Great Commission in Matt 28:18–20, and the

---

[13] For example, see John S. Hammett, *Baptist Foundations for Baptist Churches: A Contemporary Ecclesiology*, 2nd ed. (Grand Rapids: Kregel Academic, 2019), 91–116.

[14] I borrow the image of local churches as kingdom embassies from Jonathan Leeman, *Political Church: The Local Assembly as Embassy of Christ's Rule* (Downers Grove, IL: IVP Academic, 2016).

very order of Christ's command suggests that believer's baptism is normative. Jesus commands us to make disciples (evangelism), immerse them in the name of the triune God (baptism), and then teach them to observe all things (discipleship). For Southern Baptists, planting "baptistic" churches that affirm believer's baptism is an important part of consistently obeying the Great Commission.

Southern Baptists have always affirmed the principle of congregational church polity, though its application varies from church to church. Though every congregation is a "Christocracy" ruled by Jesus, he exercises that rule through the consensus of the disciples who constitute the community. Members of the church are responsible for following Christ together by applying his commands to their corporate life and witness; maintaining the church's membership by receiving and releasing members; vetting elders (pastors) and deacons according to biblical qualifications; and installing them as the church's officers. A rightly ordered congregationalism does not reject pastoral authority, recognizing that elders have been charged to lead the church through the ministry of the Word. However, congregationalism does acknowledge that elders are themselves members of the community and thus accountable to the people whom they lead. For Southern Baptists, membership is corporate ownership of the Great Commission by a local community of disciples.

Southern Baptists affirm local church autonomy, which is the belief that every congregation is fully free to follow Christ's commands without external coercion from any wider denominational body. Churches select their own officers, decide their own ministry agenda, purchase their own properties, etc. As with soul liberty, this is not freedom for freedom's sake; rather, it is communities of disciples enjoying the freedom to obey Christ in ways that are contextually appropriate to their unique locations, needs, and available resources. While some Baptist groups interpret autonomy as independence, as noted earlier, the Southern Baptist commitment to cooperative mission encourages local churches of similar faith and practice to cooperate for the sake of greater Great Commission faithfulness. Our associations and conventions are expressions of our commitment to cooperative mission. But unlike local churches, these structures are not mandated by Scripture. Rather, they are strategic arrangements, rooted in biblical principles, in which like-minded churches are free to participate to the degree they believe the Lord is leading them.

The final Southern Baptist distinctive is a free church in a free state, which is closely related to both individual soul liberty and local church autonomy. We believe that individuals and churches should not be compelled by the state when it comes to matters of belief and their implications. We further believe that the church should not seek to exercise authority over the state. Admittedly, we enjoy perhaps less consensus around this principle than we once did. American culture is characterized by a growing moral decadence. An anti-Christian secularism pervades many of our society's institutions and influencers. There is revived interest in various forms of Christian nationalism among devout believers across denominational traditions.[15] For all these reasons, many Southern Baptists are wrestling anew with the relationship between church and state. Nevertheless, we all affirm full religious freedom for all people, reject the validity of state churches, and believe that Christians ought to be actively engaged in politics for the sake of the common good. For Southern Baptists, these commitments are not rooted in Enlightenment principles or liberal democracy, though at times they may overlap in some limited ways. Rather, we affirm a free church in a free state because we believe that arrangement

[15] The term "Christian nationalism" has provoked considerable debate among Baptists and other evangelicals. For an excellent treatment of this subject, written from a Baptist perspective, see Paul D. Miller, *The Religion of American Greatness: What's Wrong with Christian Nationalism* (Downers Grove, IL: IVP Academic, 2022).

best contributes to human flourishing and unhindered obedience to the Great Commission.[16]

Conclusion: Great Commission Baptists

Pastors who are calling upon Southern Baptists to own the name Great Commission Baptists, which we approved as an alternate designation for the SBC in 2012, are growing in number. Danny Akin served on the committee that made that recommendation, and for a decade he has used both "Southern Baptist Convention" and "Great Commission Baptists" when referring to our convention of churches. I want to close by making a brief case for why Southern Baptists should embrace the Great Commission Baptists name as we move forward.

We are no longer a regional convention, yet we still retain a regional name. This is problematic for several reasons. Foremost is that our name does not accurately describe us in the way it did even two generations ago. We are not a southern denomination. Our regional name is also at odds with our national emphasis on church planting and church revitalization. A church in the Northeast or Pacific Northwest publicly identifying with Southern Baptists was not unusual during the southern migration of past generations. Today it seems odd.

Our denominational identity is less tied to southern culture than it once was. For better and worse, for most of our history we were almost as southern as we were Baptist. That is no longer the case, even for a growing number of our churches located in the South. Regional preferences and prejudices no longer define us as much as they once did (and define us less so as time goes on). We are no longer concerned with

---

[16] I expand on this theme in Nathan A. Finn, "The Separation of Church and State: A Southern Baptist Perspective," *Southwestern Journal of Theology* 64, no. 2 (Spring 2022): 51–66. See also Andrew Walker, *Liberty for All: Defending Everyone's Religious Freedom in a Pluralistic Age* (Grand Rapids: Brazos, 2021).

accentuating the differences between us and Baptists in other regions, instead emphasizing common faith and practice wherever it is found. We have repented of the role slavery played in our origins and ongoing racism has played in our subsequent history.

The key priority from 1845 that does continue to define us is our commitment to cooperative missions for the sake of the Great Commission. This thread is woven through our history and has been the glue that has held us together. Southern Baptists are a missionary people. We ought to be known by who we are, not by who we have been, even as we continue to celebrate much about our heritage. We are not a convention of Baptist churches in the South. We are a convention of North American Baptists committed to the Great Commission.

The name Great Commission Baptists better describes who we have always been when at our best, and who we should strive to be ever more faithfully, by God's grace. While I believe state conventions should retain their regional names for contextual reasons, I suggest it is time for the Southern Baptist Convention to embrace a name that better reflects our actual identity and is aspirational as we seek to be more faithful in our cooperative mission. But even if you disagree with my thoughts on this topic, let us agree to be known as Great Commission Baptists, in reputation if not in name, for the glory of God and the sake of the world he so loves.

CHAPTER ELEVEN

INTERNATIONAL MISSIONS AND THE GREAT COMMISSION

Chuck Lawless

Introduction

Jesus spoke these words at the end of the Gospel of Matthew: "All authority has been given to me in heaven and on earth. Go, therefore, and make disciples of all nations, baptizing them in the name of the Father and of the Son and of the Holy Spirit, teaching them to observe everything I have commanded you. And remember, I am with you always, to the end of the age" (Matt 28:18–20). These words became the driving force behind the writing of William Carey, known as the "founder of modern missions," as he challenged eighteenth-century believers to go to the nations.[1] To this day, the Matthew 28 expression

[1] Michael A. G. Haykin, *The Missionary Fellowship of William Carey* (Orlando: Reformation Trust, 2018), 2; William Carey, *An Enquiry into the Obligations of Christians to Use Means for the Conversion of the Heathens* (1792; CreateSpace, 2015), Kindle.

of the Great Commission is likely the best known of the five New Testament passages stating this same responsibility for believers.

These words are, according to Danny Akin, "the final marching orders for Christ's followers until He returns."[2] Indeed, Akin commonly concludes about these words, "These were his last words before ascending back to heaven and his Father. Last words are meant to be lasting words, words that leave an impression and make an impact."[3] Referring to Matthew 28, which "begins with a resurrection and ends with a commission," he states even more passionately, "These final words of our Lord are weighty, heavy, not easily digested. And they do not need an *adrenalin[e]* response. They need a *cardiac*, a heart response. They need a response that has carefully considered the King who speaks them, and the kind of servant who obeys them."[4]

Those words he has described as "weighty, heavy, not easily digested" have indeed left an impression on Dr. Akin in his own relationship with the Lord, in his role as president of Southeastern Baptist Theological Seminary, and as the father of sons he and his wife sent to the mission field in the past. Today, the lostness of the world cries out for more men and women whose hearts bleed for the sake of the nations. Indeed, as Akin has noted, "It is mind-boggling to think that in our day, with all of our numbers, resources, technologies, and wealth, there are still

---

[2] Daniel L. Akin, "The Great Commission according to Matthew's Gospel Accompanied by Insights from the Life and Writings of William Carey with the Goal of a Passionate Global Vision for Our Seminary" (sermon preached at Southeastern Baptist Theological Seminary, August 21, 2007, transcript), Daniel Akin website, accessed May 5, 2023, https://www.danielakin.com/wp-content/uploads/2007/08/matthew-2816-20-the-great-commission-according-to-matthews-gospel-manuscript.pdf, p. 4; emphasis in the original.

[3] Daniel L. Akin and Bruce Riley Ashford, *I Am Going* (Nashville: B&H, 2016), 65.

[4] Akin, "The Great Commission according to Matthew's Gospel," 13.

people throughout the world who have never heard the name of Jesus or received a clear presentation of the gospel."[5]

Needs and Challenges of the World

Even a glimpse of the spiritual condition of the world ought to be arresting. At the time of writing this chapter, the peoples of the world looked like this:

- More than 7,200 people groups are "unreached," meaning "there is no indigenous community of believing Christians able to engage this people group with church planting."[6] Generally, this classification means fewer than 2 percent of the people are evangelical Christians. These groups represent 4.7 billion people out of the world's 8 billion population.[7]
- Of the unreached people groups, 455 have one million or more people.[8]
- Every one of the fifty largest unreached people groups has more than 10 million people.[9]
- Less than 10 percent of all missionaries work among unreached people groups.[10]
- Of the 7,200 unreached groups, more than 3,100 are also unengaged, meaning there is "no church planting

---

[5] Akin and Ashford, *I Am Going*, 66.

[6] International Mission Board, "Why Are They Unreached?," PeopleGroups, updated April 3, 2023, https://www.peoplegroups.org/.

[7] International Mission Board, "Why Are They Unreached?"

[8] "Unreached?" Joshua Project, March 2022, https://www.joshuaproject.net/assets/media/handouts/unreached-peoples-overview.pdf.

[9] "Why Still Unreached?," Joshua Project, accessed April 4, 2023, https://www.joshuaproject.net/assets/media/handouts/why-still-unreached.pdf.

[10] "Why Still Unreached?"

strategy, consistent with Evangelical faith and practice, under implementation."[11]

- Of all Buddhists, Hindus, and Muslims, 87 percent "have little, if any, contact with Christians."[12]
- More than 157,000 people die every day without a relationship with Christ.[13]
- Less than one penny of "every dollar of Christian giving to all causes . . . goes toward pioneer church planting among unreached people groups."[14]
- More than 3,800 languages have no portion of the Scripture yet.[15]
- Many in the world (up to 80 percent, according to some estimates) operate as oral-preference learners; that is, they cannot read or prefer to learn by oral forms of communication—e.g., by stories, songs, proverbs, and poems.[16] Reaching them will require wise, relevant strategies.

More specifically connected to Danny Akin's theological education work is the reality that, according to the Center for the Study of Global

---

[11] International Mission Board, "Affinity Overview," PeopleGroups, updated April 3, 2023, https://www.peoplegroups.org/Understand.aspx; "Frequently Asked Questions," https://www.peoplegroups.org/294.aspx#307.

[12] "Why Still Unreached?"

[13] Chip Hutcheson, "'Lostness' Continues to Be World's Greatest Problem, Chitwood Says," Kentucky Today, updated November 16, 2022, https://www.kentuckytoday.com/baptist_life/lostness-continues-to-be-worlds-great-problem-chitwood-say/article_21bd5bcc-6536-11ed-8b29-cb66c011f6b5.html.

[14] "100 Challenge," Liebenzell USA, accessed May 5, 2023, https://liebenzellmission.org/100-challenge/.

[15] "What Work Remains to Be Done?" Wycliffe Bible Translators, accessed May 5, 2023, https://wycliffe.org.uk/about/faqs.

[16] Samuel E. Chiang and Grant Lovejoy, eds., *Beyond Literate Western Practices: Continuing Conversations in Orality and Theological Education* (Hong Kong: International Orality Network, 2014), loc. 223, Kindle; Grant Lovejoy, "Why Does Orality Matter?" *About Orality* (blog), https://orality.info/?p=1016.

Christianity at Gordon-Conwell Seminary, only 5 percent of the pastors around the world have had any formal theological training.[17] The reported percentages of pastors trained vary with each study,[18] but it seems accurate to conclude that the global church is facing what some have called a "theological famine."[19] The nations need the gospel, and the nations need training.

Then, consider this anecdotal evidence. As I have traveled the world, I have met with leader after leader who longs for more training to preach the Word and lead churches well. I have taught in places where security was such a risk that we instructed the same people in one location on one day, then moved everything to another location the second day. The leaders showed up day after day even though they took a risk every time they joined us. These leaders yearned for more training, even at an informal level, and they would listen attentively for hours if we were willing to do the training. They devoured any training they could get. Believers around the world wait for training, and the church must respond appropriately as we seek to fulfill the Great Commission.

---

[17] "What Percentage of Pastors Worldwide Have Theological Training?" https://www.gordonconwell.edu/center-for-global-christianity/researchquick-facts/. The following two paragraphs follow Chuck Lawless, "Theological Education and the Great Commission: Reflections on Our Work, with Recommendations for the Future" (faculty address delivered to Southeastern Baptist Theological Seminary, February 2, 2022), https://multimedia.sebts.edu/?p=9167.

[18] Chris Sugden, "90% of Pastors Lack Proper Theological Training, Major Conference Is Told," Virtue Online, December 17, 2020, https://virtueonline.org/90-pastors-lack-proper-theological-training-major-conference-told; "Around the world, there are 2.2 million evangelical churches. 85% are led by pastors with no formal theological training," https://trainingleadersinternational.org.

[19] "T4G Panel on Theological Training in Missions," https://missionspodcast.com/podcast/t4g-panel-on-theological-training-in-missions/.

The Global Call of the Great Commission

All four of the Gospel accounts include some statement about sending, going, or proclaiming near the end of the book, which emphasizes this calling.[20] Acts 1:8 also records Jesus calling believers to go to the ends of the earth, though at the beginning of the book rather than the end. Tim Beougher, with whom Dr. Akin and I served at The Southern Baptist Theological Seminary, has summarized these five expressions of the Great Commission in this fashion:[21]

- Matthew 28:18–20: The Authority [of Christ]
- Mark 16:15: The Objective [to preach the gospel to all creation]
- Luke 24:45–49: The Message [repentance and forgiveness via Christ's death, burial, and resurrection]
- John 20:21: The Method [Christ has sent us]
- Acts 1:8: The Power [the Holy Spirit]

Matthew 28 not only states Jesus's command to make disciples, it also emphasizes other Matthean themes, including "the authority of Christ, the universality of the gospel, the necessity of discipleship, the significance of worship and faith, and the power of the abiding presence of Christ."[22] In this passage, the one who taught like no other teacher, who calmed nature he had created in the first place, who healed the sick and freed the demon-possessed, and who broke the power of death through his resurrection gave the church its direction; after all, he had "the divine right, as ruler over all, to give all Christians their marching

---

[20] Much of this section is found in Chuck Lawless, "To All the Nations," *Southern Baptist Journal of Theology* 15, no. 2 (2011): 16–26.

[21] Timothy K. Beougher, *Invitation to Evangelism* (Grand Rapids: Kregel, 2021), 55–58.

[22] Lawless, "To All the Nations," 17. See Craig Blomberg, "Matthew," *New American Commentary* (Nashville: B&H, 2001), 429; Ian Campbell, *Opening Up Matthew* (Leominster: Day One, 2008), 176–78.

orders."[23] Note the way Christopher Wright summarizes this truth: "Jesus begins with the monumental cosmic claim, words that echo the affirmation of Moses about YHWH himself (Deut 4:35, 39), that 'all authority in heaven and on earth has been given to me' (Matt 28:18). This is the reality behind the command, the indicative behind the imperative. The identity and the authority of Jesus of Nazareth, crucified and risen, is the cosmic indicative on which the mission imperative stands authorized."[24] Thus, we may well underemphasize the imperative of Matt 28:19–20 if we simply skim over Matthew 28:18. Again, Beougher's words challenge us: "If we do not comprehend verse 18, then verse 19 will never become a reality in our life. It will not take much to stop us from sharing."[25]

The Great Commission passage in John's Gospel (John 20:21) likewise carries the authority of the risen Christ. In this case, the One the Father sent became the Sender. He who had sought to glorify the Father by doing his works and proclaiming his message would now send out his followers by his authoritative command; in the words of Merrill Tenney, "he expected them to deliver his message (John 15:27), to do greater works than he had done (John 14:12), and to give their lives in his service."[26] Jesus the Sender required that the disciples' relationship with him reflect his relationship with the Father, the one who had sent him, as Andreas Köstenberger has noted.[27] They were to be his

---

[23] A. Scott Moreau, Gary R. Corwin, and Gary B. McGee, *Introducing World Missions: A Biblical, Historical, and Practical Survey* (Grand Rapids: Baker, 2004), 44.

[24] Christopher J. H. Wright, *The Mission of God: Unlocking the Bible's Grand Narrative* (Downers Grove, IL: InterVarsity, 2006), 60.

[25] Beougher, *Invitation to Evangelism*, 56.

[26] Merrill C. Tenney, "John," in F. E. Gaebelein, ed., *The Expositor's Bible Commentary: John and Acts* (Grand Rapids: Zondervan, 1981), 193.

[27] Andreas J. Köstenberger, *The Missions of Jesus and the Disciples according to the Fourth Gospel: With Implications for the Fourth Gospel's Purpose and the Mission of the Contemporary Church* (Grand Rapids: Eerdmans, 1998), 192.

representatives, his ambassadors, his voice announcing forgiveness and freedom to non-believing peoples living in darkness (Col 1:13), blinded by the god of this age (2 Cor 4:3–4) and living under the power of Satan (Acts 26:18). They were to be light in the darkness.

The Matthew 28 command of Christ is for believers to make disciples of "all nations," a designation that likely refers to "people groups" of the world. While some view "nations" as a reference to only Gentiles, the book of Matthew emphasizes reaching both Jew and Gentile alike. This gospel does indeed focus on God's love for Israel (Matt 9:36; 10:5–6; 15:24), and it presents Jesus as the fulfillment of the promise to bless the nations of the world through Abraham (Gen 12:3). At the same time, it portrays God's plan and work through Gentile women in the genealogy of Jesus (Matt 1:5), magi (Matt 2:1–12), a Roman centurion (Matt 8:5–13), and a Syrophoenician woman (15:22–28).[28] Indeed, the universality of this call is clear in these additional Great Commission texts:

(1) Mark 16:15, "Go into all the world and preach the gospel to all creation."
(2) Luke 24:47, "repentance for forgiveness of sins will be proclaimed in his name to all the nations."
(3) Acts 1:8, ". . . and to the ends of the earth."

The command of the Great Commission is to make disciples—a process that includes leading a nonbeliever to turn from sin and trust Christ, baptizing him or her, and directing that new Christian in the lifelong task of walking with Christ in obedience. Followers of Christ are, in fact, to obey everything Jesus commanded, and this objective demands we teach one another to do so and then hold each other accountable for that commitment. Making disciples is thus decidedly a relational and

[28] See Lawless, "To All the Nations," 19–20.

corporate task that is the "heart of the Great Commission."[29] It is also an ongoing process for as long as God gives us life.

"Making disciples" is the only imperative in Matt 28:19–20, but that fact does not diminish the force of the participle "go" in these verses. D. A. Carson's analysis is helpful at this point. Not only does the participle translated "go" in this verse carry the sense of a command, but "in a context that demands that this ministry extend to 'all nations,' it is difficult to believe that 'go' has lost all imperatival force."[30] Commenting on the interpretation of "go" (Matt 28:19) as "as you go," Akin, Merkle, and Robinson are even more pointed in their conclusion: "Those who prefer to translate the text 'As you go' misunderstand the original Greek and are thereby weakening the force of Jesus's commission, which requires the church to go."[31] Given who Jesus is and what he has commanded believers to do, Akin's conclusion and application are thus neither surprising nor wrong: "There is no need to pray and ask God if we should go and take the gospel to the nations. We have been told to go."[32]

Going to and reaching the nations is not an easy task, however. Over the years, I have worked with and prayed with missionaries dealing with much more than we might think it possible to handle. In some cases, sickness invades bodies as soon as the workers hit the ground in their new place of service. Language and cultural barriers seem insurmountable. Loneliness captures the heart geographically distanced from family. The spiritual soil is so hard at times that even getting started feels impossible; as one missionary told me even after years of service,

---

[29] Daniel L. Akin, Benjamin L. Merkle, and George G. Robinson, *40 Questions about the Great Commission* (Grand Rapids: Kregel, 2020), 193.

[30] D. A. Carson, "Matthew," in *Expositor's Bible Commentary Matthew, Mark, Luke,* ed. F. E. Gaebelein (Grand Rapids: Zondervan, 1995), 595. See also Lawless, "To All the Nations," 18.

[31] Akin, Merkle, and Robinson, *40 Questions about the Great Commission*, 154.

[32] Akin, "The Great Commission according to Matthew's Gospel," 8.

"Dr. Lawless, we're still trying to pick up rocks rather than planting seeds." Meanwhile, a very real supernatural enemy seeks to devour any workers who have taken the gospel to the front lines (1 Pet 5:8).

Had the Great Commission passages of the New Testament ended with just the command to go and make disciples, the tasks would surely seem overwhelming. But the commands come with the promise of God's presence and power. Craig Ott describes this undeniable truth in discussing Matt 28:20: "The same Jesus to whom all authority is given promises to accompany the disciples on this daunting mission—they neither go on their own authority, nor do they go alone. One can hardly overlook the comprehensiveness of Matthew's formulation: all authority, all nations, all that Jesus commanded, who is always with them."[33] Indeed, he goes so far as to conclude that the command to disciple all nations is "a truly staggering proposition that would verge on the ridiculous were it not for the accompanying authority and promise of the risen Christ, who gives the commission."[34]

That promise echoes throughout Great Commission passages in the New Testament. In Matthew, the disciples would find that hope in the first and last chapters of that Gospel: the Redeemer named "God with us" (Matt 1:27) would be with them to the end of the age. Wherever the Lord compelled them to go, he would be with them; never would they be alone. As the famous Southern Baptist missionary Lottie Moon wrote in a letter about her work, "As you wend your way from village to village, you feel it is no idle fancy that the Master walks beside you, and you hear His voice saying gently, 'Lo! I am with you always, even unto the end.'"[35]

---

[33] Craig Ott, Stephen J. Strauss, and Timothy C. Tennent, *Encountering Theology of Mission* (Grand Rapids: Baker, 2010), 92; italics in the original. Ott wrote this chapter of this book.

[34] Ott, Strauss, and Tennent, 92.

[35] Lottie Moon letter to Dr. Tupper, May 10, 1789, quoted in Keith Harper, *Send the Light* (Macon, GA: Mercer University Press, 2007), 89.

The account of the Gospel of Luke is equally confirming. Jesus mandated that his disciples preach "repentance for forgiveness of sins" to all the nations, but they were not to do so in their own ability. Rather, they were to wait in Jerusalem until they were "empowered from on high" with the Spirit God has promised (Luke 24:49). They were not to make any plans or launch any efforts apart from the power of God's Spirit. The task for these ordinary "nobodies" was to call for repentance and offer forgiveness, but, as Darrell Bock has stated, "It is not to be carried out in mere human strength. . . . God's intimate, indwelling presence is necessary to make it work."[36] In Luke's second volume, Acts, that Spirit would fall on the disciples and empower them to be Christ's witnesses in Jerusalem, Judea, Samaria, and the ends of the earth (Acts 1:8; 2).

In addition, the Gospel of John's expression of the Great Commission includes the image of Jesus's breathing on the disciples and saying, "Receive the Holy Spirit" (John 20:22). The disciples, hiding behind a door for fear of the Jewish leaders who had killed Jesus, needed assurance and empowerment—and Jesus provided both. Twice he sought to reassure them with the words, "Peace be with you" (John 20:19, 21), and he strengthened their faith by showing them his hands and his side in between the repeated words. In breathing on them the Holy Spirit—likely an act "foreshadowing the bestowal of the Spirit to take place on the Day of Pentecost"[37]—Jesus reminded them they could not accomplish their Great Commission task apart from God's power. More important, he assured them of his presence in their work.

It is significant that these same disciples had previously struggled in their walk with God. They often did not understand what Jesus

---

[36] Darrell L. Bock, "Luke," *IVP New Testament Commentary* (Downers Grove, IL: InterVarsity, 1994), 390.

[37] Colin G. Kruse, "John," *Tyndale New Testament Commentaries* (Downers Grove, IL: InterVarsity, 2003), 376.

had taught them (Mark 4:10–13). They failed at times in ministry (Mark 9:14–18). They argued among themselves about who was the greatest (Mark 9:33–34). All of them fled when Jesus was arrested, even after they had said no such thing would ever happen (Mark 14:31, 50). Some then doubted the resurrection (Matt 28:17; Mark 16:11; Luke 24:13–27; 36–39). As Robert Coleman has described them:

> By any standard of sophisticated culture then and now they would surely be considered as a rather ragged collection of souls. One might wonder how Jesus could ever use them. They were impulsive, temperamental, easily offended, and had all the prejudices of their environment. In short, these men selected by the Lord to be his assistants represented an average cross section of society in their day.[38]

They were, in fact, "not the kind of group one would expect to win the world for Christ."[39] On the other hand, the Spirit would fill them, and they would join other believers in being God's witnesses. The Jesus who commanded them to undertake the Great Commission empowered them to fulfill that command. He continues to be with us today as we seek to reach the nations.

Application in the Great Commission Task

Danny Akin is a theologian-practitioner, a seminary president who both stands on the Word of God and sets a practical example for being a Great Commission leader. Indeed, he has written that "faithful and effective theological schools" will produce students and graduates who

---

[38] Robert E. Coleman, *The Master Plan of Evangelism* (Grand Rapids: Revell, 1993), 23.

[39] Coleman, 23.

are pastor-theologians and missionary-evangelists.[40] These roles are, he says,

> complementary. They naturally go together. We should continually remind ourselves that the greatest theologian who ever lived was also the greatest missionary who ever lived. His name was Jesus. And the greatest Christian missionary who ever lived was also the greatest Christian theologian who ever lived. His name was Paul. Faithful theological schools can impress this fourfold assignment biblically, theologically, historically, and practically on their students.[41]

With that balance in mind, I conclude this chapter with practical steps for church leaders and their congregations to commit themselves to the Great Commission call to get the gospel to the nations.

First, we must be uncompromisingly committed to believing and preaching the Word of God. John Piper, in his well-known book *Let the Nations Be Glad*, argues that answering three questions is "crucial for the missionary task of the Christian church":[42]

1. Will anyone experience eternal conscious torment under God's wrath?
2. Is the work of Christ the necessary means provided by God for eternal salvation?
3. Is it necessary for people to hear of Christ in order to be eternally saved?

---

[40] Daniel L. Akin, "Theology for Church, Worship, and Ministry," in David S. Dockery, ed., *Theology, Church, and Ministry* (Nashville: B&H, 2017), 392.

[41] Akin, 392.

[42] John Piper, *Let the Nations Be Glad!* (Grand Rapids: Baker, 2010), 157. The following questions are found on pages 159–60. Italics in the original.

His conclusion is that the Scriptures compel us to a positive response to each question, and those responses increase the urgency of the missionary task. Based on his reading of Romans 10:13–15, Piper rightly asserts that "effective calling presupposes faith in the one called . . . faith presupposes hearing Christ in the message of the gospel . . . hearing Christ in the gospel presupposes a proclaimer of the gospel."[43]

In Danny Akin's words, "The Bible is a missionary book."[44] It is indeed the story of the Creator–Redeemer who pursued Adam and Eve hiding in their sin; raised up a people through whom would come the Messiah; came himself in Christ to pay the penalty for sin and break the power of death; called forth his church to proclaim the message to the nations; and will ultimately gather together "a vast multitude from every nation, tribe, people, and language, which no one could number, standing before the throne and before the Lamb" (Rev 7:9). You and I have the privilege—and the Christ-mandated responsibility, according to the Scriptures—to proclaim that message to the ends of the earth.

Second, the church must regain a wonder over Jesus. The gospel accounts are replete with examples of people amazed by Jesus, who taught like no one else had ever taught, worked miracles like others had not seen, and offered forgiveness they had not experienced. The general pattern (albeit with exceptions) was that people amazed by Jesus tended to talk about him; for example, those astonished over Jesus's teaching and his authority over demons in Mark 1:21–27 spread the news about him "throughout the entire vicinity of Galilee" (v. 28). Even those Jesus commanded not to speak about him did so, almost as if they could not help but speak about the one who dramatically changed their lives (Matt 9:23–26; Mark 1:39–45; 5:36–43).

---

[43] Piper, 195.

[44] Danny Akin, "Baptist Faith & Message 16: Evangelism and Missions," Daniel Akin website, March 16, 2010, 3, https://www.danielakin.com/wp-content/uploads/2010/03/16-Evangelism-and-Missions-Manuscript-kh.pdf.

As I have written elsewhere, "That's the way the Great Commission works: believers who are amazed by Jesus tell others, and they in turn are amazed. When we lose our amazement, however, our Great Commission passion disappears."[45] The church that desires to reignite this passion would be wise to hear and apply Akin's concluding words in "Worthy Is the Lamb!," a sermon based on Rev 5:1–14: "If the governor walks in, it is appropriate to stand. If the president walks in, it is appropriate to stand and applaud. But if Jesus, the Lamb, walks in, to stand is inadequate, to applaud is arrogant. The only proper response to *who* He is and *what* He has done is to fall down and worship!"[46]

Third, we must see our neighbors and the nations as "sheep without a shepherd"—and pray for more laborers. In 2009, Dr. Akin challenged the faculty and students at Southeastern Seminary with these heartfelt words: "Let's cry for our nation and all nations, let's pray for the persecuted church, the unreached peoples, the dictators and despots. Let's pray as Jesus taught us in Matthew 9:38, 'Therefore pray the Lord of the harvest to send out laborers into His harvest.' We fail to reach the nations because we fail to pray for the nations."[47] We simply will not make a dent in global lostness apart from prayer.

More recently, Akin reorganized the seminary's leadership team to create a vice-presidential position to lead the seminary to be not just a Great Commission seminary, but also a praying seminary. Our goal is

---

[45] Chuck Lawless, *Nobodies for Jesus: 14 Days toward a Great Commission Lifestyle* (Franklin, TN: Rainer, 2014), 12.

[46] Daniel L. Akin, "Worthy Is the Lamb!" (sermon preached at Southern Baptist Theological Seminary, August 31, 2000, transcript), Daniel Akin website, https://www.danielakin.com/wp-content/uploads/old/Resource_519/Revelation%205.1-14%20Worthy%20Is%20The%20Lamb%20Manuscript.pdf.

[47] Daniel L. Akin, "A Great Commission Theology for Life" (sermon preached at Southeastern Baptist Theological Seminary, February 19, 2009, transcript), Daniel Akin website, 4, https://www.danielakin.com/wp-content/uploads/2009/02/1-timothy-21-7-a-great-commission-theology-for-life-outlineand-manuscript-ds.pdf.

this: "We who seek to reach our neighbors and the nations must confess both our love for God and our dependence on him through our praying. We want our graduates to be the best equipped servants they can be, but we want them leading from their knees."[48] In this task, faculty and students pray weekly for unreached people groups and missionaries.

Fourth, we must teach believers to obey all that Jesus commanded. That is, our Great Commission efforts at making disciples must include not only evangelizing nonbelievers but also equipping believers to follow Christ fully. This commitment is a both/and proposition, not an either/or focus. Evangelism not accompanied by discipleship leads to baby believers leading other baby believers; discipleship that does not lead to ongoing evangelism can be inward focused and head centered. Craig Blomberg's words, in fact, express this reality most clearly: "If non-Christians are not hearing the gospel and not being challenged to make a decision for Christ, then the church has disobeyed one part of Jesus's commission. If new converts are not faithfully and lovingly nurtured in the whole counsel of God's revelation, then the church has disobeyed the other part."[49]

Fifth, we must "train the trainers" around the world. One of Akin's legacies at Southeastern Seminary will be the "Global Theological Initiatives" program that focuses on raising up and equipping Great Commission leaders around the world. GTI emphasizes training "national leaders, teachers, pastors, and missionaries who covenant to take what they have been given and entrust it to the next generation of faithful church members and leaders."[50] National graduates thus take

---

[48] Chuck Lawless, "Prayer in a Season of Crisis," *Southeastern Perspectives*, January 11, 2021, https://www.sebts.edu/news-and-events/headlines/2021/01/fa20_chuck_lawless/.

[49] Craig Blomberg, "Matthew," *New American Commentary* (Nashville: Broadman & Holman, 1992), 432.

[50] Global Theological Initiatives, "What Makes Us Unique," https://www.sebts.edu/academics/gti/default.aspx.

the responsibility to teach others, who then teach others, multiplying training efforts around the world. These labors have resulted in training offered on six continents, with emphases in Hispanic, Persian, and East Asian leadership development. Seminaries may be uniquely situated to carry out this work, but our responsibility is to challenge pastors and local churches to engage this critical task as well.

Finally, we must call out the called—even if that call means we send our best to the nations. Our Christian universities and seminaries must not only partner with churches to train the next missionaries, but we must also equip pastors with a Great Commission burden. Because the lead pastor is the "most visible" leader, he must be "viewed as the lead evangelist, disciple-maker, and mission advocate. . . . [and] the Great Commission needs to permeate all that he says and does."[51] The pastor must faithfully preach the message of a globally minded God; obediently live his own life from a place of brokenness over lost neighbors and nations; and continually challenge church members to consider their own roles in going to the nations. Indeed, he must (as must all of us, beginning with me) be open to God's calling us first to people like those William Carey described in his day as "lost in ignorance and idolatry."[52]

Whether speaking to the child first learning about missionaries, the teenager or college student facing life decisions, the married couple questioning their own place in life, or the senior adult determining how to use discretionary time and income, the pastor has opportunities to turn believers toward the nations. That responsibility is not optional for church leaders—and the peoples living in darkness need our brightest to consider going where the gospel has not taken root. We pastors and our congregations must send our best with celebration and anticipation, not with reservation and reluctance.

---

[51] Akin, Merkle, and Robinson, *40 Questions about the Great Commission*, 320–21.

[52] Carey, *An Enquiry*, Kindle loc. 57.

Conclusion

Almost forty years ago, it was a Women's Missionary Union president in the local church I pastored who first challenged me to consider the nations.[53] It was not until I became a seminary professor, though, that international missions truly grabbed my heart. Under the influence of colleagues like George Martin and John Mark Terry, I could not help but face the lostness of the world—and then push my students to do the same. Great Commission-focused professors made a significant difference for me.

With that personal history in mind, perhaps the best way for me to conclude this chapter is to let Danny Akin speak for himself, challenging potential students to consider Southeastern Seminary:

> I do not mind telling you, right from the very beginning, that Southeastern is a dangerous place to attend seminary. It is dangerous because we will challenge you—I will challenge you—to consider afresh your calling and what it is God wants you to do for His kingdom and His glory. At Southeastern, we do not primarily ask, "Why should I go carry the Gospel to the nations?" Rather, we ask, "Why should I stay in my homeland when there are so many who have not heard?"[54]

You and I must ask—and answer—the same question.

---

[53] See the WMU website at https://wmu.com.

[54] "Our Leadership: Daniel L. Akin" Southeastern Baptist Theological Seminary website, accessed July 10, 2023, https://www.sebts.edu/about/our-leadership/.

CHAPTER TWELVE

CHURCH PLANTING AND THE GREAT COMMISSION

Ed Stetzer

Introduction

Of all the amazing wonders and oddities of the world, one of my favorites is the relatively unknown forest of Fishlake, Utah, called Pando. While not as well-known as the Grand Canyon or Great Barrier Reef, Pando is incredible because it is home to the single heaviest organism in the world, weighing 13.2 million pounds. On the surface, Pando appears to be a forest of over 47,000 trees. But underneath the ground, scientists have uncovered that every tree is connected to the same root system. This is why Pando got its name, from the Latin "I spread." The single organism has spread tens of thousands of trees over 106 acres. If stretched out, it would go halfway around the world.

Pando Forest can give us a vivid picture of the church. The church is not a bonsai planted meticulously in its curated pot, cultivated to a particular shape and formed over time. The universal church is a living forest, an interdependent collective ecosystem in a divided and polluted world. Each individual local church looks from the surface like its own organism, completely self-sufficient and distinct from all others. Yet underneath, all these churches are connected as one living organism that intertwines, strengthens, and enlivens each expression as part of the greater whole. And like Pando, the church spreads. New churches go out as distinct ventures to form communities of discipleship and outreach, yet they are never disconnected from the whole. The call of church planting is to advance the enduring and animating mission of the collective church.

Early in my ministry, I was blessed to experience church planting's dual nature of connectedness and spread. In 1988, a time when very few people talked about church planting, Donna and I moved to the inner city of Buffalo, New York, to start a church. We were long on zeal and short on training. Yet as I pastored on the weekends and worked as an insulation contractor during the week to pay the bills, I developed a love and vision for the city that outgrew even my own church. I forged deep relationships with other pastors in the neighborhood, community leaders, and even other Christian ministries across the city. My love for these people ignited a love for the mission of the church to show and share the love of Jesus to a lost and hurting world. God used this season of ministry to expand my passion for church planting to a holistic love for church multiplication.

With the steady increase of church planting in America and the powerful industry that supports it[1]—for better and for worse—we

[1] JR Woodward and Dan White Jr. describe the broader cultural lens of popular Christianity in America as industrial complex, expressing the reality that the church in America has been profoundly shaped by the concept of American success and that the imagination that shapes that movement is deeply impressed upon the hearts and minds of leaders in American Christian industries. See Woodward and White, *The Church as Movement: Starting and Sustaining Missional-Incarnational Communities* (Downers Grove, IL: IVP, 2016). As you will see, church planting is no different.

desperately need a renewed vision for God's mission that shapes our praxis and strategy when it comes to planting churches. We need a mission-shaped strategy rather than an industry-enforced model or a church-centered paradigm. To quote Danny Akin from a statement called "Axioms for a Great Commission Resurgence," "Mission is not a ministry of the church but is at the heart of the church's identity and essence. We must encourage our churches to see themselves as the missionary bodies that they are."[2]

This begins with a biblical understanding of mission. It is not the church that has a mission in the world; rather, it is God's mission that has a church in the world.[3] Evangelistic zeal is the fuel of a God-shaped mission that should propel church multiplication movements. In his address at InterVarsity's 1976 Urbana Conference, John Stott spoke to the importance of a mission-shaped faith that is anchored to the Scriptures and in the nature of God himself:

> It is essential, therefore, for Christians to understand the grounds on which the Christian mission rests. Only then shall we be able to persevere in the missionary task. . . . More precisely, biblical Christians need biblical incentives, for we believe the Bible to be the revelation of God and his will. So we ask: has he revealed in Scripture that "mission" is his will for his people? Only then shall we be satisfied. For then it becomes a matter of obeying God, whatever others may think or say.[4]

---

[2] Daniel Akin, "Axioms for a Great Commission Resurgence" (presented at Southeastern Baptist Theological Seminary, Wake Forest, NC, April 16, 2009), https://bit.ly/3kjg9U6.

[3] Christopher J.H. Wright describes the biblical metanarrative of the *missio Dei* in his magnum opus, *The Mission of God: Unlocking the Bible's Grand Narrative* (Downers Grove, IL: IVP, 2006).

[4] John R. W. Stott, "The Living God Is a Missionary God" in *Perspectives on the World Christian Movement*, ed. Ralph Winter and Steven C. Hawthorne (Pasadena: William Carey, 2009), 3.

Stott is right: we need to rediscover the Great Commission's importance and relevance in church planting and church multiplication movements today.

In this chapter,[5] I contend for this broader vision of church multiplication as the central and animating strategy for church planting. First, I will survey the growth of church planting beginning in the early 1990s to where we are today, paying attention to the incentives, tools, and theology that shaped and advanced church planting across denominations and traditions. Only after understanding how we got to this point can we turn our attention to the challenge of cultivating a healthy and full theology and strategy of church planting that advances the church's mission. We seek a vision of church planting that simultaneously upholds the unity and facilitates the spread of the church through unique local bodies.

From Church Planting to Planting Industries

Consider the historical development of church planting in the West, particularly North America. With some exceptions, churches have planted churches. This ecclesiocentric model dominated American evangelicalism and was in some ways fueled by the prominent church growth movement promulgated by Donald McGavran before the rise of church planting in the late 1980s and early 1990s. The method for this approach depended on local churches within a particular denomination to identify the area of the country that needed a church and send a group to start a church. Informed by the homogeneous unit principle popularized by McGavran, the catalytic impact of church planting in the 1990s laid the foundation for the development of today's church planting industrial complex.

---

[5] Andrew MacDonald, Todd Korpi, Desmond Henry, and Auburn Powell assisted with this chapter.

The church planting boom of the 1990s was built upon a systems approach that became prominent the decade before. At its core, this approach shifted the primary catalyst in the planting process from the local church to the denominations who oversaw those local churches. This came with a lot of clear benefits, the foremost being the professionalization, centralization, and systemization of church planting as denominations worked to equip and support church planters with the best available knowledge of the practice. What started out as a faith community's mission to plant another congregation quickly morphed into a professional paradigm, where trained practitioners were assessed, equipped, and dispatched to offer more support to local church planting initiatives. Churches were largely cut out of the equation as denominations directly trained, resourced, and commissioned individuals to plant churches. The systemization of denominational church planting was hitting its apex in the early 2000s, just as I began writing my dissertation on the development of church planter support systems.

This approach shifted yet again with the rise of immensely influential churches (who were newly planted churches themselves) like Willow Creek in Chicagoland and Saddleback in California. The influence of these churches (and others that would follow) brought about the advent of the *entrepreneurial planter.* This model of planting churches was built upon the previous professional paradigm that had fueled evangelical church planting, but surpassed the denominational hierarchies that brought the professional paradigm to the forefront. The sources of wisdom and best practices for planting and growing vibrant churches shifted away from church growth experts, denominational leaders, and seminaries to the entrepreneurial megachurches who were training and resourcing new church planters at a rapid pace.[6] Many of these

---

[6] A study of Protestant pastors undertaken by the Wheaton College Billy Graham Center with Lifeway Research conducted in 2017 discovered that

entrepreneurial churches launched their own networks aimed primarily at resourcing church planting, including groups like Acts 29 and ARC.

In our book *Viral Churches*, Warren Bird and I summarized the shift with these points:

- Recent years have seen an aggressive increase in the number of new churches launched across the United States.
- Not since the pioneer days of settling the West has this country seen such a focus on planting.
- The pace of church planting now exceeds the number of churches being closed annually.
- There are more books, conferences, and other resources than ever for planters.[7]

In a matter of a few decades, church planting went from something of nominal importance in the American church scene to creating systems and priorities that turned planting into its own industry. Things have changed since 1988 when I planted a church in Buffalo, New York. If you had asked me then what the future of church planting would look like, I would have not imagined the current magnitude of overall importance church planting has today.

Church planting has likewise undergone a market revolution during my lifetime, transforming from the informal and underappreciated work of a few to a professional system of networks, denominations, gurus, conferences, and resources. Funding networks, recruitment approaches, coaching activities, and more form a businesslike approach, which at some level was inevitable since church planting is now a multimillion-dollar industry. But this brings with it some unintended consequences.

---

two-thirds (66 percent) of pastors looked to nationally known pastors or large churches for help with ministry practices.

[7] Ed Stetzer and Warren Bird, *Viral Churches: Helping Church Planters Become Movement Makers* (San Francisco: Jossey-Bass, 2010), 17. Kindle.

Church planting has become a career more than a calling. Another unintended consequence is the lessening attention to evangelism that can happen in an industry-approach to church planting. Evangelism is essential to church planting movements as blood is to our body because evangelism is defined by the central message of the gospel and is the means through which the gospel is communicated to both Christians and non-Christians.

There is certainly reason to be frustrated at the current state of the church planting industry. The era of church planting as an informal movement is over. What once was a movement is now a marketplace. In *Viral Churches* we documented the remarkable shift in emphasis to church planting and argue that the need of the hour is for multiplying church planting movements. But near the conclusion we also add a warning:

> However, if the multiplication of church planting is to become truly movemental, it will require an evangelistic intensity that is still not widespread or deep enough. In most cases, the majority of new attendees at new churches are still believers—either transfers from other churches or dropouts from previous churches. To truly shift to a movement, church plants—and the people who are part of such plants—must make intentional evangelism a defining and ongoing aspect of their new church.[8]

The call to renew evangelism in church planting is both timely and timeless. It is simultaneously a return to our New Testament roots and a proven strategy for effective church growth. Many years ago, Peter Wagner stated that the most effective evangelistic method is church planting.[9] This is true if church plants are intentionally evangelistic

---

[8] Stetzer and Bird, 199–200.

[9] E.g., C. Peter Wagner, *Church Planting for a Greater Harvest: A Comprehensive Guide* (Eugene, OR: Wipf & Stock, 2010), 11, 22.

in their disciple making. At first thought, emphasizing the need for greater evangelistic focus in church planting sounds unnecessary. After all, aren't church plants, by virtue of their very existence, inherently evangelistic? Ideally, this would be true. But when we consider how much church growth happens because of transfers from other, established churches—and how much of the church's life and ministry can be unintentionally geared toward generating that transfer growth—we see the need for evangelistic renewal more clearly than ever. In addition, as churches become established, evangelism often gets pushed more to the margins without those churches even realizing it. Ironically enough, the Great Commission gets lost in the hectic efforts of doing church ministry. How can we maintain and even grow in a focus on evangelistic church planting in an age of industry domination?

Shifting Gears to Multiplication

Church planting has shifted several times over the last few decades. Church planting methods shifted from churches planting churches, denominations planting churches, to parachurch organizations planting churches. Where once planting a church was a leap of faith that was supported by very little training or scant resources, it is now a multimillion-dollar enterprise designed to equip entrepreneurial planters with the tools and funds needed to start and grow a large church.

With these changes, we have gained much and we have also lost much. Church planting that is devoid of evangelism and disciple making, centered on personality, and propped up by the brand of denomination/network will not provide the gospel growth to strengthen the future of the church in America. To address the current issues in church planting, we must shift toward an evangelistically driven multiplication approach to planting. But what does multiplication even mean? Isn't the act of planting churches multiplication? Not exactly.

By multiplication, I don't simply mean the act of multiplying (i.e., just planting more churches, though we certainly need more churches planted). Multiplication requires a shift to a new mindset that possesses two important characteristics.

First, a shift toward multiplication requires a return to an ecclesiocentric model of church planting. Eddie Gibbs explains the organizational challenge of adopting a denominational-driven approach over more ecclesiocentric models to church planting:

> Today, we live in a cultural of discontinuous and often unpredictable change. When things happen suddenly and unexpectedly, the church needs organizational structures that are flexible and flat—that is, capable of adjusting to changing needs and circumstances to allow for timely and appropriate responses. This is a challenge faced by every institution, including those within business, politics, education, health care, and the military, as well as the church.[10]

In other words, churches must be trained and equipped to handle and respond to what is happening in their unique context and how the Holy Spirit is leading them to respond. Rather than merely curating best practices, systems, and processes from a denomination or network far away, ecclesiocentric church planting in the twenty-first century requires that we apply a localized approach to discern and empower churches to minister with the truth of the gospel.

Denominations and networks can come alongside planters and pastors by shifting training efforts from simply teaching planters what to do (i.e., executing pre-built systems) to how to discern (i.e., identifying where the Lord is already at work and how best to join him). Reintegrating local churches into the church planting process would

---

[10] Eddie Gibbs, *Church Morph: How Megatrends Are Reshaping Christian Communities* (Grand Rapids: Baker Academic, 2009), 12.

also aid in this ecclesiocentric shift so that new church planters can learn, be accountable to, and be supported by established churches who have been around for years.

A second characteristic of a movement mindset is an increased innovation. The same period that saw the rise of the church planting industry also witnessed a significant shift in the church's place in North American culture. In many ways, we have lost our home field advantage in the culture. While historically it is true that Christianity has flourished best (and been corrupted least) when it lives as a prophetic voice on the margins of a society, this continuing trend brings about extraordinary challenges for churches who seek to multiply through evangelism.

One of these challenges is in the waning effectiveness of the attractional model of church ministry. While still the predominant model of church engagement with culture in the United States today, it is quickly becoming less and less viable. In the attractional model, everyday Christians participate in the Great Commission by inviting their friends to church—whether a Sunday morning service that has been planned with seekers in mind or an event designed to entice them to return and, eventually, be integrated into the lifeblood of the church community.

While this approach to evangelistic ministry has undoubtedly borne fruit over the years, it relies upon a broader cultural system that is nominally Christian. In fact, many of the contexts in which attractional churches have flourished best are in places like the American South, which possesses a deeply engrained, nominally Christian identity. But as nominally Christian culture wanes in North America, the effectiveness of the attractional model wanes as well. We must be effective in our evangelism. Increasingly, churches and church planters will have to adopt more innovative models and practices that pair the unchanging truth of the gospel with the needs and longings of the culture to which God has called the planter.

Helping the church move from simply planting churches to a multiplication mindset is the reason Warren Bird and I wrote *Viral Churches*: "Our 'viral church' idea is about falling in love with multiplication and abandoning what seems to be an addiction to addition."[11] It is time we shifted the focus from church growth or church planting, as vital as they are, to church multiplication and even what I would call healthy church propagation, which carries with it the potential for exponential and movemental gospel impact over time.[12] The way we point to God in the world is by proclaiming the gospel message in which God reveals his character and works through the life, death, and resurrection of his Son.

The missional imperative described above is pivotal to creating movemental mindset in church plants. In an era obsessed with church planting industry standards, we need to choose:

1. Missional purpose over pragmatism
2. People over programs
3. Multiplication over addition
4. Healthy propagation over meaningless multiplication
5. Gospel-centered evangelism over brand-centric evangelism

Planting too often becomes conflated with the end or purpose of mission rather than as one of its fundamental tools. Meaning that we often mistakenly believe our mission is "to plant churches" when our true mission is "to plant churches to reach lost people with the gospel." Charles Van Engen put it this way: "As the anticipatory focal point of Christ's reign, missionary congregations are called to spread throughout the world the knowledge of the rule of the King. This means local churches cannot be ends in themselves, for the church is not the final goal of mission. Local churches are, rather, the instruments of something

[11] Stetzer and Bird, *Viral Churches*, 36.

[12] Woodward and White express this idea in *The Church as Movement*.

much greater than themselves. They are tools of the kingdom of God."[13] Thus, when we understand planting as multiplicative propagation, the framing changes from overemphasizing numerical growth—which gets most of the attention in church planting discussions—to the underlying and primary mission that compels, animates, and accomplishes this growth. The "why" must come before the "how" because ultimately, we cannot manufacture growth and not all growth is healthy. Pragmatism, best practices, and rugged entrepreneurial individualism have become the gods of the church planting industry, and we need to change the narrative. Our focus must be on the mission of multiplicative propagation—and God handles the results.

Building Great Commission Churches

Central to the church's role in God's reconciliatory mission in the world is the Great Commission—the mandate to go and disciple others with the transformative truth of the gospel of Jesus Christ. The gap between the "go" and "make disciples" is where evangelism takes place. Therefore, evangelism is a crucial component to any church, or any Christian, responding obediently to the Great Commission. I suggest four ways we can keep evangelism central to our church planting endeavors and increase our evangelistic temperature in a world that seems cold and harsh. Here are the 4 Cs that will help change the culture around evangelism in our church planting movements:

1. Calling and identity
2. Communication of the gospel
3. Contextualization
4. Coupling our efforts with God's power

[13] Charles Van Engen, *God's Missionary People: Rethinking the Purpose of the Local Church* (Grand Rapids: Baker, 1991), 111.

First, we need to embrace our calling and identity as intentional evangelists. Church planters are multipliers of the kingdom, not recyclers of church members. Or, to borrow from the widely attributed saying, planters are fishers of men, not keepers of the aquarium! Sadly, the latter has become the norm in our church planting efforts. For evangelism to thrive in our church planting movements, we need to rediscover our calling as gospel witnesses. Scripturally, every disciple of Jesus is called to be a witness (Acts 1:8). Some are called to be evangelists (Eph 4:11–12), to equip the body, proclaim, and spread the good news of Jesus. Not everyone may possess the calling of an evangelist, but all of us are called to evangelism by virtue of our responsibility to be Christ's witnesses. John Stott establishes the calling of every Christian to be a witness:

> Our mandate for world evangelization, therefore, is the whole Bible. It is to be found in the creation of God (because of which all human beings are responsible to him), in the character of God (as outgoing, loving, compassionate, not willing that any should perish, desiring that all should come to repentance), in the promises of God (that all nations will be blessed through Abraham's seed and will become the Messiah's inheritance). In the Christ of God (now exalted with universal authority, to receive universal acclaim), in the Spirit of God (who convicts of sin, witnesses to Christ, and impels the church to evangelize) and in the church of God (which is a multinational, missionary community under orders to evangelize until Christ returns).[14]

Second, evangelism needs to be defined as gospel proclamation that seeks a response to the gospel message. The Lausanne Covenant defined evangelism as the work "to spread the good news that Jesus Christ died for our sins and was raised from the dead according to

[14] Stott, "The Bible in World Evangelization," 22.

the Scriptures, and that, as the reigning Lord, he now offers the forgiveness of sins and the liberating gift of the Spirit to all who repent and believe."[15] Church planters need to be faithful in prioritizing and proclaiming the gospel message, knowing that proclamation and demonstration will bring about growth in the new plant. Too often, church plants get established and grow through the recycling of disgruntled Christian consumers from other churches. Much like Pando Forest, the propagation of the gospel message needs to be rooted in the ground of the good news itself. Stott encourages us to combine fidelity to the Scriptures with sensitivity. Stott states, "Only then can we hope with faithfulness and relevance to relate the Word to the world, the gospel to the context, Scripture to culture."[16]

One topic worth clarifying is "seeking a response." In many churches, seeking a response to evangelism has been reduced to someone "making a decision." But decisions do not equal disciples. A movemental posture regards seeking a response to the gospel message as beginning with a decision but being followed by a pattern of transformation. Paul Hiebert puts it this way:

> We need to return to a biblical view of transformation, which is both a point and a process; this transformation has simple beginnings (a person can turn from wherever he or she is) but radical, lifelong consequences. It is not simply mental assent to a set of metaphysical beliefs, nor is it solely a positive feeling toward God. Rather it involves entering a life of discipleship and obedience in every area of our being and throughout the whole story of our lives.[17]

---

[15] "The Lausanne Covenant," Lausanne Movement, 1974, https://bit.ly/3XnQlEX, par. 4.

[16] Stott, "The Bible in World Evangelization," 23.

[17] Paul Hiebert, *Transforming Worldviews: An Anthropological Understanding of How People Change* (Grand Rapids: Baker Academic, 2008), 310.

So, part of what it means to plant Great Commission churches is for churches to view evangelism and discipleship as discernably different—but deeply connected—activities. Evangelism is "reaching the lost," and discipleship is "raising the reached." Yet, Great Commission churches must also see those two missional responsibilities as being inextricably linked to one another. They are both part of that Great Commission. One task of seeking a response to evangelism is discipling our congregations in how to walk with people in their first steps of responding to the gospel. After all, the Great Commission is principally concerned not with decisions, but with disciples.

Third, Great Commission churches prioritize a contextualization of the gospel message that bridges cultural and worldview gaps without misrepresenting Christ. Too often church plants in the United States assume that people they seek to reach have a basic biblical framework in their minds. That is often not the case. There are cultural bridges to cross that make the context of the gospel increasingly important. As Akin writes:

> Different contexts demand diverse strategies and methods. We must think like missionaries and ask, "What is the best way to reach the people I live amongst with the gospel?" Various ethnic believers and social/cultural tribes will worship the same God, adore the same Jesus, believe the same Bible, and preach the same gospel. However, they may meet in different kinds of structures, wear different kinds of clothes, sing different kinds of songs, and engage in different kinds of ministries. We must treat the United States missiologically and do so with the same seriousness that our international missionaries treat their foreign people groups.[18]

But contextualization seeks to communicate a gospel message in a context the hearer can relate to. The systems, processes, pipelines, etc., of

[18] Akin, "Axioms for a Great Commission Resurgence."

churches today are not as "one size fits all" as we might have hoped, and as the culture around us continues to change, the need for contextualization in our Great Commission efforts will only become more dire.

A fourth characteristic of Great Commission churches is the recognized partnership between God's leading and power and the human effort to sustain true, exponential impact. The Great Commission starts with a statement of Jesus's position and power (Matt 28:18). Then, predicated on God's ability, Christians are commissioned to make disciples. The truth is that we need God's abiding power to carry out that task. No church planting machine can operate for long without the fuel of God's power and presence. We need God's power to help us break through the defenses of the human heart that often stand guard in our culture of outrage, anger, and isolation. We need God's power to move us forward in mission against the powers of this world that darken the minds of unbelievers (2 Cor 4:4). It is terrifying how easily, in a well-intentioned effort to do the work of the ministry, we can lose sight of the object and aim of that ministry: Jesus. Equally terrifying how often those of us working in church planting get so busy working for Jesus that we forego a desperate and abiding reliance upon him—a recognition that unless he is building the church, we who labor in church work labor in vain (see Ps 127:1).

Conclusion

Central to shifting the vision away from the church planting industry and toward evangelistic fervor for church multiplication is reclaiming the Great Commission vision as central to the church's mission and work in church planting. The Great Commission must be central to the focus of our church planting efforts if we desire to become stewards of multiplication rather than mere managers of church maintenance. We cannot relegate evangelism and discipleship to the margins of God's mission—they are as foundational to Christ's mission through the church today as they were in the church's infancy.

We face increasing external pressure from the proliferating influence of secularism and relativism, which pushes the faith toward the periphery of society. And we face internal pressures of polarization, division, and sin among churches that threaten to disrupt their primary mission of reaching lost people and raising them in the community of faith—truly, their *only* mission. At its core, the church must recognize that we are not called to create competing organizations that contribute to division or that glorify ministers, but to multiply the church of Jesus through evangelism and discipleship.

Like the trees of the Pando Forest, the vibrancy of the church of tomorrow rests upon our vision for multiplication—a vision that prioritizes healthy and vigorous growth through engagement in the Great Commission, rather than simple numeric addition. We need to return to the basic motivation that brought church planting to the forefront of North American Christianity—a desire that all would come to know Christ and his saving power.

But also like the Pando Forest, there is an interconnectedness and interdependence that must permeate our culture of multiplication. The Pando is strong because it is interconnected. The church is strong for the same reason. In a world increasingly hot-tempered, xenophobic, and ideologically polarized, the mutuality of the church is more than sharing resources across denominational boundaries. It is, rather, a testimony to the unifying power of the gospel, which breaks down the walls of hostility to unite across cultures (see Eph 2:14).

We have before us a great opportunity to reignite the heart of church planting for the twenty-first century. We can empower planters to discern where God is calling them, what relationships they need along the way, and how they might best reach the place of their calling with the transformative power of the Great Commission.

CHAPTER THIRTEEN

THEOLOGICAL EDUCATION AND THE GREAT COMMISSION

Keith S. Whitfield

Introduction

Times are hard for institutions of higher education. They face significant challenges resulting from massive market changes and disruptions. Enrollment declines, changes in student preferences, emerging alternatives, and diminished public perception of higher education are just a few of the threats. Schools struggle to find sustainable revenue sources to keep pace with the changes in enrollment patterns and increased operational costs. Christian institutions are not immune to these broader trends impacting higher education; they must also navigate additional challenges specific to faith-based schools. This chapter focuses on the mission of graduate theological education, which presents its own distinct challenges.

Much has changed in how individuals envision fulfilling their ministry calling. Formerly, those called to ministry relocated to a seminary and studied to become a pastor, serve in a church staff position, or go to the mission field. Now there are more diverse roles for serving the church, not all of which come with the expectation of theological training. Churches also are seeking to develop, engage, and equip a broader base of ministry leaders. They are not thinking only about equipping people to lead churches but also considering how to advance the church's mission creatively and develop strategies for marketplace ministry. As a result, churches recruit and develop leaders from numerous professional backgrounds with varied perceptions about their ministry training needs.

All this raises an important question: Where is theological education heading? The answer provides direction and leadership, clarifies purpose, and establishes a mindset for how best to address the challenges before us. While there are some specific challenges that need specific innovative solutions, in this chapter I suggest the foundational way to navigate the future is to recall our purpose as the people of God and to see how this purpose determines the vocation, mission, curriculum, cooperation, and commission of theological education. This commitment will provide missional direction from which creative answers to today's challenges can be pursued.[1] Faithful theological education participates in God's mission to call men and women from all nations to be disciples of Jesus Christ, our Lord.

The ultimate purpose of theological education is not the spiritual or academic formation of students, nor is it primarily about preparing people to fulfill ministerial roles. While these are important functions

---

[1] For a helpful article on innovative and practical solutions, see Ed Stetzer and Andrew MacDonald, "How Can and Should We Reach and Train Our Future Pastors and Christian Leaders?" *Christian Education Journal* 17 (2020): 160–76.

of theological education, its chief purpose comes from, in the words of Dr. Danny Akin, "the last words" of King Jesus. The best-known expression of his final words is found in Matthew 28:19–20, where the church is called to make disciples by baptizing people from all nations and teaching them to obey all that Jesus taught. Jesus commissioned his followers to this enduring task just as he ascended into the heavens. If these words are supposed to guide the mission of his people, they should also direct the preparation of ministry leaders to serve his church faithfully under his Lordship. The purpose for theological education is to equip students to be disciple-makers and to train others to do the same.

This chapter will begin by reflecting on two moments in the history of Southeastern Baptist Theological Seminary. Each instance represents an institutional response to the question, Where is theological education heading? The chapter will then recount how the Lord providentially prepared Dr. Akin to lead Southeastern to grow as a Great Commission seminary. This section reminds us that theological schools are not led by slogans or marketing campaigns, but by leaders with conviction and clarity who set the right direction for theological education. The chapter closes by exploring how the Great Commission should shape theological education.

Where Are We Heading? An Urgent Question

Quo vadis? is a Latin phrase that means "Where are you going?" This question has been asked twice at Southeastern Seminary. Together, these two moments illustrate how institutions have viewed the purpose of theological education. The first instance was in 1974, during Randall Lolley's inaugural address as the third president of Southeastern Seminary. Lolley described the seminary sitting in crosscurrents that impacted the school. The first current was external: the moving stream of Southeastern's constituency—its supporters, the seminary community, and the churches of the Southern Baptist Convention. Each had interest in the seminary pursuing its task in a particular way. The second current was internal: the task of theological education and the challenges associated with navigating the educational endeavor's demands and the students' needs.

Lolley's address represents the recurrent discussion over the purpose of theological education and what determines it. Educators have proposed two primary options over the last seventy-five years.[2] Some contend theological education should be viewed as vocational, training ministers to serve in particular church positions. Others believe theological education should be understood as formative, focusing on students' spiritual and academic formation. Lolley tried to navigate how the respective forces pulling the institution in each direction impact the way a theological school envisions its purpose. He wanted the seminary to navigate both streams without getting swept up by one current over the other.

---

[2] Daniel O. Aleshire, *Beyond Profession: The Next Future of Theological Education* (Grand Rapids: Eerdmans, 2021); Mud Flower Collective, *God's Fierce Whimsy* (New York: Pilgrim Press, 1985); Edward Farley, *Theologia: The Fragmentation and Unity of Theological Education* (Philadelphia: Fortress, 1983); Edward Farley, *The Fragility of Knowledge: Theological Education in the Church and the University* (Philadelphia: Fortress, 1988); Justo L. Gonzalez, *The History of Theological Education* (Nashville: Abingdon, 2015); Hugh Hartshorne, "What Is Theological Education?" *Journal of Religion* XXVI (1946): 235–42; H. Richard Niebuhr, *The Purpose of the Church and Its Ministry* (New York: Harper & Row, 1956); H. Richard Niebuhr, Daniel Day Williams, and James M. Gustafson, *The Advancement of Theological Education* (New York: Harper & Row, 1957); Joseph C. Hough Jr., and John B. Cobb Jr., *Christian Identity and Theological Education* (Chico, CA: Scholars Press, 1985); David H. Kelsey, *Between Athens and Berlin: The Theological Education Debate*, repr. ed (Eugene, OR: Wipf and Stock, 2011); David H. Kelsey, *To Understand God Truly: What's Theological about a Theological School* (Louisville: Westminster/John Knox; Grand Rapids: Eerdmans, 1993); Max L. Stackhouse, *Apologia: Contextualization, Globalization, and Mission in Theological Education* (Grand Rapids: Eerdmans, 1988); and Charles Wood, *Vision and Discernment* (Atlanta: Scholars Press, 1985).

Thirty-two years after Lolley's address, *Quo Vadis?* was posed again at Southeastern Seminary. In the second year of Dr. Akin's tenure as president, as the faculty completed a curriculum revision, the Board of Trustees adopted a new mission statement for the school. This time, the answer did not focus on navigating external and internal currents, or on the dueling purposes of preparing students for vocational ministry, or on engaging in a formative academic process. These factors were not and should not be ignored, but the address took a different approach. It set forth a Great Commission purpose for theological education, demonstrating how it participates in the mission God gave the church. The address provided a truly theological purpose by focusing theological education on God's mission and the centrality of the church in it.

Before Akin became Southeastern's president, the school was already known for its commitment to missions. In 1990, Lewis Drummond, the fourth seminary president, laid out a vision for a center for Great Commission studies, which was established in 1992 by the school's trustees.[3] In 2001, the school constructed a building to house the center and further emphasize the urgency of world evangelization.[4] In the fall of 2006, Southeastern became known as "a Great Commission Seminary" and began promoting its motto: "Every Classroom a Great Commission Classroom." These slogans reflect the mission statement adopted in 2006: "Southeastern Baptist Theological Seminary seeks to glorify the Lord Jesus Christ by equipping students to serve the Church and fulfill the Great Commission." This statement directed Southeastern as a missionally focused institution with a curriculum, faculty, and student body that would be shaped by and embody this mission.

---

[3] The official name of the center is The Lewis A. Drummond Center for Great Commission Studies.

[4] This information is recorded on a plaque that hangs in the Jacumin-Simpson Missions Building on Southeastern Baptist Theological Seminary's campus.

How God Prepared Dr. Akin to Lead Southeastern to Become a Great Commission Seminary

This chapter explores the connection between the Great Commission and theological education. The foundation for this relationship is based on biblical convictions. At the same time, this book celebrates the Great Commission legacy of Dr. Akin and the way God prepared him to cast a Great Commission vision for Southeastern Seminary.

Akin arrived at Southeastern resolved to build on its strong commitments to biblical preaching, evangelism, and missions. He elevated the school's focus on these ministries by prioritizing commitment to the Great Commission. Akin has often recounted how he became inspired to beat the Great Commission drum to which Southeastern Seminary would march.[5]

He describes it as a clarion call that came to him through a series of providential events. The first of these occurred at the beginning of 2006. Two long-time friends and committed supporters of Southeastern Seminary, Richard and Gina Headrick, invited Dr. Akin and his wife Charlotte to visit Southeastern students serving international missions as they completed their degrees. On this trip, the Akins witnessed the immense spiritual need, and grieved the reality that men, women, boys, and girls around the world had little, or no, access to the gospel.

The second providential event occurred when the Lord called two of the Akins' sons, Tim and Paul, and their families to serve overseas. During these years, the Akins continued to visit Southeastern students, and visit their sons' families, around the world. The overwhelming

[5] For an expanded version of this story, see Chad Burchett, "Why the Great Commission Matters in Theological Education: A Journey with Danny Akin," Southeastern Baptist Theological Seminary website, September 13, 2022, https://www.sebts.edu/news-and-events/headlines/2022/09/fa22_wgcm/.

reality of global lostness stirred the Akins' hearts for the nations and focused Dr. Akin's conviction that the Great Commission must be the mission driving Southeastern. The third event came from his personal encounter with God's heart for the nations while reading the Scriptures. The clarity of the Great Commission in the Bible established a guiding principle for him: "if [the Great Commission] matters that much to God, it should matter to us."[6] He embraced that who God is and what he is doing in the world must direct how believers live their lives and how churches understand their mission, and if the Great Commission is central to God's heart and the mission of the church, it must be central to theological education.

The Great Commission Shape of Theological Education

God created to have a people who know and worship him (Exod 7:16; Eph 1:9–10; Rev 4:11). He accomplished his redemptive mission by sending his Son into the world. The Triune God revealed himself and reconciled humanity in Jesus Christ (John 1:18; 2 Cor 5:18–19). Participation in God's redemptive mission extends to the church, as the Holy Spirit empowers Christians (Acts 1:8). Jesus says in John, "As the Father sent me, I also send you" (20:21). In Matthew's account, the commission's essence is to participate in God's mission by making disciples—the process by which Jesus's followers make new followers of others through leading them to follow Christ, baptizing them, and teaching them to obey everything Jesus commanded. Theological education's mission is to train Christian leaders to equip the church to be disciple makers. In this way, theological education participates in God's mission.

---

[6] Burchett.

The Great Commission "Vocation" of Theological Education

While "vocation" has several definitions, I use it to speak of "calling" in its most basic sense. In this section, I answer: What is theological education's responsibility? Or, to ask it differently, What is theological education's summons? To be summoned means to be called to a duty. While God did not ordain the formation of theological institutions in the Bible, the ministry of theological education nevertheless has been divinely summoned.

God calls his church to make disciples by baptizing and teaching them to follow all that Jesus commanded (Matt 28:19–20a). In the Great Commission, baptism signifies that one has heard and responded to the gospel and converted to following Christ. It is the sign that one has been identified with Christ and the church, his body. The instruction to teach demonstrates the centrality of leading, training, and instructing disciples on how to live as members of Christ. The vocation to teach is essential to the church's Great Commission calling. Teaching is the duty to participate in God's work to form the mind of Christ in his people (Phil 2:5–11). Christian teaching is a theological task because it calls people to give honor and glory to Jesus Christ by obeying his commands, sharing the good news that is in his name, and depending on his power as they follow him. The call to theological education supports the church's call by preserving all that Christ taught us to obey *in* the church and *for* the church and its mission. The idea that God is teacher, and what he teaches is himself and his ways, is central to the nature of Scripture as divine revelation. God's self-revelation summons us to know him and to make him known (2 Cor 5:14–21), which requires effective teaching and training (Eph 4:7–16).

Teaching ministry helps others understand truth and live by it. We find this model in Peter's sermon at Pentecost. He shares facts about who Jesus is and what he accomplished. He uses that information as reasonable evidence to establish the truth about who Jesus is.

Peter proclaims this message to provoke a response because the message of Christ requires a response. Truth is not merely a principle to ascertain, but a reality to live. This understanding of what it means to know reflects the biblical expectation that knowledge changes how we relate to God and live our lives. Thus, someone cannot claim to know truthfully yet not live by what they claim to know. Jesus confronts the Pharisees with this concept of knowing when he says: "Why do you call me, 'Lord, Lord,' and do not do what I say?" (Luke 6:46 NASB1995).

The ministry of teaching has been summoned because in every generation Scripture must be expounded and its content on the being and works of God must be explained and proclaimed. We are reminded afresh of this summons in every generation as the church faces distinct challenges to our faith. Our day is no different, and in fact, today, we may be in more need of theological education for the health and witness of the church. The cultural infusion of secularism has led our society to renounce the classic foundation of reason and moral judgments. The Christian faith calls us to recognize and embrace that all of reality is from and for God. This truth is the foundation that orients our lives. We are creatures dependent upon our Creator, and he has a good purpose for all things.

The Great Commission "Mission" of Theological Education

"Mission" and "vocation" can be used interchangeably if both concepts communicate the purpose for someone or something. However, above, I defined the vocation of theological education narrowly as a divine summons to teach. The mission of theological education identifies the "why" for this divine summons. The "why" is simple. It is so that theological education may participate in the mission God has given to the church.

God's mission is for his people to know him. God sent his Son into the world to accomplish this mission through the life, death, and resurrection of Jesus Christ (John 8:19; 14:6–7). Indeed, through Jesus, he "reconcile[s] all things to Himself" (Col 1:20 NASB1995; see 2 Cor 5:18–19; Eph 1:10). Through sacrificing his Son for us, he purchased a people from every tribe, tongue, people, and nation (Rev 5:9–10). God then sent his people into the world to participate in his purposes (John 20:21). God's people seek to follow Jesus by conforming their hearts and minds to him and obeying him by joining his mission to multiply followers of Jesus.

Ephesians 4:11–16 lays out the responsibility of Christian leaders to edify the church, cultivate maturity among God's people, and guide them to be united in Jesus. Ultimately, these aims are pursued that the gospel of peace may be known among the nations (Eph 6:15). If spreading the gospel of peace is the charge of the church, this purpose must also direct the tasks of theological education. Leaders need to be equipped to edify and lead the church to pursue its mission. Theological education equips church leaders with knowledge about the Bible's teaching and trains them to study the Bible for themselves and teach the people they are called to serve. It cultivates in church leaders a theological mind, establishing them in what they believe and why they believe it. It prepares ministers to teach and train others to know God and live lives that honor him. Theological education is instrumental to the church's mission to make disciples.

The Great Commission "Curriculum" of Theological Education

If both the vocation and mission of theological education are shaped by the Great Commission, the theological curriculum must also be molded by it. The curriculum in theological education represents the educational strategy to prepare people for ministry. It entails the scope and sequence of courses required to earn a degree. A key assumption in this chapter is that the essence of Christian ministry is the Great Commission call to make disciples. Thus, central outcomes for a Great

Commission curriculum must be establishing a conviction to obey Jesus in his call "to go and make disciples" and equipping people to be disciples and make disciples. Another component of a Great Commission curriculum is a fitting "pedagogical pattern" that reinforces the disciple-making outcomes. The Great Commission directs both the urgency and practicality of theological education by clarifying that its purpose is to make disciples.

When it comes to scope and sequence of the theological curriculum, church leaders and missionaries must be trained in the message and theology of Scripture and trained to faithfully interpret and apply it. To do this well, students must be trained in biblical hermeneutics and methods for determining the meaning of a text. These disciplines help us identify blind spots in both our understanding and that of others as we interpret biblical texts. Studying the history of interpretation helps us discern how the Bible can be applied to one's context by seeing how it was applied in previous contexts.

In addition to learning the message of Scripture, a Great Commission curriculum should teach students to think along with the Scriptures. This is the task of theology—learning to think the message of Scripture in a coherent and comprehensive way and apply biblical truths to the questions in one's own context. Church history helps us learn how the church has lived out the Christian faith and faithfully engaged its calling as witness of the good news of Jesus Christ. Theological education's goal is to edify God's people in the clarity and conviction of what we believe and how to live our faith.

Along with biblical, theological, and historical knowledge, Great Commission students also must be trained in missiology and Christian philosophy. Few people put these disciplines together, and many see one as academic and the other as practical. Both disciplines, though, aim to confront ideas that oppose the Christian faith and provide a clear, credible defense for its truthfulness. Christian ethics joins philosophy and missiology as a discipline that offers public witness to the goodness and moral foundations of the Christian faith. As the ideological debates in the West shift from the reasonableness of truth claims to rejecting moral order and embracing relativity grounded in individual rights, the missiological importance of Christian ethics to aid our witness will become more significant. Finally, several ministry-focused disciplines (evangelism, preaching, and counseling) equip students for ministry engagement so that the gospel may be communicated, defended, and applied effectively.

God has called his people to make disciples, so ministry preparation must include disciple formation focused on shaping the convictions, competencies, and character of students. The scope and sequence of the curriculum develops convictions and competencies. Great Commission theological education seeks to cultivate the specific character of a disciple. The biblical picture of a mature disciple is a person who: (1) possesses Christlike character (fruit of the Spirit), (2) is obedient to God's will, (3) serves others out of love, (4) shares his or her faith, and (5) responds to conviction with repentance. Christian leaders must model a Great Commission life if they intend to lead others to give their lives to fulfill the Great Commission.

In Rom 12:1–2, Paul provides a pedagogical pattern for the formation of a disciple. Teaching a Great Commission curriculum should follow his pedagogical pattern. Romans 12:1–2 is not typically associated with the Great Commission. However, given that Romans is a letter from a missionary raising money to advance the mission, it is reasonable to connect Paul's instructions to the Great Commission. In the center of this letter, Paul presents a framework for living the Christian life. Life for the Christian is to be a response to who God is and his mercies (v. 1). We recognize that to live this way, we face a battle. Paul defines this battle as seeking to resist conformity to the patterns of the world by having our minds renewed (v. 2). A "renewed mind" manifests itself through what Augustine called rightly ordered "loves": love for God and love for neighbor. These loves result from knowing God and what he has done to reconcile us to himself. By this transforming work, we become wise and can determine what is acceptable to God and live our lives as an act of service (vv. 1–2).

The Great Commission "Cooperation" in Theological Education

Cooperation in theological education is the strategic recognition that the church and its theological institutions cannot fulfill the vocation and mission of theological education isolated from one another. We acknowledge that the church receives the Great Commission and God empowers the church to fulfill it. Thus, theological education operates as a servant to the church, strengthening it and advancing its mission by equipping the church's leaders. Daniel Aleshire was right when he said, "The church could live without the seminary, but the seminary could not live without the church."[7] Yet we should not dismiss the strategic role of theology schools.

The question, "Where should theology be taught?" has received renewed attention in recent years. As more local churches do their own training for ministry, calls have increased to return theological education to the context of the church. Local churches no longer look to institutions exclusively to provide formal theological education, as they did in the past. One reason for this shift is disenchantment with the classical approach to theological training. Classical ministry training has been perceived as ineffective to prepare church leaders in the twenty-first century. Even so, most churches cannot provide theological education at an appropriate level for ministry preparation. Church leaders and ministers recognize as they encounter increasing ministry

---

[7] Quoted in Daniel L. Akin, "Theology for Church, Worship, and Ministry," in *Theology, Church, and Ministry*, ed. David S. Dockery (Nashville: B&H Academic, 2017), 289.

challenges that they need substantial biblical, theological, philosophical, ethical, and missiological training. To explain and defend the faith—in the face of cultural and social objections and in response to complexities of secular worldviews—requires expertise in disciplines that most church leadership does not possess.

The church and theological institutions should maintain a symbiotic relationship. Most churches are unable to provide the educational resources and expertise that theological schools can offer. Theological schools have professors with advanced training and understanding that offer a richness to theological reflection, instruction, and equipping. While these schools may fill the mind with knowledge and develop critical thinking, they are less effective in nurturing passion for ministry, the need for personal godliness in caring for others, and the resolve to love others the way we are called (Matt 22:39). This is not because they do not value or aspire to cultivate these dispositions. Rather, these qualities develop best through ministering to real people in the context of the church. Most theological schools cannot provide the in-the-field, contextualized learning and practice a church can offer. Students preparing for ministry need churches to apply what they learn and encourage their passion for ministry. Theological schools also need to understand developments in the ministry context to sharpen their teaching and refresh their approach to issues addressed in the classroom. Being in relationship with churches helps theological educators and schools learn from the church. The best cooperative model between schools and churches balances the valuable attributes of theological schools and of churches for theological education and ministry preparation.

The Great Commission "Commission" of Theological Education

Theological schools come alongside the church to help prepare people whom God has called to serve and whom his people recognize as gifted and called for ministry leadership. When students complete their ministry preparation through theological education, the church expects that the education equipped them for the ministry to which God has called them. To do this, schools set forth learning outcomes for each degree program and commit to see their graduates achieve those outcomes. At Southeastern, we have additional institutional core competencies that shape every program of study. The core competencies provide a rubric for implementing the institution's mission statement into the curriculum. However, these learning expectations reflect educational competencies rather than missional duty. Equipping students to fulfill the Great Commission requires those competencies, but the "commission" of a Great Commission theological education suggests there are certain expectations, a "missional duty," for the students. We expect our students to graduate consumed with a global focus, committed to be disciple-makers, and equipped to endure a lifetime of faithful ministry. These characteristics are distilled in our four marks that present what a Great Commission seminary "commissions" its students to be and do. The descriptions of the characteristics were initially written for use in the Southeastern Seminary's viewbook, which introduces to prospective students the Great Commission of Southeastern Seminary and the academic programs offered:

- **Love God:** The first of the great commandments is that we love the Lord our God with our heart, soul, and mind (Matt 22:37). We are committed to seeing Southeastern students grow in their love and knowledge of God, so they will worship, trust, hope, and delight in him more. Our love for God and others, the Bible tells us, is based first on God's love for us (1 John 4:19). We believe when we are captivated by the love of God (2 Cor 5:14–15), we are compelled and directed to live for his glory and for the salvation of all peoples.
- **Love the truth:** Jesus says, "I am the way, the truth and the life. No one comes to the Father except through me" (John 14:6).

Because God is truth, we believe his inspired Word is true. By God's Word, he makes himself known to us, sustains our faith in him, provides a light for our lives, and transforms us. We train students to understand and to trust the sufficient Word of God. We cherish his enduring and unfailing Word because it is the message of salvation for all those who believe (Rom 1:16). We are committed to seeing Southeastern students love and know the truth, so they may faithfully teach and share it.

- **Love the church:** The Scriptures call us "to care for the church of God, which he obtained with his own blood" (Acts 20:28 ESV). We love the church because God loves the church and identifies with the church as his body (Eph 1:23). The church is central to God's work in the world—a redeemed people called to be devoted disciples of Christ and ambassadors of the gospel. We equip students to serve the church and fulfill its mission.
- **Love the world:** The Scriptures say, "For God so loved the world, that he gave his only Son, that whoever believes in him should not perish but have eternal life" (John 3:16 ESV). We are committed to seeing Southeastern students love what God loves and to participate in his redeeming work in the world. Southeastern is a Great Commission seminary. We are consumed with a global focus because we are called and commissioned by Jesus "to make disciples of all nations" (Matt 28:19).

Conclusion

After sending out his disciples, Jesus assured them that their mission's success did not depend on them alone. He pledged to them that he would be with them always until the end of the age (Matt 28:20). The church was also given these words, and a similar promise: "I will build my church, and the gates of Hades will not overpower it" (Matt 16:18). These promises were not given to theological schools as such. But in the face of the uncertainties that graduate theological education must navigate, these assurances are applicable if a school's mission aligns with and serves the church's mission. The school's work will be needed until Jesus returns. Jesus will enable his church to train its leaders in one form or another until that day. Through these leaders, he protects his people from the gates of hell and prepares them to assail those gates to rescue others from the kingdom of darkness and transfer them into the realm of Jesus Christ (Col 1:13).

Connecting the Great Commission to the task of theological education gives the proper focus to this ministry. It calls the people to give honor and glory to Jesus Christ by obeying his commands, sharing the good news of salvation in his name, and relying on his power and protection. It focuses the ministry of theological education on serving the church's mission. It directs the seminary to focus on—above all other good endeavors—the mission that our Lord Jesus sent his church to pursue: to make disciples among the nations through gospel proclamation and biblical exposition. For this reason, the Great Commission should shape the vocation, mission, curriculum, cooperation, and commission of theological education.

We are grateful to the Lord for how he worked in Dr. Akin's life to help him see with clarity and conviction how Jesus's "last words should be lasting words," even for the mission of a theological school.

CHAPTER FOURTEEN

THE FAMILY AND THE GREAT COMMISSION

Todd Unzicker and Ashley Unzicker

Introduction

The Great Commission brings up many images and thoughts for Christians.[1] Men resembling Indiana Jones dressed for a safari in a dark jungle, but with a worn-out King James Bible instead of a braided whip. Modestly dressed women serving in dense, poor urban neighborhoods in South Asia. Single young adults spending a summer vacation or a couple of years after college sharing the gospel with an unreached people group. But rarely do our minds go to a family doing mission work together. When we talk of the Great Commission, every Christian demonstrating and declaring to all peoples the hope that is only found

[1] For a helpful introduction to the Great Commission, see Daniel L. Akin, Benjamin L. Merkle, and George G. Robinson, *40 Questions about the Great Commission* (Grand Rapids: Kregel Academic, 2020).

in Jesus Christ, without involving the entire family, we miss a vital witness and strategic resource.

Admittedly, our story became "our story" because of the Great Commission. God literally wove our paths together while we were each living on mission for him. For the two of us, we do not know any other way of living our lives for the name and fame of Jesus, whether across the street or to the ends of the earth. We thank God that even before we were followers of Jesus, he put people in our paths who stressed that the call to mission life was not something special for a sacred few but a mandate for all. Our prayer for you is that our story, and some of our mistakes and efforts along the way, will show you that your family has a vital yet simple role to play in fulfilling the Great Commission.

Our Story

Todd's Testimony

In the fall of 2005, I was a sports reporter who had heard the gospel throughout my life. Providentially, God put several men in my life who began shaping me. These included pastor James Merritt, who is a fellow contributor to this volume; Mark Richt, the head football coach at the University of Georgia (UGA); Kevin "Chappy" Hynes, who worked with the Fellowship of Christian Athletes at UGA; and Sky Pratt, the pastor of college and missions at Prince Avenue Baptist Church in Athens, Georgia. Dr. Merritt, Coach Richt, and Chappy all stressed God's love for all peoples, but it was Sky who insisted that I go with him on a short-term mission trip to Honduras.

Little did I know that this one-week trip would change the trajectory of my life. I surrendered my life to Christ on September 25, 2005. Soon after, I sold my home and quit my dream job as a sports reporter for UGASports.com/Rivals.com. I boarded a plane to become a full-time missionary in Honduras. For the next two years, I spent most of my time starting a seminary, preaching and teaching in rural mountain villages, providing clean water, and leading short-term teams much like the one the Lord used to transform my own life. My goal during those trips was always to provide every team member a small glimpse of God's redemptive work in the world—tangible evidence that would stick with them after they returned home. I did not want them to remain the same. I was praying for change! This was never truer than when I picked up a small family team from Connecticut one Saturday afternoon.

Ashley's Testimony

It was 2007. After an astounding number of terrible life choices, I can say without any hyperbole that it was a miracle I was still alive. Not only was I alive, but I had somehow graduated from college, had an apartment, and held a steady job at a hospital. But I still had this nagging little habit of choosing bad relationships, bad habits, and somehow always managing to be in the wrong place at the wrong time. Each day was lived in a way to avoid pain and have fun. In the back of my mind, I knew there had to be more to life!

One Connecticut-cold February morning, my dad asked if I would consider going on a medical mission trip to Honduras with him and my mom. Surprisingly, I only had one question at first: What will we be doing? My mom was a nurse at the time, so her going made sense. But I worked on the administrative side of things and would be little to no help—at least medically speaking. He told me we would be sharing the gospel. I now had one more question: What is the gospel?

That question sparked a quest to find an answer. I agreed to the trip and boldly darkened the doors of a nearby church. That same day, they announced a conference on the topic "How to Share Your Faith." Since I didn't have faith, I thought it would be a good idea to get some before I shared it with others on my upcoming mission trip. The conference was the day before I left for Honduras, so there was very little time to study, but it would have to do. At the conference, they gave me a Bible and a gospel tract. I took them with me on the plane ride to Honduras and walked through all the verses leading me through the gospel message. Halfway through, I realized I had a big problem and needed Jesus to rescue me. I gave my life to him on the airplane and walked off that plane a believer, follower, and daughter of God.

Ashley in Honduras

The first person I met in Honduras was Todd. He was wearing an old blue shirt, beat-up khakis, and flip flops. He obviously did not care how he looked. It was funny, but also intriguing. He seemed to live without burdens or limits—like he had God on his side or something! The woman who began the trip with two questions now had 827 questions, and they were all about God. Todd would smile and patiently walk me through the answer. When I asked what to read next, he was ready to give me a passage or a book in the Bible that might be helpful. He also showed me how God has given each of us a purpose. Following him was not about receiving forgiveness and then going back to my old way of life, but it was about a lifetime of discipleship. Another crucial thing Todd taught me was that the Great Commission is not for the spiritual elite or the seasoned believer. It is for me, too. I needed to share with others the same good news that God used to change my life.

When it was time to go back to the States, I was terrified to face my old life. I did not have Christian friends or godly community. Todd was returning on the same flight to Miami. Oddly enough, without any (human) intervention, the airline assigned us seats next to one another. We chatted, we laughed, and we exchanged phone numbers. Over the next few months, we stayed in contact. Todd continued to help me understand the Scriptures more, and I grew to like him more. I told him that I didn't want to date him—by then, I was over all that mess.

But I did want to marry him! I told Todd that if he didn't want to marry me, he'd have to let me know so I could go looking for someone just like him. He did not accept my quasi-proposal, but he proposed to me shortly after that. We were married later that same year, 2007.

Moving to Florida

While we were engaged, and Todd was still living in Honduras, a team from Holmes County, Florida, came down for a one-week trip. On that trip was Shelly Chandler, a pastor from First Baptist Church of Bonifay. He spoke with Todd about an open position in his county association as director of missions. Having never heard of a director of missions before, Todd asked Shelly what it was. Shelly replied, "Instead of telling you what it is, let me tell you what I think it could be." He explained how Todd could help lead the churches in the county in obeying the Great Commission.

With our wedding right around the corner and the possibility of moving to northwest Florida on the horizon, I was job hunting again. Again, Shelly Chandler approached us about a possible job. He asked if I would consider becoming the children's minister at First Baptist Bonifay. What an honor! I felt spiritually unqualified, but they graciously interviewed me and gave me a chance. First Baptist had deep convictions about the Great Commission. It was part of the church's DNA. Everything they did seemed to filter through going and making disciples. Although I was in a leadership role, many of the children's families welcomed me into their homes and patiently discipled me.

Being around People and Pointing Them to Jesus

Because we both worked for Christian organizations, it's easy to think, "Well, of course you did these things. You were paid to." But we did things that people working in secular environments could do, too.

Our goal was simply to be around people and point them to Jesus. We believed that every individual should do everything they do for the glory of God and do it all strategically for the mission of God. Anyone can do that, whether he or she is a teacher, banker, construction worker, or homemaker.

In our little town of Bonifay, we taught kids and rallied pastors and their congregations. Sure, we hung out together and did things that brought us closer, but our main objective was to go out into our communities and beyond.

We spent time each week showing children how to make disciples in schools, on sports teams, and with friends. Our church group took kids to a convalescent home each month to sing, bring gifts, and share Jesus. When the local high school football team needed a chaplain, Todd stepped up, connecting with players and coaches to demonstrate the power of Jesus's transforming work. As a couple, we did work in the prisons, pregnancy centers, and under-resourced parts of our community, and we led short-term mission trips.

Mission trips are often associated with the Great Commission. It's not so unusual to see a photo of a mission group with children in need, or in the airport, wearing cargo pants and matching T-shirts with Scripture (or the occasional PFG fishing shirt). Trips like these have advanced the gospel in the last thirty years. The lost have been saved, the needy have been served, and churches have been planted. But in leading many short-term trips, we also discovered that they often produce even greater fruit among the team members once they return home.

Short-term trips are like discipleship microwaves: they provide Great Commission "sparks" that heat up believers to give themselves more permanently to disciple making. Short-term trips can transform entire congregations, since members spend more time thinking about those in need outside the church rather than their own preferences inside the church walls. The heat first sparked by a short-term trip can even grow to a call to full-time missionary service. Today, we know at least five people from that one-traffic-light Florida county who serve as full-time missionaries with the International Mission Board. All of them took their first trip with us during our season in the Florida Panhandle.

The Great Commission Call

The Call to Make Disciples

Jesus commanded us in Matthew 28:19–20 (ESV) to "Go therefore and make disciples of all nations, baptizing them in the name of the Father and of the Son and of the Holy Spirit, teaching them to observe all that I have commanded you. And behold, I am with you always, to the end of the age." In these two verses, we are told to make disciples (not just converts) of all nations, baptize them, and teach them all God has commanded us. Although we typically think of missionaries when we think of these two verses, this is a command for everyone who has placed his or her faith in Christ.

The Great Commission is not the calling of a select few. Rather, as our friend Danny Akin likes to say, these verses are Jesus's final marching orders for all of his followers until he returns.[2] God has given believers the gift of salvation, by grace alone through faith alone, and not because of our good works. But one fruit of our salvation is that he calls and equips us for good works that glorify him and bless others—including disciple making. Our disciple making begins with evangelism, which is sharing the gospel, in the power of the Holy Spirit, for the sake of seeing unbelievers trust King Jesus alone as their Lord and Savior. The new believer then follows Christ publicly by being baptized.

---

[2] Daniel L. Akin, *Ten Who Changed the World* (Nashville: B&H, 2012), 3.

But if new converts are to become disciples—followers of Jesus—they also must be discipled. Discipleship is maturing believers investing in believers who are less mature in their faith to help them grow in their walk with Christ and become more faithful in their obedience to his commands. This includes the command to share the gospel with others. An important part of discipleship is helping believers see the value in investing in others themselves, thus fulfilling Paul's vision of "disciple-making disciples" in 2 Tim 2:2.

Disciple making ought to take place everywhere Christians live and everywhere we go. We are surrounded by lost people whom God wants to be his disciples. Great Commission obedience begins in the home, with parents making disciples among their children. But it also takes place in church buildings and in our neighborhood, at work and at the ball field, in the classroom and the boardroom, in small towns and big cities, among people who look like us and speak our language, and among people of other ethnicities who speak other languages. Healthy churches make disciples and then send them out to make other disciples.[3] This brings us to cross-cultural missions.

The Missionary Call

There is a myth common among many believers, at least in our circles, that goes something like this: God mostly calls single people to serve as missionaries. If they are young singles, preferably right out of college, that is even better. Single people make the best missionaries because they do not have spouses or children, meaning they have maximum freedom to do their missionary work.

We understand why this myth is so popular. Many of us know singles who serve faithfully as long-term missionaries. Also, some of

[3] See J. D. Greear, *Gaining by Losing: Why the Future Belongs to Churches That Send* (Grand Rapids: Zondervan, 2015).

the most famous missionaries in our tradition have been single men like Bill Wallace and single women like Lottie Moon. Even the apostle Paul reminds us that some believers should remain single because of the greater freedom to serve the Lord (1 Corinthians 7). So, we thank God for the single men and women who have answered God's missionary call upon their lives. They play a strategic role in fulfilling the Great Commission.

Thankful as we are, we still need to explode this myth. God also calls young married couples to serve as missionaries. And he calls our believing children to serve as missionaries. And he calls empty nesters to serve as missionaries. And he calls retirees with grandchildren to serve as missionaries. God's call to Great Commission faithfulness applies to all believers. So, all of us ought to live with our "yes" on the table to share the good news cross-culturally among unbelievers in underreached and underserved places.

The Great Commission is not for the spiritual elite. It is not even for those whose life circumstances seem especially convenient or flexible. The Great Commission is for every man, woman, and child who has placed their faith in Christ alone for salvation. And that means the Great Commission is also for families of every size and shape and season of life. The Great Commission provides all believers with our ultimate purpose as followers of Jesus.

Churches on Mission

Every-Member Ministry

True faith in Christ is always accompanied by kingdom purpose, which includes good works that glorify the King. This faith leads the believer into action. We serve our King by serving one another. We define "work of the ministry" as "service accompanied by God's message." Paul called every saint, each follower of Jesus, to do the work of ministry to build up the body of Christ into the likeness of Jesus, to the glory of God, and by the power of the Holy Spirit (1 Cor 12; Eph 4:11–13). Like most Baptists, we believe God calls individuals to serve as pastors and other ministry leaders, but we affirm the vision of "every-member ministry" modeled in the earliest churches.[4]

This body of Christ, the church, is a movement of God that calls every Christian to participate, whether single, single again, or with a family. We participate in God's movement primarily through meaningful involvement, or membership, in local congregations. These local churches are regional, contextual expressions of the one universal church. From the earliest chapters in the book of Acts, the Great Commission is given and obeyed in close connection with local churches, resulting in the worldwide advance of the universal church.

In Acts 1:8, Jesus reiterated his command for his followers to be his witnesses, both locally and across cultures, promising they would do so in the power of the Holy Spirit. Shortly thereafter, the disciples began to gather into a local church. According to Acts 2:42–47 (ESV), the Jerusalem church "had all things in common," gave generously, loved well, and praised God—and the Lord added to their number those who were being saved. Then, in Acts 3, Peter and John saw the lost (v. 4), shared the gospel (vv. 14–18), and called people to repentance (vv. 19–20). Evangelistic urgency was evidence of what God was doing in and through the church.

The message of the gospel was so powerful that nothing could stop it. Through the gospel message, shared in the power of the Holy Spirit, God provided his followers with boldness and courage even in the face of persecution. "We cannot but speak of what we have seen and heard"

[4] A significant part of Todd's ministry as the executive-director of the Baptist State Convention of North Carolina is investing in pastors so that they can lead their churches to embrace every-member ministry more faithfully for the sake of Great Commission obedience.

(Acts 4:20). This is how each believer, not just leaders, should view his or her life. Acts 5:42 says the disciples "did not cease teaching and preaching that the Christ is Jesus" (ESV). As Dr. David Black writes of the earliest disciples, "It seems to me, then, that bearing witness to Christ is absolutely and unavoidably necessary and obligatory for the believer."[5] They were ordinary people sharing an extraordinary message.

The gospel still knows no limits. It is for murderers of God's people, as we see in the example of Saul, who became the apostle Paul (Acts 9). It is for both Jew and Gentile, as we see in Peter's vision and the conversion of Cornelius (Acts 10). And it is for entire families who follow Jesus together (Acts 2:38–39; 10:24–48; 16:11–15). We must be faithful to participate in the work of the ministry through humble acts of service accompanied by proclamation of the gospel.

The Example of Stephen

Many forms of ministry may seem less grand than the call to relocate and share the gospel in some far-off land. But many seemingly mundane works of the ministry are used mightily by God for his kingdom purposes. Take, for example, the act of simply distributing food to those in need, as we see with Stephen in Acts 6:1–3. Stephen was an ordinary layperson whom the Jerusalem church appointed to help provide food to the Hellenistic Jewish widows. Stephen's works of the ministry attracted the attention of many people in his community, some of whom came to Christ.

Stephen also attracted the attention of the unbelieving Jewish priests. He was brought before the Jewish Council, where he was able to share the gospel publicly. They were enraged at his accusations that they had killed Jesus, so they stoned him. But on the same day that this table-waiting servant of Christ was stoned, Acts 8 tells us that the

---

[5] David Alan Black, *The Jesus Paradigm* (Gonzalez, FL: Energion, 2009).

gospel left Jerusalem—for the first time! This was not because of the apostles. It was because an ordinary layperson was doing common work to serve the church, which God used to fan the gospel flame. "Stephen's service provoked the trial. Stephen's testimony provoked the riot. And of those who left preaching the word, Luke goes out of his way to note that not a single apostle was included," said preacher J. D. Greear.[6]

Like the earliest disciples, we are ordinary servants called to bear an extraordinary message. So how can we keep quiet? How can we be still? We have been given eternal purpose, and nothing can stop this purpose. Not stones. Not imprisonment. Not kings on their royal thrones. God is worthy of all glory, and we glorify him by doing the work of the ministry in obedience to Jesus's Great Commission. This brings us back to the family.

Great Commission Parenting

The Great Commission played an important role in our own individual spiritual journeys, our marriage, and our respective calls to the ministry of the gospel. Christ's command is for individuals. And the more we studied the Bible, the more convinced we became of the relationship between the Great Commission and the local church. Christ's command is for churches. But as we have hinted throughout this chapter, we also believe that Great Commission faithfulness is very closely tied to God's vision for the family. Christ's command is for families.

As we became parents, traveling domestically and internationally for the Great Commission became more difficult to navigate logistically. We knew that the Great Commission was not simply for singles or those without children. As parents, we wanted our children to

[6] J. D. Greear, "We Send Every Member" (sermon preached at The Summit Church, September 20, 2020), available online at https://summitchurch.com/message/we-send-every-member.

understand our family's role in God's global purposes. In an affluent and comfort-driven culture, we realized that keeping this message central in our family was a must.

First we worked to show our children that motivation *to do* in the Christian life comes from being soaked in what Jesus did for us. His perfect life, sacrificial death, and victorious resurrection compel us to live with gratitude and love for the Savior first and foremost. We worked (and continue to work) hard to teach our children that the Great Commission is less about what we do and more about what he has done for us. This is why we serve him and serve others for him.

We wanted our children to see such acts of service firsthand. Since before they could talk (and sometimes even walk), we simply brought our children along and involved them in local Great Commission work. We realized we could be on mission strategically for God's glory, even in the smallest of things.

We had three children under four years old. Anyone who has had small children knows that some days, just getting out of the house is like going on a vacation. Like many parents before us, we would start the space shuttle launch that is getting kids packed up and dressed to meet up for a playdate at a local park. The days we could sit and talk with other moms about life, marriage, hobbies, or anything other than *Mickey Mouse Clubhouse* or *Super Why!* were a much-needed break. It was during this time that we realized even something as seemingly insignificant as this could be used for the glory of God and his mission.

Several families from our local church realized that instead of going to the park right near our neighborhoods, we could go to a park nearby that was frequented by refugees. We had read reports of hundreds of refugees from war and persecution being resettled in an apartment complex in our city. We began meeting there for our playdates, and for several years those playdates turned into purposeful days of Great Commission obedience. We met women from other cultures who were in the same stage of life that we are. Our children played with their children. While our backgrounds, experiences, and views of God were wildly different, we shared common interests in our families.

During these weekly outings, we helped those refugees acclimate to a new culture. Eventually, doors opened to share the gospel, resulting in many of our new friends coming to faith in Christ and even the beginning of a new church among an unreached people group right here in our city. Honestly, this would not have happened if it had not been for our family and something as seemingly mundane as a playdate. We realized that our family is a tool God wants to use to obey the Great Commission by reaching the nations relocating right to our backyard. And like the earliest disciples, our family obeys the Great Commission in connection with our local congregation for the global advance of the universal church.

Conclusion

For the Unzicker family, the Great Commission is not an option, but a mandate. We believe the same is true of your family. The Great Commission provides the purposeful glue behind all a family's endeavors. In an age that completely redefines what the family means, the Great Commission serves as a living, breathing witness to the love of Jesus Christ. Couples declare and demonstrate Jesus's love for the church and his rescuing work in part by serving on mission together. Parents and children model God's love for his redeemed while ministering in the name of Jesus.

We hope you have seen from our life stories that family and the Great Commission go together like peanut butter and jelly: each unique, but also much better together. Our goal as parents is not to raise church kids. Rather, our desire is to raise young disciples in our home who grow with a white-hot love for Jesus's work of redemption in their own lives and in the lives of people from every nation, tribe, and tongue.

Our prayer for our kids and yours is that they will embrace this vision of Great Commission families, champion that vision with their own children one day, and that all of us will reunite around the throne one day, countless families who answered the call to make disciples from among all peoples.[7]

[7] A helpful resource for helping children learn to pray for unreached people groups is Jason Mandryk and Molly Wall, eds., *Window on the World: An Operation World Prayer Resource*, rev. ed. (Downers Grove, IL: InterVarsity, 2018).

CHAPTER FIFTEEN

WOMEN AND THE GREAT COMMISSION

Amy C. Whitfield

I can still remember distinctly what could only be described as a call to ministry, although it was more of a gradual process than a lightbulb moment. After starting college with a very specific career path in mind, when the time came to select an internship, I could not bring myself to walk through the door I had always expected. Despite great opportunities, all I wanted was to do an internship working with the youth group at my church. I didn't understand why I was choosing that, but I never regretted one day spent with those girls. I followed up with another internship the next year, and then another. At some point, I finally admitted to myself that the only thing I wanted to do was serve the church.

This experience was probably common to many young people, both men and women alike. But as a female, wondering what options even existed for me was overwhelming and disorienting. In the end, the answer came from simply trusting the Lord and letting him direct my paths, which he did through the encouragement of others who found a seat for me at their tables. I have worked in ministry spaces full-time, part-time, and as a volunteer. I have taken mission trips to the other side of the world and walked across the parking lot to teach a senior adult ladies' Sunday School class at the church next to my house; both have shown me that the mission is everywhere. My passion for communication enabled me to meet a need, which in turn lets me wake up every day and do what I do best for my church. Being on mission is what I love.

I am not alone in this, but among some of my dearest friends in all the world. One of life's greatest delights is to see women flourishing as they follow the call of Jesus to make disciples.

According to the Religious Landscape Survey, women compose 51 percent of the membership in Southern Baptist churches.[1] In other words, women make up more than half the church. God's mission was given to the entire church, and as image bearers, we find our greatest flourishing when we are living in and for him.

Scripture consistently demonstrates women's important role in redemptive history. The four women named prominently in Christ's genealogy shows how God used women like Tamar, Rahab, Ruth, and Bathsheba in his divine plan to bring rescue through the Savior. Men and women may have distinct roles in particular contexts that are pointing to something beautiful, but those roles do not diminish worth or dignity or standing before the Creator. Even within complementary gender relationships in the home and the church, God calls women to

[1] "Religion in America: U.S. Religious Data, Demographics and Statistics," Pew Research Center's Religion & Public Life Project, June 13, 2022, available online at https://www.pewresearch.org/religion/religious-landscape-study/religious-denomination/southern-baptist-convention/.

a variety of roles in the church and on mission for his kingdom. That mission began with Jesus's last—and lasting—words to his disciples.

In Matthew 28, Jesus proclaimed "All authority has been given to me in heaven and on earth. Go, therefore, and make disciples of all nations, baptizing them in the name of the Father and of the Son and of the Holy Spirit, teaching them to observe everything I have commanded you. And remember, I am with you always, to the end of the age" (Matthew 28:18–20). This command to "go" was given to his eleven disciples, but it was clearly not intended to stay only with them. It was a command for the church that was to come, and one that we must continue to obey today.

Whether our call is across the street or around the world, we are all called to be disciple-makers. According to Article XI of the Baptist Faith and Message, "It is the duty and privilege of every follower of Christ and of every church of the Lord Jesus Christ to endeavor to make disciples of all nations."[2] If God calls all his people to be on his mission, it must be concluded that women are called to fulfill the Great Commission alongside their brothers. This is also evident in Article VI, which acknowledges that the office of pastor is for qualified men, but also affirms that "both men and women are gifted for service in the church."[3]

The Great Commission was not the first time Jesus told someone to "go" after his resurrection. Before appearing to the disciples, he first appeared to Mary Magdalene and Mary the mother of James, as they both feared and rejoiced over the empty tomb. When he met the women, they immediately began to worship. He told them not to be afraid and to "Go and tell my brothers to leave for Galilee, and they

[2] The Baptist Faith and Message 2000, Article XI: Evangelism and Missions, available online at https://bfm.sbc.net/bfm2000/ (accessed January 21, 2023).

[3] The Baptist Faith and Message 2000, Article VI: The Church, available online at https://bfm.sbc.net/bfm2000/ (accessed January 21, 2023).

will see me there" (Matt 28:10). When the disciples received the Great Commission at Galilee, they were there because Jesus had already told two women to "go and tell." As a result of the women's testimony to the resurrected Christ, the disciples were ready to receive their marching orders from King Jesus.

Women in service of God's mission is also described in the book of Acts, when on the day of Pentecost, the Holy Spirit was poured out on both men and women. From then onward, we read of women who were instrumental in the development of the early church. Priscilla worked alongside her husband Aquila, hosting and supporting the apostle Paul in his ministry. When Apollos came and spoke boldly but without full understanding, Priscilla was right there with Aquila as "they took him aside and explained the way of God to him more accurately" (Acts 18:26). Their help prepared Apollos as the church grew through his teaching. Lydia was a well-connected, established businesswoman who feared God and gathered with women by the river for prayer. When she heard the gospel from Paul, she believed and was baptized along with her household—the first convert in Europe. She hosted Paul and Timothy and was instrumental in establishing the new church at Philippi. Phoebe was known as a servant of the church at Cenchreae, and Paul trusted her enough to take his message to the church in Rome. She financially supported the spread of the gospel and traveled on her own journey to visit and encourage the church.

While this picture is clear in the earliest days of the church, the modern church has wrestled with how brothers and sisters work alongside each other to further the Great Commission. Questions about how women fit into ecclesiological and missional models, as well as denominational structure, have played out in various settings.

While the Southern Baptist Convention began under controversial and even deeply regrettable circumstances, missions were (and still are) at the heart of its purpose. And although women were active members of local churches, the pathways for them to contribute in a cooperative system were murky at best. In the early years of the Foreign Mission Board, married couples were sent to the mission field, with wives serving courageously alongside their husbands. But Southern Baptists did not have a clear category for a woman pursuing a call to the Great Commission outside of that model.

The term of the first single female missionary, Harriet Baker, did not go well. Despite dedication to her calling and a desire to serve, there was turmoil and drama among the missionary community in the brief time she was on the field. Facing mistreatment from others and a lack of support from her peers, she ultimately returned home. Baker had served as something of a test case, as many in the field and in leadership debated the role of single women in a missionary context.[4] After such a negative experience, more than twenty years would go by before leaders were willing to try again. Eventually, the benefit of women reaching other women became clear, and the 1870s brought with it the women's missionary movement. Lula Whilden and Edmonia Moon paved the way for the Southern Baptist Convention's most famous missionary, Edmonia's sister Lottie.[5]

Back home, women started to see how they could participate in the Great Commission even if they weren't taking a ship to the other side of the world. The formation of the Woman's Missionary Union opened the door for them to work together and to financially support other women in the field. The auxiliary organization was founded during an era when American women were mobilizing for causes they believed in, such as the temperance movement and social justice, and

---

[4] Keith Harper, "Let the Dead Bury Their Dead?!? Issacar Jacox Roberts and the Shaping of Southern Baptist Foreign Mission Efforts," *J. H. Spencer Historical Society Journal* 1 (2009): 11–20, http://baptisthistoryhomepage.com/spencer.jornl.roberts.i.j.html.

[5] Tessa Sanchez, "IMB Commemorates the Service of Single Female Missionaries," International Mission Board (December 17, 2020), https://www.imb.org/2020/12/16/imb-commemorates-service-single-female-missionaries/.

Southern Baptist women determined that they could stand together for missions. Even if they could not go to the nations themselves, this collective effort gave them the opportunity to offer instrumental help to others. They could support the women who were going, and through their efforts at home, they could impact the women who were being reached.

Although the women were beginning to make a significant impact for missions in fundraising, it took time before they could be fully involved in convention deliberations.[6] In 1885, debate broke out on the floor of the annual meeting over the eligibility of women to serve as messengers. The presence of Mrs. J. P. Eagle and Mrs. M. D. Early among the delegates from Arkansas sparked what could only be described as a constitutional crisis.[7] Mrs. Eagle and Mrs. Early were not the first women to participate in convention proceedings. Myra Graves, the widow of Baylor University president Henry Graves, had twice previously registered as a messenger without incident. But in 1885, the matter eventually made it to the floor.

The female delegates' credentials were immediately challenged. A committee was quickly drafted and produced both majority and minority reports, from opposing sides. The crux of the argument was a reference in Article III of the constitution to the Convention consisting of "members." The Arkansas delegation argued that Mrs. Eagle and Mrs. Early met the constitutional requirements because the category was not gender-specific, and they should be welcomed. Opponents argued that the constitution never intended to include women, and they should be dismissed on that understanding. Others

---

[6] David Roach, "Women & the SBC: 100 Yrs. of 'Extraordinary' Input Noted," Baptist Press (March 22, 2018), https://www.baptistpress.com/resource-library/news/women-the-sbc-100-yrs-of-extraordinary-input-noted/.

[7] In 1885, states would send groups of delegates to the Southern Baptist Convention. They would later be identified as messengers.

argued that they didn't agree with the notion of women as messengers, but the wording in the constitution did not prohibit their participation.[8]

One floor speech proclaimed, "The question before this convention is, shall the Baptist ladies of this country, who have sent more money into the vaults of this Convention than the men, be excluded from a part in its deliberations?"[9] For the SBC meeting in 1885, the answer was yes. To cool the heated situation, the women in question withdrew their names from the delegation and the president ruled that all reference to the debate specifically surrounding them should be removed from the record.[10] However, the argument sparked the later decision at that same Convention to amend the SBC Constitution by changing the word "members" to "brethren." Since the debate had centered around the intention of their governing documents, the majority of those who were left determined, by a vote of 131 to 42, to make clear that only men should be involved in decisions regarding the cooperative work of Southern Baptist churches.[11] It would take thirty-three years to change this disposition. At the 1918 Southern Baptist Convention meeting in Arkansas, the constitution was amended to use the term "messengers," for the express purpose of opening the door for women to participate. This was just two years before the Nineteenth Amendment to the Constitution of the United States granted women's suffrage.[12]

In 2018, the SBC Annual Meeting in Dallas commemorated that constitutional amendment with a resolution "On the Dignity and Worth of Women on the Occasion of the One Hundredth Anniversary

---

[8] "Southern Baptist Convention," *Tennessee Baptist*, May 16, 1885, 6–7.

[9] "Southern Baptist Convention," 7.

[10] "Southern Baptist Convention," 7.

[11] 1885 Southern Baptist Convention Annual, 30.

[12] Roach, "Women & the SBC."

of Women as Messengers to the Southern Baptist Convention."[13] This statement of support for the participation of women and the affirmation of their gifts echoed the growing involvement of women in various areas of service. That same year, one-third of the 9,632 registered messengers were women. Many participated in floor discussion, with others serving on the platform in various capacities. In multiple seminary reports, a clear theme was the affirmation of women and their gifts, as well as an eagerness to equip them for service in the kingdom.

In the Southeastern Baptist Theological Seminary report at that same meeting, President Danny Akin explained on behalf of the institution, "We are committed to a complementarian understanding of gender roles in the church and in the family. But at the same time, we are also committed to inviting women to come as equal image bearers of God, as women who have been trained and equipped and gifted by God to be deployed to the ministry assignments that God has for them."[14] This dedication to training women for service has opened more doors for women to be equipped and has also served as a model for churches to pursue the same commitment within their own local bodies.

Women have many avenues for service within the body of Christ. They are called to prayer and to prophecy. Older women are specifically

---

[13] Resolution "On the Dignity and Worth of Women on the Occasion of the One Hundredth Anniversary of Women as Messengers to the Southern Baptist Convention," Southern Baptist Convention (June 12, 2018), available online at https://www.sbc.net/resource-library/resolutions/on-the-dignity-and-worth-of-women-on-the-occasion-of-the-one-hundredth-anniversary-of-women-as-messengers-to-the-southern-baptist-convention/. The text of the resolution is included at the end of this chapter.

[14] "SBC18 - Joint Seminary Reports - Wednesday Morning," Baptist Press (July 14, 2022), available online at https://www.youtube.com/watch?v=sqn1ufBRUNE&feature=youtu.be.

assigned to mentor and disciple younger women, just as older men mentor and disciple younger men. Beyond that, and within a biblical framework, there should be countless avenues of service for women in the church. In a "Casual Conversation" panel discussion at Southeastern Seminary on October 3, 2019, Jen Wilkin stated that "we often send the message that the gifts given are nice but not necessary. The gifts of women are essential and indispensable to the mission of God." President Akin affirmed her statement and addressed the goal of Southeastern Baptist Theological Seminary: "The big challenge is to be rigorously biblical and not allow our traditions or the pressures of the culture to dictate how we flesh out biblical truth. We are asking the question of what women can do."[15]

It is of utmost importance that the church pursue and maintain a strong commitment to foundational biblical doctrines. But it is also crucial that within that commitment, we continue to build up and encourage the gifts and contributions of women. Southeastern Seminary has worked to maintain a balance in this area. Akin recently explained:

> My complementarian convictions do not mean men are superior or more spiritual than women, or that women are incompetent or unable to serve the Lord with distinction and faithfulness. Far from it! Southeastern welcomes women to come and study with us. Women's gifts are essential to the health and building up of the Church. I am so encouraged by my sisters in the faith who, throughout Church history, have served Christ faithfully in the roles he has appointed for them. Moreover, I am also challenged by my sisters who have served in these roles with

[15] "Casual Conversation with Jen Wilkin," Southeastern Seminary (October 3, 2019), available online at https://www.youtube.com/watch?v=GyQF2P5U-70&feature=youtu.be.

> unrivaled sacrifice, resolve and faithfulness and helped to fulfill the Great Commission of King Jesus.[16]

The mission of Southeastern Seminary is to glorify the Lord Jesus Christ by equipping students to serve the church and fulfill the Great Commission. The institution and its leaders desire that churches be filled with men and women who live out the marching orders of Jesus and have an eye toward taking the gospel to the ends of the earth. This value is handed down in every forum, from the classroom to the graduation platform. One strategy that Akin has specifically used is to present a yearly chapel message to students, highlighting missionaries as models. In over a decade of annual chapel messages, an overwhelming number of them have highlighted women's service around the world in response to the call of the Great Commission.

- **Ann Hasseltine Judson** was known as "the mother of modern missions," serving with her husband Adoniram in Burma. On her way to the mission field, she wrote in her journal, "Endeavoured to commit myself entirely to God, to be disposed of, according to his pleasure . . . I do feel that his service is my delight. Might I be but the means of converting a single soul, it would be worth spending all my days to accomplish."[17] She died young on field, but her writings inspired countless others—particularly young women—to

---

[16] Danny Akin, "FIRST-PERSON: The Pastor and Biblical Complementarianism," Baptist Press (November 14, 2022), available online at https://www.baptistpress.com/resource-library/news/first-person-the-pastor-and-biblical-complementarianism/.

[17] Danny Akin, "'The Lord Is My Refuge' Plainly Put on Display in the Life of Missionary Ann Hasseltine Judson—Psalm 142.1–7," Southeastern Baptist Theological Seminary Convocation, Wake Forest, NC (August 22, 2019), available online at https://www.danielakin.com/wp-content/uploads/2019/08/Psalm-142.1-7-The-Lord-is-My-Refuge-Plainly-Put-on-Display-inthe-Life-of-Missionary-Ann-Hasseltine-Judson-manuscript-mjh.pdf.

give themselves for the cause of Christ by taking his gospel to the nations.

- **Sarah Hall Boardman Judson** served faithfully alongside two husbands in Burma for more than twenty years. It was difficult to leave her family behind, but she simply could not shake her desire to go to the nations, and the fruits of her labor can be seen even today in Myanmar.[18]
- **Betsey Stockton** was born a slave and became the first single woman to go to the nations. She established schools for children in the Sandwich Islands, Maui, Canada, and in the US. Even in a life filled with hardship, she wrote, "Though sorrowful, yet I rejoice. The missionary's sorrows and the missionary's joys are mine. The missionary's grave and perhaps the missionary's heaven will also be mine."[19]
- **Lottie Moon** has perhaps the most storied legacy of any Southern Baptist. Her commitment to the people of China shone through in the many letters she wrote and messages she sent to the churches, imploring them to support the work and to send more. She believed that women could work together and mobilize to collect a Christmas offering for foreign missions. That offering continues to this day and raises millions, providing most of the annual budget for the International

[18] Danny Akin, "God Knows What He Is Doing Beautifully Exemplified in the Life of Sarah Hall Boardman Judson Psalm 138:1–8," Southeastern Baptist Theological Seminary Chapel, Wake Forest, NC, n.d.), available online at https://www.danielakin.com/god-knows-what-he-is-doing-beautifully-exemplified-in-the-life-of-mary-bordon-judson-psalm-1381-8/.

[19] Danny Akin, "Find Your Contentment in Christ: The Life and Missionary Ministry of Betsey Stockton, the First Single Woman to Go to the Nations," Southeastern Baptist Theological Seminary Convocation, Wake Forest, NC (August 19, 2022), available online at https://www.danielakin.com/find-your-contentment-in-christ-the-life-and-missionary-ministry-of-betsey-stockton-the-first-single-woman-to-go-to-the-nations/.

Mission Board, the largest missionary-sending organization in the world. Lottie Moon heard the call to go, and she did. But she was not satisfied with just going. She used her voice to implore others to send.[20]

- **Bertha Smith** was at the center of the great Shantung Revival in China, which began as an awakening among the missionaries serving on the field. Just before she left, she wrote, "My heart rejoices that I am on the way to China. I feel unworthy of the privilege of going . . . but I am trusting that God shall use me to do a great work for Him there."[21] Bertha Smith was a woman of prayer and evangelism who changed the world and inspired many.
- **Eleanor Chestnut** was a medical missionary who loved the people of South China and saved countless lives and was known for her sacrificial love. Her example inspired others to go.[22]
- **Harriet Newell** only lived to age nineteen, and never got to live out the mission she believed she was called to. Though she died on the way to India, her passion for reaching the world lived on in her journal. She wrote a year before she died, "O that I

---

[20] Danny Akin, "The Power of a Consecrated Life Lived Out in the Ministry of Miss Lottie Moon - Romans 12:1," Southeastern Baptist Theological Seminary Chapel, Wake Forest, NC (December 4, 2007), available online at https://www.danielakin.com/wp-content/uploads/2007/12/romans-121-the-power-of-a-consecrated-life-lived-out-in-the-ministry-of-miss-lottie-moon-manuscript-kh.pdf (accessed January 10, 2023).

[21] Danny Akin, "Galatians 2:20 & Bertha Smith, A Soul-Winning Missionary," Southeastern Baptist Theological Seminary Convocation, Wake Forest, NC (August 19, 2014), available online at https://www.danielakin.com/galatians-220-bertha-smith-a-soul-winning-missionary/.

[22] Danny Akin, "How the World Will Know We Belong to Jesus: The Life of Missionary Eleanor Chestnut – John 13:34–35," Wake Forest, NC (August 18, 2015), available online at https://www.danielakin.com/how-the-world-will-know-we-belong-to-jesus-john-1334-35/.

had a thousand pious relatives well calculated for the important station of missionaries . . . I would say to them, 'Go and let the destitute millions of Asia and Africa know there is compassion in the hearts of Christians. Tell them of the love of Jesus and the road to bliss on high.'"[23]

- **Darlene Diebler Rose** suffered much for the Lord in a Japanese internment camp, losing her husband and experiencing abuse. Through it all, she bore witness to the gospel and for the rest of her life proclaimed, "I would do it all again for my Savior."[24]
- **Betty Stam** was martyred alongside her husband in China. Their courageous example of faith and unwavering trust in the sovereignty of God inspired many to become missionaries and to be willing to give their lives for the cause of Christ.[25]

The stories of these women demonstrate the glory of God working through his people to carry out his mission. They demonstrate the

---

[23] Danny Akin, "Precious in the Sight of the Lord Is the Death of His Saints: Harriett Newell – Psalm116," Southeastern Baptist Theological Seminary Convocation, Wake Forest, NC (August 21, 2012), available online at https://www.danielakin.com/precious-in-the-sight-of-the-lord-is-the-death-of-his-saints-harriet-newell/.

[24] Danny Akin, "The Lord Is My Light and My Salvation: Darlene Diebler Rose (Fall 2016 Convocation)—Psalm 27," Southeastern Baptist Theological Seminary Convocation, Wake Forest, NC (August 18, 2016), transcript, Danny Akin (blog), https://www.danielakin.com/wp-content/uploads/2016/08/Psalm-27-The-Lord-Is-My-Light-and-My-Salvation...Darlene-Diebler-Rose-Convocation-Fall-2016-kh.pdf.

[25] Danny Akin, "The Missionary Psalm: Beautifully Obeyed in the Life and Martyrdom of John and Betty Stam – Psalm 67," Southeastern Baptist Theological Seminary Convocation, Wake Forest, NC (August 23, 2011), available online at https://www.danielakin.com/wp-content/uploads/2011/08/Psalm-67-The-Missionary-Psalm-Beautifully-Obeyed-in-the-Life-and-Martyrdom-of-John-and-Betty-Stam-Manuscript-ds.pdf.

humility and sacrifice of women responding to the call of Christ. They also represent the impact that comes from a leader championing the contributions of his sisters who have gone before him, implying encouragement and advocacy for the work of his sisters listening in the pews.

Women make up more than half the church. Their service to the Great Commission is indispensable. My call to ministry was gradual, but the realization that I could use my gifts fully in service to the church came through the encouragement and affirmation of a long line of leaders. The first leader in that line was Danny Akin, more than twenty years ago. By God's grace and for his glory, that has made all the difference.

RESOLUTION ON THE DIGNITY AND WORTH OF WOMAN ON THE OCCASION OF THE ONE HUNDREDTH ANNIVERSARY OF WOMEN AS MESSENGERS TO THE SOUTHERN BAPTIST CONVENTION

WHEREAS, The Bible presents the Lord God as creating both the man and the woman by His own hand and in His own image and likeness, crowning them with essential and inestimable dignity and worth (Genesis 1:26–27; 2:7, 21–22; 1 Peter 3:7); and

WHEREAS, The Bible consistently demonstrates that women played a significant role in ministry, evangelism, and disciple making (Mark 16:1–8; Luke 2:36–38; 8:2–3; 24:10; John 4:39; 11:20–27; 20:18; Acts 1:14; 16:40; 18:24–26; Romans 16:1–2; 2 Timothy 1:5); and

WHEREAS, God calls and gifts women for a variety of roles within the biblical framework of complementary gender relationships; and

WHEREAS, Women were valued servants of the early church, many martyrs in the post-apostolic era, and heroic missionaries of the historic Baptist movement, such as Lottie Moon and Annie Armstrong; and

WHEREAS, Women have served in a variety of ways throughout the history of the Southern Baptist Convention, including elected offices, service on committees and boards, missions education, ministry through entities and agencies, and positions in higher education, as well as within local churches; and

WHEREAS, Women continue currently to serve in a wide range of ministry roles within Southern Baptist life; and

WHEREAS, May 15, 2018, marked the one hundredth anniversary of women serving as messengers to the Southern Baptist Convention; now, therefore, be it

RESOLVED, That the messengers to the Southern Baptist Convention meeting in Dallas, Texas, June 12–13, 2018, honor the immeasurable contribution of women to our cooperative mission of Great Commission work; and be it further

RESOLVED, That we thank God for women who have contributed in biblically appropriate ways through discipleship, missions, education, evangelism, service, leadership, and working for advocacy and justice; and be it further

RESOLVED, That we affirm the gifts of women in their distinctive God-assigned roles, even as we continue to witness to Scripture's teaching (Genesis 2:18, 21–24; Ephesians 5:22–33; Colossians 3:18–19; 1 Timothy 2:9–14; Titus 2:3–5; 1 Peter 3:1–7) in a culture increasingly confused in matters of gender and sexuality; and be it further

RESOLVED, That we call upon women to serve in diverse capacities to advance the gospel in their homes, local churches, communities, the marketplace, and within our denomination; and be it further

RESOLVED, That we call upon older women to invest in younger women for the sake of developing them into godly followers of Christ consistent with Paul's admonition in Titus 2:3–5; and be it finally

RESOLVED, That we call upon all Southern Baptists to encourage, cultivate, and celebrate the diverse gifts, callings, and contributions of women in biblically appropriate ways.

CHAPTER SIXTEEN

KINGDOM DIVERSITY AND THE GREAT COMMISSION

Walter R. Strickland II

Introduction

> "May they all be one, as you, Father, are in me and I am in you. May they also be in us, so that the world may believe you sent me. I have given them the glory you have given me, so that they may be one as we are one. I am in them and you are in me, so that they may be made completely one, that the world may know you have sent me and have loved them as you have loved me." (John 17:21–23)

Jesus's prayer for his followers is that they would be one (John 17:21). This unity extends far beyond joint affirmation that Jesus is Lord. It resembles the depth of unity between Father and Son within the Godhead. For Christians, oneness is predicated upon believing the "good news," and like the Father and Son, believers follow the divine example of being one in purpose and love. Brotherly love is not an end unto itself; it is so "the world may know you have sent me and have loved them as you have loved me" (v. 23). In short, oneness is about mission.

Jesus, in his omniscience, is fully aware of the challenges that His people would face to remain in one accord through the centuries. Therefore, Jesus does not pray for an unimaginable display of power, but the simple act of remaining unified in Christ and being of a single missiological purpose. The breadth of the Great Commission encompasses gospel proclamation to the ends of the earth, and the missiological task includes the whole people of God comprising believers from "every nation, tribe, people, and language" (Rev 7:9). The unity of God's people in the Great Commission task bears witness to the peace and harmony made possible by the message we bear.

Despite the clear charge for God's people to be unified in mind, heart, and mission, in the mid-twentieth century, Martin Luther King Jr. famously said that one of the most segregated hours in Christian America was 11:00 a.m. on Sunday. In fact, he was certain it was probably *the* most segregated hour.[1] According to Lifeway Research, this unfortunate claim remains true well into the twenty-first century.[2] In a world continually looking for a means of bringing people together with substantive cultural, ethnic, economic, and political differences, the church has an opportunity to take the lead as a rich communion on mission.

Diversity Strategies among Christians

Among Christian organizations, there have been attempts of various kinds to embody Jesus's prayer of being one (John 17:23). This

[1] Martin Luther King Jr. on *Meet the Press*, April 17, 1960.

[2] Bob Smietana, "Sunday Morning in America Still Segregated—and That's OK with Worshipers," Lifeway Research, January 15, 2015, https://research.lifeway.com/2015/01/15/sunday-morning-in-america-still-segregated-and-thats-ok-with-worshipers/ (accessed October 31, 2022).

brief survey of methods employed to bring about unity amid diversity within God's people highlights their utility and surveys their weaknesses, beginning with the pursuit of quotas and percentages. Initial efforts to diversify Christian organizations were based upon the inherent value of every image bearer. The goal was to incorporate believers from every background as a demonstration of God's saving power over all people. These efforts were energized by the hope that adding people of different backgrounds would undoubtedly change the ministry's internal dynamics and make it more effective to reach a broader swath of people with the gospel. This desire drove Christian organizations to develop numerical goals to demonstrate this biblically motivated desire.

The most significant factor in the success or failure of these efforts is the strategies and ethos of those pursuing such goals. While it is ill advised to establish arbitrary numeric goals, aspirations to better represent and serve a church or ministry's constituency are appropriate. Pursuing an enhanced ability to reach stated goals can edify an organization, but this is not always the case. Efforts to pursue numerical equity can quickly devolve into a heavy-handed exercise to reach personnel quotas above all else. A myopic focus on numerical equity rather than the missiological fruit of a diverse yet unified organization pursuing the Great Commission together can quickly become a deterrent to the mission. Pursuing quotas and percentages while overlooking a healthy team dynamic is based on the mistaken notion that numbers alone will achieve the oneness that Jesus prayed for in John 17.

Another common method of pursuing Jesus's vision of oneness is making robust biblical arguments that lay the groundwork for unity. Common lines of biblical logic begin with an affirmation that all people are made in God's image (Gen 1:27) and are therefore worthy of dignity and respect. Other Old Testament passages that demonstrate God's desire to gather a multicultural people include Rahab and Ruth's incorporation into God's people and ultimately into the genealogy of Jesus (Matt 1:5).

Examples abound in the New Testament because God's spiritual family transcends a single people. Matthew's account of the Great Commission makes it evident that the gospel is for all (Matt 28:19). The book of Acts describes the gospel transcending ethnic and cultural barriers and making inroads from Jerusalem to Judea, to Samaria, and to the ends of the earth (Acts 1:8). Most explicitly, Ephesians 2 highlights unity in Christ between ethnic groups because the dividing wall of hostility between Jew and Gentile is no longer standing (Eph 2:11–22). Finally, John's eschatological vision in Revelation 5 captures a picture of the Christian's destiny when God's multiethnic people gather in his kingdom forever (Rev 5:9).

For Bible-believing Christians, Scripture is our chief source of motivation and guide to pursue unity amid God's diverse people. Within Christian organizations, it is common to devote intense attention to crafting biblical unity statements, but at times, those efforts do not translate into action. Biblically grounded unity statements are essential in a culture where there is confusion about the word "diversity" and because methods that range from abusive to biblical have been employed for diversity's sake. However, a theologically robust public declaration alone cannot generate the oneness Jesus prayed for in John 17. Public statements must be followed by intentional and sustained efforts that value what an organization could be if it were a diverse yet unified people.

Cultural assessment is another method deployed to make Jesus's vision of oneness a reality. No single culture has perfected faithfulness to Christ. As a result, every culture must be refined by Scripture. This necessary process is both rewarding and challenging but is most effectively executed when voices from inside and outside of the culture are included. Within any organization or society, the dominant culture is inescapable—this is nothing to lament. However, the dominant culture garners the most attention because its ideals can do the most good or harm to the surrounding cultures. For this reason, contemporary society tends to fixate on the dominant culture to the near exclusion of surrounding people groups.

Cultural assessment has a place in pursuit of oneness, but it should not be led from a desire for retribution. When revenge is the motive, the dominant culture sinks deeply into shame, caused to bear in perpetuity the burdens of generations past, or made to feel their culture is inherently broken. Cultural assessment of present and past should not produce despair, but biblical lament that motivates corrective thought and action. Initiatives that exclusively feature cultural assessment focused on the dominant culture do not motivate God's people to persevere through the challenges that bear the fruit of unity and are prone to stall out in hopelessness.

The most effective means of pursuing unity on mission begins with sharing the beauty of each culture's contribution to the faith. The respect, understanding, and love that flow from this kind of sharing is the first step toward a rich communion. As the superstructure of unity is built, to varying degrees, the best versions of the methods surveyed are deployed in pursuit of the prayer Jesus prayed two millennia ago.

A Rich Communion

In the fall of 2014, Derek Hicks delivered a lecture in Binkley Chapel titled "The Gumbo Pot: Christian Community as a Complex Brew." Hicks explained how the sophistication of gumbo should mirror the people of God. He insisted that

> gumbo is not a tidy dish but is an assortment of flavors and colors that oddly come together and create a glorious taste. Unlike the melting pot, gumbo represents the colorful expressions of

> given communities and does not disguise the robustness of the elements. Gumbo is not only profound unto itself . . . [gumbo] must be shared because in its essence the dish exudes a posture of fellowship and cooperation.[3]

Like gumbo, the oneness of God's people is accentuated by the cultural and ethnic differences of those who constitute Christ's body. Such unity highlights the powerful force that binds them, enhancing the church's public witness.

The unity and diversity of God's people is based on the gospel's universal message that saves particular people and those people demonstrate his Lordship in their daily lives. This is the distinction between the good news of the gospel (Christ dying and resurrecting to rid all of creation from the stain of sin) and gospel stories (the testimonies of the redeemed in Christ as they walk in faithfulness to God's commands). The gospel is not captive to any culture, but it manifests in enculturated people. Christ is the believer's primary identifier, no matter their culture, so there is a family resemblance among the people of God. This rich communion is not unified by superficial homogeneity, but by the Savior, who is the ultimate reconciler.

The cultures that comprise God's family are rich with differences. Cultures are distinguished by nonbiological characteristics that shape common behaviors and thought patterns associated with a people group. Culture helps elucidate humor, guide food preferences, and determine norms, such as what it means to be "on time."[4] Culture also frames

---

[3] Derek Hicks, "The Gumbo Pot: Christian Community as a Complex Brew" (lecture, Southeastern Baptist Theological Seminary chapel, Wake Forest, NC, November 4, 2014).

[4] Walter R. Strickland II, "General Introduction" in *For God So Loved the World*, ed. Walter R. Strickland II and Dayton Hartman (Nashville: B&H Academic, 2020), xix–xx. Culture is not to be confused with ethnicity or race. *Ethne*, translated "ethnicity" (sometimes "nations"), is a biblical term used to describe the "peoples" of the earth. Two of the widely known occurrences of *ethne*

biblically appropriate worship styles and patterns, and the language used to express lament and adoration to God. The joys and sorrows believers endure on their faith journeys cause them to develop spiritual strength in unique areas that allows them to walk in faithfulness within their life circumstances.

Since every believer is being sanctified to navigate their family of origin, social context, vocational situation, and ecclesial environment, they have gained a unique aptitude for traversing their life circumstances that enhance the people of God with whom they fellowship. God's diverse people live through various trials, and saints sharpen one another as through the journey with Christ (Prov 27:17). Scripture suggests that iron sharpens iron most effectively across the lines of difference. This dynamic is evident in 2 Tim 2:2 (older and younger men) and in Titus 2 (older and younger women) as they benefit from the age gap. In the contemporary American church, learning from older generations is held in higher regard compared to gleaning from those of a different culture. Unfortunately, believers rarely reap the benefits of this mutual sharpening because of the unconscious yet prideful assumption that those from different cultures have nothing insightful to offer each other.[5]

---

are Matthew 28:19 and Revelation 7:9. Ethnicity refers to the biological origins of a person's birth and is part of God's good creation (Gen 1:31). Together, humanity's numerous ethnicities reflect the fullness of God's intention for his image bearers. Likewise, contemporary discussions of race do not reference the human race as a whole, but a socially constructed reality that attributes negative or positive meaning to biological characteristics and cultural manifestations that are used to categorize people. Racialization simultaneously fosters belonging for some and antipathy for others.

[5] Due to social dynamics, minority cultures must engage other cultures (for example, the minority culture seminarian has a cross-cultural encounter when reading most of his textbooks and interacting with the lion's share of his professors and fellow students). For the majority culture, there must be a proactive choice to interact beyond their average book, professor, or classmate because the value of such interaction is often overlooked. Social dynamics notwithstanding, learning from one another is a fruitful undertaking.

Contemporary culture often frowns upon people from different cultures admonishing each other. But among the people of God, communion with Christ supersedes any cultural affiliation. Believers can arrive at a place where cross-cultural sharpening is mutually beneficial if care is given to understanding and appreciating a culture's language, expression, and disposition. Steven Bevans says:

> A person can participate in another context to some degree. In some cases, an outsider may be more in tune with a particular culture than many of those who are born within it. If a person approaches a culture or context openly, is willing to learn the necessary language or languages, and is willing to read and appropriate sociological and anthropological literature about a particular culture, he or she can understand much of what a particular culture is about.[6]

This dynamic of cross-cultural sharpening is only effective if believers are calling others to embody Christlike characteristics in their life circumstances and cultural framework. It is beneficial to be sharpened by believers from various backgrounds, but when a particular expression becomes the standard by which others are judged, it is problematic. This leads to Christianity within a specific cultural framework becoming the rubric by which every other believer is judged. No single demographic, of any kind, is at the center of the Christian narrative—Jesus is.

Attempts to manifest the oneness that Jesus prayed for fails when a set of cultural trappings is the prerequisite for participating in Christ's body. It is God's design that the textures of Christian faithfulness enhance the communion of the saints. Textured culture in the church benefits the Church's public witness, enhances the edification

---

[6] Steven Bevans, *Models of Contextual Theology* (Maryknoll, NY: Orbis, 2002), 19.

of the saints, and is necessary to pursue God's mission more effectively together.[7]

A Rich Communion on Mission

In fulfillment of Jesus's prayer, God's people should endeavor to be a rich communion pursuing the Great Commission together. A united pursuit of God's mission sharpens God's people in their Bible reading, theologizing, and in church life because they do so as a unified community.

Bible Reading

Seeking God is essential to the Christian life. Humanity witnesses God in creation, by the Holy Spirit, but most clearly through biblical exegesis. Scripture dramatically describes God's world, his design for it, and his redemptive action within it. Biblical engagement is essential for a Christian to flourish because God's inspired and authoritative Word is a wellspring of life and hope for believers. Through voluntary and glad submission to Scripture, the faithful are transformed into Christlikeness. As Christians are sanctified unto Christ, they read Scripture more accurately.[8] For example, the Christian who allows Scripture to restore a

---

[7] William H. Bentley recalled African American preachers in the middle of the twentieth century mimicking the culturally contextualized ministry practices modeled by their seminary professors. He specifically noted Black ministers rolling their r's like Scottish pulpiteers because these ministers in training were not able to distinguish exemplary ministry practices from their cultural trappings. William H. Bentley, *The National Black Evangelical Association Reflections on the Evolution of a Concept of Ministry* (Chicago: William H. Bentley, 1979), 16.

[8] Growing in biblical understanding also requires an increasingly refined implementation of biblical interpretation practices. Robert Plummer's *40 Questions about Interpreting the Bible*, 2nd ed. (Grand Rapids: Kregel Academic, 2021) is a broadly accessible and widely read resource that introduces healthy practices in biblical hermeneutics. For a more scholastic treatment of helpful hermeneutical methods, see Grant Osborne's *The Hermeneutical Spiral:*

biblical understanding of possessions will continually understand the implications of the Bible's teaching on stewardship more accurately. In the same way, believers must continually assess their cultural assumptions to ensure that those presuppositions do not obscure the meaning of the text.

After acknowledging the divinely endowed characteristics of the Bible, it is essential to recognize how our enculturation influences Bible reading. It is critical for believers to understand what cultural assumptions and values they might project onto Scripture that may obscure its meaning. Said differently, human presuppositions can either illuminate or obscure biblical teaching. The believer's philosophical assumptions, emotional disposition, family of origin, and religious past must be interrogated by Scripture to ensure they are not clouding the biblical message. These factors can cause Bible readers to mis-exegete Scripture and eisegete personal desires that misshape the faith into our own image. Because human assumptions are like the "air we breathe," it is imperative to read Scripture in a community seeking the Bible's meaning and significance together to encourage one another away from our cultural presuppositions that overrun biblical interpretation.

Christians committed to biblical authority and authorial intent from individualist versus collectivist cultures provide a vivid example of how reading Scripture in community can help discern the author's intended meaning.[9] Unlike many individual inerrantists, those from communal cultures are unlikely taken aback by the importance of reading Scripture

A Comprehensive Introduction to Biblical Interpretation, rev. and exp. (Downers Grove, IL: IVP Academic, 2006). My emphasis on transformation in the hermeneutical process is highlighted because transformation and sanctification occur most effectively in community, which is the focus of the essay.

[9] The distinction between individualist and collectivist cultures is that individualists see to their own well-being first, then the community's. Collectivists are the inverse; they seek the well-being of the community before their own because their fate is bound up with their broader community.

in community as a helpful means of understanding it. Bible readers from individualist cultures often gravitate toward themes of penal substitution and highlight the righteousness/justice that results from Christ's finished work. In addition, believers from a communal environment with an honor/shame orientation are likely to insist that Jesus died and rose for justification, but also for the shame believers bear for their own sin or the sin that was committed against them (Heb 12:2). With a shared desire to discover the author's intended meaning, a rich communion of diverse believers can employ proven biblical interpretation methods with more accuracy together than they can apart.

Theologizing

The work of theology is the work of every Christian disciple to apply the Word of God to daily life. This process traverses the common Western chasms between orthodoxy (right thought), orthopraxy (right action), and orthopathy (right affection) because theologizing is a holistic endeavor that requires more than an intellectual ascent to knowledge. Theology is often reduced to producing timeless statements about God. This is good and necessary, because theologizing certainly includes engagement with the divine, but that theological process is commonly abstracted from its human authors on the one hand, and its implications for daily living on the other. Theology that is reduced to a purely intellectual exercise causes the illusion of understanding without its substance, namely, adhering to "the weightier matters of the law" (Matt 23:23 ESV).

Theology is a task undertaken by people, in the messiness of life, with our eyes fixed on Christ as we make our pilgrimage down a path of sanctification. Thus, theological exploration is enriched by compounding lines of inquiry produced by myriad questions forged in a variety of cultural contexts. While Christian thought is not captive to any cultural experience, obedience occurs where God calls us into Christlikeness. People are born and live amid a specific set of cultural and circumstantial realities. It is in those circumstances they are called to "walk in newness of life." This results in unique theological inquiries as believers from various contexts submit themselves to biblical authority.

Christ is Lord overall and his reign is manifest among the redeemed. Testimonies to Christ's universal saving work are born around the world as Jesus encounters image bearers salvifically in the particulars of their lives. Jesus is the only way to salvation (John 14:6), and sinners are drawn to him in various ways—largely based upon their emotional and spiritual needs. The result is that believers are captivated by the saving Lord for reasons pertinent to their story and are subsequently discipled into a fuller understanding of Christ and his lordship in their lives.

"Appropriate" theological inquiry has been disproportionately driven by those who maintain the power of the press, perches in the academy, influential pulpits, and denominational authority. In evangelicalism, the cohort of ecclesiastical and theological leadership has been culturally homogeneous. It follows that the doctrinal questions and concerns held by the dominant culture have become "normal" in formal theological discourse. Since Jesus is Lord over all and theology is a task undertaken to ultimately live out the wisdom of Christ, believers should be able to bring God's Word to bear on the joys, sorrows, questions, and concerns of all people, to his glory. Unfortunately, theological inquiry from nondominant cultures is often deemed "acceptable" insofar as it matches the dominant culture. As a result, theologizing in a rich communion on mission will produce new lines of theological inquiry.

As God's people theologize together, one fruitful methodology between "traditional" Western theology and theology from the cultural margins is the distinction between a theology from "above" and theology from "below." Undertaking the theological task together will bear productive fruit. Believers who approach the theological task in these distinct ways are not commonly in fellowship, but a rich communion on mission provides a constructive environment for this kind of sharpening to occur.

Since the Protestant Reformation, the most published approach to theology in the West has focused primarily on the identification and exposition of the primary *loci* (or heads) of doctrine. The loci first appear in Philip Melanchthon's *Loci Communes* in 1521. Melanchthon's loci, which include God, creation, free will, sin, law, gospel, and grace, are part of the framework of what is often called "systematic theology." This method of theology begins "above" with a doctrinal inquiry, such as, Who is Christ? What is humanity? or What is the church? The method then explores it exegetically and explores relevant philosophical and historical theological considerations along the way towards developing a summary of Scripture's teaching on the matter. Only after this thought exercise takes place is the significance of that doctrinal summary applied to daily life "below."

A theology from "below," on the other hand, begins by believers seeking God's face in their daily lives. This method of conducting theology is considered "from below" because of its orientation to God. Amid daily circumstances, Christians are compelled to "cast their cares upon the Lord" (1 Pet 5:7) and discover divine encouragement, wisdom, and guidance. While theology from below has not been the primary means of conducting academic theology in evangelical institutions, it parallels the patterns of life more closely than a theology from above. After assessing life circumstances and inviting divine help, the believer lives in accordance with divine wisdom amid daily life.

When theologizing in community, those who conduct theology from above and below shore up each other's weaknesses. Those who explore theology from above tend to conduct exegetical, philosophical, and historical exploration of doctrine and lack prolonged integration into daily life. However, in a robust theological community, those conducting theology from below would insist upon thinking theologically about daily life. Explorers of theology from below also tend to construct theological reflection with a passionate desire to be useful to an individual or community. As a result, doctrinal expression can become detached from historical considerations and any organizational framework meant to aid novice Christian theologians to be thorough in their theological engagement.

In addition to conducting theology with mixed complementary methods, a rich communion on mission will more comprehensively bring the gospel to bear on life's challenges. Believers who fellowship and theologize in a community are empathetic to circumstances beyond their own experience because they have loved a friend through their circumstances. Bringing biblical truths to bear in the lives of both believers and unbelievers from a variety of backgrounds makes the rich communion more effective in taking, proclaiming, and demonstrating the restorative power of Jesus Christ wherever the curse of Genesis 3 is found.

Church Life

The value of a rich communion on mission extends beyond individual sharpening, Bible reading, and theologizing. It enhances the culture of worship gatherings, preaching, and shepherding the flock. Considering others (Phil 2:3) is a Christlike characteristic that should permeate the Christian life, much like Paul's concern with Peter in Galatians 2, when he insisted that his fellow Jews were putting too many Jewish cultural customs on Gentile converts. Because of Christ's fulfillment of the Law, matters of circumcision, Sabbath, and food are features of Jewish cultural customs, not the means of entering God's family.

In the Christian family, belonging in our worship and church life is not predicated on keeping dominant cultural customs. When participation in the people of God is not dependent upon knowing "insider" language, worship styles, songs, or preaching styles, it is ready to incorporate believers from various cultural backgrounds.

A rich communion on mission also extends the reach of preaching to believers from various backgrounds. The sacred preaching moment consists of a preacher heralding the gospel's cosmic, communal, and personal implications. The gospel's cosmic scope offers hope of a coming kingdom and salvation to anyone who cries out to Jesus as Lord; this message is immediately relevant to all believers. In contrast to proclaiming the gospel's cosmic implications, discerning the gospel's communal implications for a specific church is contextual. This task requires knowing the specific challenges that threaten a particular body of believers. At the personal level, the gospel restores a biblically appropriate view of self in the face of satanic lies that threaten each image bearer in unique ways. Thus preaching, like the gospel, is three-pronged: it is (1) cosmic, and it is contextual in that it is both (2) communal and (3) personal. Upholding preaching's full scope is complicated when a diverse body of believers takes gospel's contextual implications seriously.

The preacher's background functions as the primary cultural reference point for the church because it is the immediate context through which Scripture is understood and most readily applied in sermons. It follows that every preacher communicates most intuitively to people whose lives resemble their own. These dynamics subtly announce the kind of people who feel shepherded most naturally in a church's environment. Even the most experienced expository communicators default to shepherding as if parishioners will endure the same issues, hardships, and concerns the preacher has personally encountered.

Although every believer is encouraged by the cosmic implications of Christ-centered teaching, enthusiasm is tempered for those on the church's cultural margins because the redemption story is rarely applied to their concerns on a personal level. If illustrations, anecdotes, and application seldom make biblical faith concrete, a parishioner's feelings of functional pastoral abandonment are difficult to navigate. Over time, a lack of spiritual guidance amid life's greatest struggles makes a listener ask, "Is this the church for me?" While preachers and teachers of the Bible naturally bring something of themselves to the teaching moment, a rich communion on mission allows ministers to know, understand, and impart the implications of God's Word to a variety of people more intuitively because they have linked arms pursuing God's mission together.

The principle of self-awareness and understanding of struggles beyond your own is not only relevant for preaching, but immediately applicable to counseling and shepherding within a diverse body. Being able to "bear the burdens of others" (Gal 6:2) is essential in an increasingly diverse communion. Believing communities will bear a variety of burdens that will significantly expand as people of different vocational, socioeconomic, ethnic, and cultural backgrounds join the movement. While burdens foreign to a shepherd's life might be outside their experience, if they have helped another bear that burden, they will be able to recognize their burden, even if they have not borne it themselves.

Conclusion

The culmination of Jesus's prayer for oneness is a rich communion that pursues God's mission more effectively together than apart. A diverse communion provides ample opportunity to practice considering others, which develops an individual's spiritual maturity. As God's people achieve Jesus's vision for oneness (coupled with gospel clarity), their corporate witness that extends beyond the world's superficial unity brings glory to God. The kind of cultural awareness forged when pursuing the Great Commission together reduces Christian belonging from specific cultural trappings to Christ alone, which makes a missional community poised to pursue and welcome people from every cultural background. A rich communion on mission will more easily navigate cultural pitfalls in interactions with people of every background and deploy various methodologies to meet people with the gospel in their cultural context. In short, true oneness that mirrors the diversity of God's kingdom is the result of pursuing Christ and the Great Commission together.

AFTERWORD

Mike Buster

I will never forget the day in December 1980 when God allowed me to cross paths with Danny Akin. When I met Danny, he spent much of the time grilling me about whether I was qualified to serve as a youth director at Northlake Baptist Church in Dallas, where he served as associate pastor. He asked me a series of questions that I had never been asked, nor knew the answers to, as a twenty-two-year-old graduate fresh out of Ouachita Baptist University. I was not prepared to spell inerrancy, much less articulate my position on the topic. Danny had just graduated from Criswell College and was more than prepared for theological debates.

Fortunately, Danny did what Danny does. He showed mercy and grace with my ignorance and then began to teach me theology! We would spend the next three years doing ministry together and carpooling from Dallas to Southwestern. From that first encounter with Danny until this day, I have had a front row seat to the "Danny, Charlotte, and the boys show." A few years later, Danny would be my best man when I married Joanie. Forty years later, he is still the best man I know.

Danny and Charlotte have raised four of the finest young men I have ever known in Jonathan, Nathan, Paul, and Tim. Each one of these men has been called to ministry and missions with hearts for serving God's people. Each is uniquely gifted, and all have become some of our greatest leaders in the Southern Baptist Convention. In addition, they have given fourteen grandchildren to the Akin team as of this writing.

Growing up in Atlanta, Georgia, Danny loved to play baseball more than he loved God. But, at the age of ten, the Lord transformed him, and he surrendered his life to serving King Jesus. It was as though God said, "You think I did a lot with a couple of fish and few loaves of bread? Watch this!"

Danny is one of the humblest individuals I have ever known, and he has never forgotten whence he came. This is why, throughout his ministry, he has been able to ward off what he refers to as "the green monster of pride that sneaks into our lives with an attitude of entitlement that transforms a once humble servant into a Hulk-like prima donna who less and less resembles a simple carpenter from Galilee." What an example to follow.

Danny was called to ministry in July 1977 and has steadfastly served in churches and seminaries. For the past two decades, he has served faithfully as the President of Southeastern Baptist Theological Seminary. What God has done through Danny at Southeastern Seminary is simply astonishing. He is the author of thirty books and countless articles—all while remaining faithful to his commitment to expository preaching and the Great Commission. He has the prowess of a great theologian, the sensitivity of a pastor, and the prophetic voice of a preacher. His passion for training the next generation of pastors and missionaries is unceasing.

You cannot outgive Danny and Charlotte. They are both givers in numerous ways. Charlotte is truly Danny's helpmate in their family life and in her role as the First Lady of Southeastern. She enjoys hosting many events at the beautiful Magnolia Hill for seminary wives,

Southeastern trustees, and cabinet members. She has the heart of a sweet servant seeking to minister to all those the Lord places in her path. To know Charlotte is to love Charlotte. They make an incredible team for the Lord.

Danny is well known for his passion for servant leadership. He is a humble leader who walks with God as a husband, father, and friend. Although revered as "Dr. Daniel L. Akin" in the wider world, he is still simply "Danny" to many of us. Through his Christian walk, Danny reminds us that there are no superstars, but lowly shepherd-servants of the great Shepherd, and that we are on this planet for a few short years to honor King Jesus and seek to fulfill the Great Commission.

Joanie and I join with thousands of others in congratulating Danny on twenty incredible years as president of Southeastern Baptist Theological Seminary. We love Danny and thank God for him, Charlotte, and the entire Akin team!

NAME AND SUBJECT INDEX

SCRIPTURE INDEX

Mark

Luke

Romans